1947	1953	1964	1968
Minor White	Paul Strand	Sylvia Plachy	Jim Marshall
Nude Foot, San Francisco	*Tailor's Apprentice,* Luzzara, Italy	*Hungarian Wedding* or *Marika's Wedding*	Johnny Cash at Folsom Prison, California
P. 127	P. 51	P. 92	PP. 114–115

1949		1965	1969
Minor White		Bruce Davidson	Graham Nash
Sandblaster, San Francisco		*The Welsh Pony*	Joni Mitchell
P. 32		PP. 78–79	PP. 110–111

1971

Stephen Shore

Amarillo, "Tall in Texas"
PP. 68–70

1977

Paul Berger

Mathematics #57
P. 142

1984

Robert Adams

Pawnee National Grassland,
Colorado
P. 75

1988

Eugene Richards

Blind Elder,
Guinea, West Africa
P. 105

1990

Carrie Mae Weems

Untitled, from the
"Kitchen Table" series
P. 47

1991

Sylvia Plachy

Swann's Way,
Prague
PP. 94–95

1993

Elinor Carucci

Two Eyes
GATEFOLD,
PP. 120–121

1994–1997

Jeff Dunas

David "Honeyboy" Edwards
P. 43

Seeing Being Seen

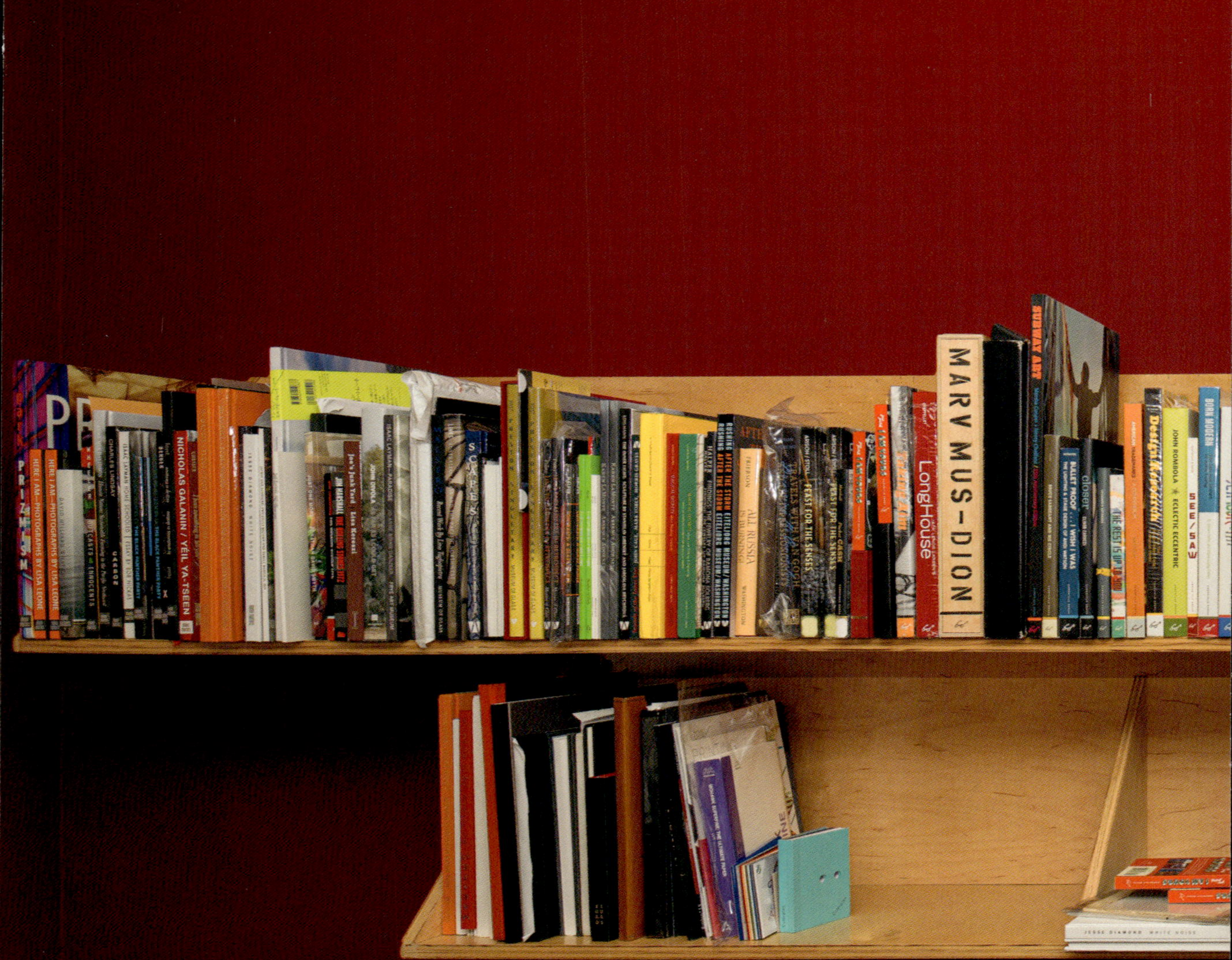

PRISM
PRIZMISM
HERE I AM
HERE I AM—PHOTOGRAPHS BY LISA LEONE
OUTCASTS and INNOCENTS
THE BLACK PANTHER PARTY
CHARLES LINDSAY
ISAAC LAYMAN
NICHOLAS GALANIN / YÉIL YA-TSEEN
JESSE DIAMOND
JIM MARSHALL
THE BEIJING TREES 1972
WHITE NOISE
SCAPES
NICHOLAS GALANIN
ALL RUSSIA
FEAST FOR THE SENSES
AFTER THE STORM
RUSHING
LongHouse
MARV MUS-DION
SUBWAY ART
DESIGN
BORN MODERN
JOHN ROMBOLA ★ ECLECTIC ECCENTRIC
BULLET PROOF
... I WISH I WAS
closer
THE REST IS UP TO YOU
SEE / SAW
JESSE DIAMOND   WHITE NOISE

Seeing Being Seen

A Personal History of Photography

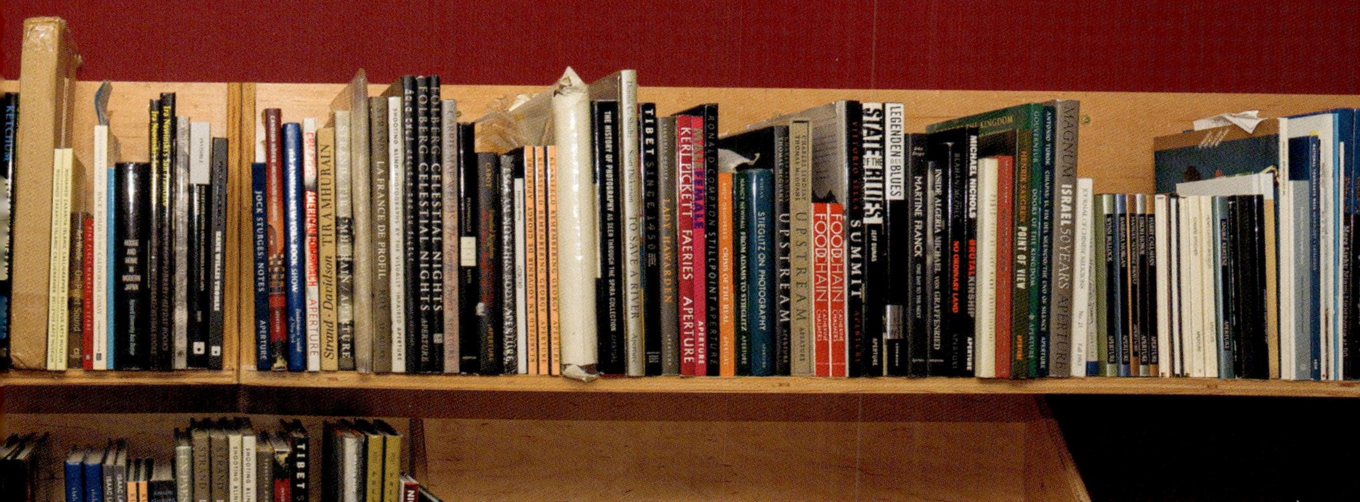

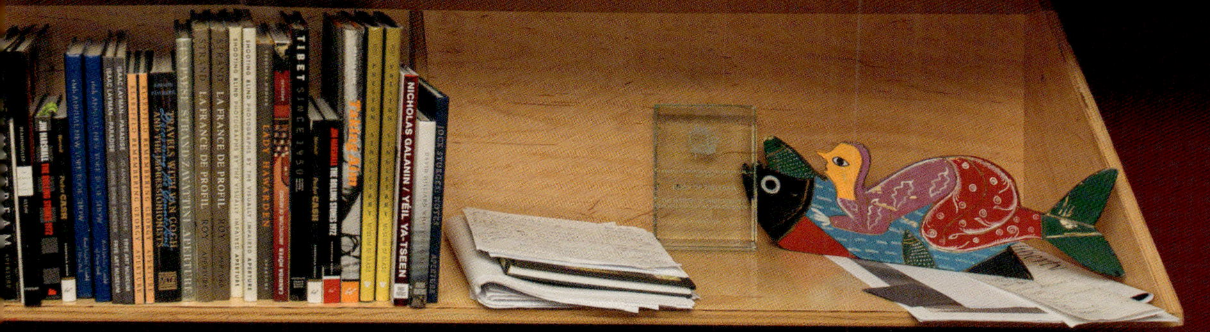

MICHELLE DUNN MARSH

Afterword by Nancy Salguero McKay,
Executive Director, Highline Heritage Museum

MINOR MATTERS BOOKS, SEATTLE AND NEW YORK minor matters.

Pages 2–3: My office shelves, inherited from G. Gibson Gallery, Seattle (the top shelf includes copies of all the books I've worked on), 2020. Photographed for Peggy Roalf's Design Arts Daily (DART) newsletter, March 2020.

Contents

There are a few points through which we could enter this history—my history, that of a girl who started out reading picture books, and went on to publish them—but this warm September evening in 2009 is an appropriately magical one to start.

I was backstage at the Grandstand of the Puyallup Fairgrounds. Whiffs of nearby cattle cut the cotton-candied air as I filled a plate from a modest buffet, and sat down with Graham Nash. We had just reviewed *Taking Aim*, a book I edited of Graham's all time favorite rock and roll photographs. Over dinner with the project's catalyst, Jasen Emmons, and me, Graham shared how happy he was with the book, and his thoughts on the forthcoming exhibition.

As Graham excused himself to prepare for his performance, my thoughts turned to where I was. I'd grown up seeing Ray Charles, The Beach Boys, Alabama, and countless other musicians (along with rodeos and even a Catholic mass) at The Fair's multipurpose arena. Eighteen years earlier, I received my high school diploma on the very stage that would in moments hold Crosby, Stills, and Nash. One of those stars was now my colleague and friend. *How was this my life?*

Nearly a decade later, after reading a *Seattle Times* Sunday feature about my career, then-curator Nancy Salguero McKay posed a similar question to me and pushed me to offer up some answers. My eventual response was *Seeing Being Seen*, an installation of books I've worked on and photographs I own inaugurating a rotating space within the newly opened Highline Heritage Museum (see pp. 156–157). This publication serves as a catalog to and expands upon that installation.

I did not particularly want to write this book; I'd much rather be working on someone else's. But when I saw in the exhibition a distillation of the amazing people I've known and projects I've been a part of, I realized that our stories, the stories of the workers behind the scenes in the arts, are also worth telling, so those who seek this beautiful path of cultural collaboration know the joys and challenges of following through on that endeavor.

Since 1996 I have made a living as a designer, editor, and publisher; an educator and producer of cultural programs; and an arts administrator. Nearly all of those roles shared an overarching goal to expand audiences for exceptional American photographic practitioners and their photographs.

As a visual delineation of reality, photography is an art form that I find both unique and universally accessible. My love affair with photography developed as a by-product to my early devotion to books. I started writing books as soon as I could form letters; those first forays often included images. In my late teens I was introduced to photographic books. They felt like a secret enclave for children who grew up but still wanted to read pictures. I had no desire to construct an alphabet by making images; the photographers I kept discovering were doing a stellar job of that. The more their photographs transformed me, the more I read within their work.

As the number of images made and shared expands exponentially today, photography's voracious present sometimes seems to be consuming its brief past. Anyone with wi-fi access can contribute thoughts and images to global archives online, and anyone can support or refute that data. As a result, our "histories" are being adjusted daily,

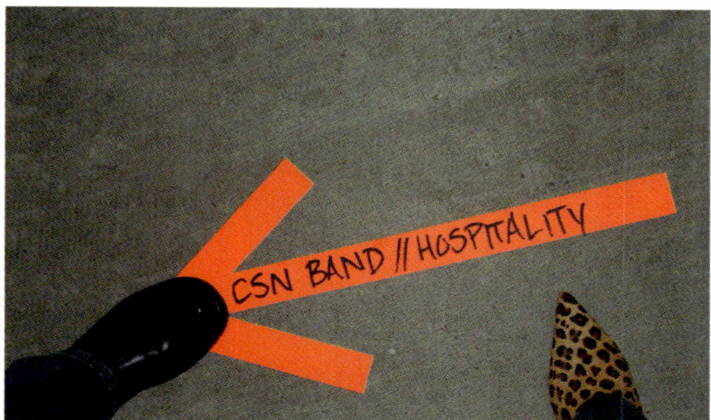

broadening awareness of previously unknown visionaries, and diversifying the narratives of tangential fields. There is more to wade through, experience, and question, all through a backlit screen that is both portal and barrier. While some people comfortably engage with the world from a virtual distance, I prefer the messy unpredictability of direct and personal interactions—with books, with prints, and with humans, especially the humans who perceive the world through some form of a viewfinder.

Photography and history are exercises in time travel, and time travel is not linear. Neither is *Seeing Being Seen*. It moves from 2009 to 1980, 1997 to 1905 with the turn of the page and the discovery of a photograph as it came into my purview. The most recent photograph is the 2019 wet-plate collodion tintype by Will Wilson (cover); it is one of three contemporary photographs included in this volume made from nineteenth-century processes.

Of the imagemakers featured through their capital "P" photographs, I have worked with all in some capacity, except for the five I arrived too late on the scene to know personally. Those five—Minor White, Paul Strand, Edward Steichen, Barbara Morgan, and Dorothy Norman—were humans known to the humans I know. It is a continuum I am proud to be a part of and seek to extend, by introducing others to the photographers who have influenced me. The photographs presented are objects I live with, selected from an archive of prints acquired through my work. The prints span seventy-five years; the images extend further, and are listed chronologically by year of exposure or construction on the endpapers.

Photographs have many layers. Each viewer will enter them to the depth of their choosing, inevitably infusing the images with a bit of themselves in the process. That exchange is particularly powerful in photography because of the mysteries of how photographs stimulate our emotional and cognitive functions. The process I developed to read photographs is presented separately, and can be used with this book for those who wish to learn more.

Seeing Being Seen is drawn from my past, but it is also my contribution to the future—presenting in one volume internationally known and soon to be known practitioners from different generations, genders, ethnicities, geographies, and educational backgrounds who, from my vantage point, well represent this modern medium. They are included here because of who they are. They are also included here because of who I am.

Shoe selfie backstage at the Grandstand of the Puyallup Fairgrounds, 2009

Seeing

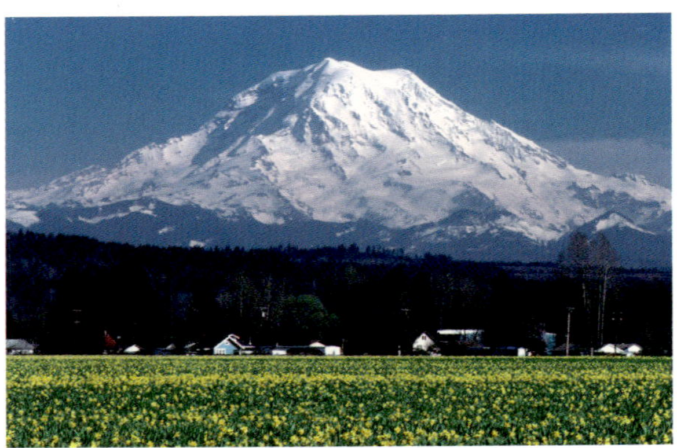

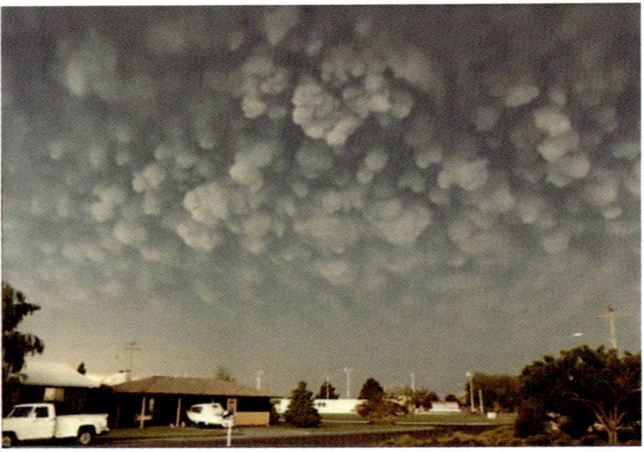

Top: Tahoma (Mount Rainier) from the Puyallup valley, 1989.
Bottom: Ash plumes from the eruption of Louwala-Clough
(Mount St. Helens), 1980

I was shy as a child, preferring to observe my environment from behind barriers—a favorite blanket, the gentle height of an apple tree, or the limbs of my parents and two older siblings. My awareness of the granular place I occupied in the universe was stimulated by the natural beauty of the Pacific Northwest, the region I was born into, specifically by the elusive views of Tahoma (Mount Rainier). This 14,411-foot peak can be seen, when it happens to present its majestic face, from nearly every route into the Puyallup valley from the North Hill area where we lived. I have never had ambitions to reach its summit, or even hike its lowlands, but still gaze upon it whenever I have the chance, knowing that at any point it could disappear for days behind cloud cover.

When I was seven years old, Louwala-Clough (Mount St. Helens), a long-dormant volcano in Washington state not visible from where I grew up, erupted, and an ash cloud appeared in the sky. If at the time someone had said, "that isn't real, you just imagined it," I would have believed them. A hallucination would have been preferable. Disbelief at what I had witnessed occurred again years later when a tower evaporated in front of me on a sunny September day in 2001.

From early on I held sight as experiential, and yet I doubted it. The imagery of my subconscious did not assist in resolving those two states. I don't recall at what age my recurring nightmares began, but they were always the same—black, thickly drawn stick figures of people plodding along in an endless line, with flashes of fluffy loose-lined Michelin-like men and women floating. They frightened me to the point that I did not want to go to sleep. A pediatrician told my parents that I had an "overactive imagination," and suggested that more physical activity might tire me out and foster sound rest. Running around made no difference. In addition to the dreams, I began talking in my sleep, and occasionally sleepwalking.

My sister, who shared a bedroom with me, found my nocturnal condition both annoying and entertaining. The eventual solution came in two parts: a "write on/wipe off" board and pen to record the thoughts that sometimes possessed me during slumber, and a nightly routine with my father to plan out my dreams for that evening. It is possible that my inclination toward visual storytelling began then, as we discussed subjects and sequences to hold the nightmares at bay.

My father was good at stories. He had long connected us to his mother using photographs to remind him of anecdotes, which he shared while we all sat around her gravestone. I was both fascinated by and fearful of this relationship between photography and memory. At seven or eight years old, I was already asking myself if I actually remembered my third birthday, and the epic Winnie the Pooh cake the neighbor made for me, or if I only *thought* I remembered it, because I'd seen photographs marking the occasion? I wanted memory to retain authenticity. I don't recall ever expecting authenticity from the photographs.

My siblings were each adopted, and I was a surprise conception after their arrival. My parents were of different ethnicities, but all five of us shared one physical feature:

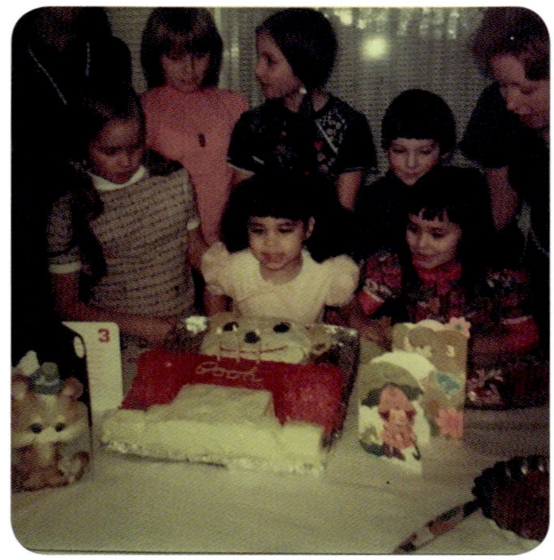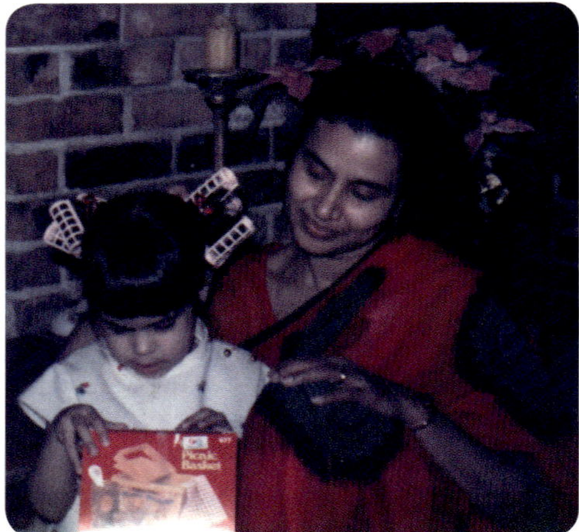

dark hair. Beyond that, our similarities and distinctions were very much a matter of inter-pretation, often dependent upon what people did or didn't know about our family.

When people commented on the ways we children looked alike, my siblings and I agreed with them. And when others noted how very different we looked from one another, we agreed with them, too. In public, I was sometimes subject to an overt line of questioning depending on the time of year, and my fluctuating skin tones. "Where are you *really* from?" "What *are* you?" Saying "I'm from Puyallup" was never enough. The fear and sense of displacement those questions fostered in me as an already shy child heightened an existing desire to observe, rather than participate, in what was going on around me.

When I was twelve years old, over two feet of my hair had to be cut off to manage what I now know is an inherited health condition. It was a radical, unexpected shift toward androgyny in the early stages of adolescence. I was often mistaken for a boy, particularly when shopping for shoes or clothing. Too tall to hide behind my siblings or parents anymore, I had to find some new armor to protect myself. I decided that if people were going to keep staring at me, I was going to give them something to look at.

One day I could be a twin to my father in jeans, t-shirts, and matching Kangol slouch caps as we sought spark plugs at the local auto parts store; that same evening I might summon the 1980s gender-bending looks of Duran Duran or Boy George in dressing for a church dance. My mother was alarmed. My father was amused, and worked out a daily inspection of my outfits. Clothing as performance became essential for me to move comfortably in the world, an opportunity to direct some aspect of how I was seen. This was particularly useful when I later entered public-facing professional roles.

My mother, who immigrated to the United States from Burma when she was twenty-eight, descends from a Catholic community of intermarriage between people of

 Left: My third birthday with siblings and neighbors, 1976 *Right:* Age two, with my mother, 1975

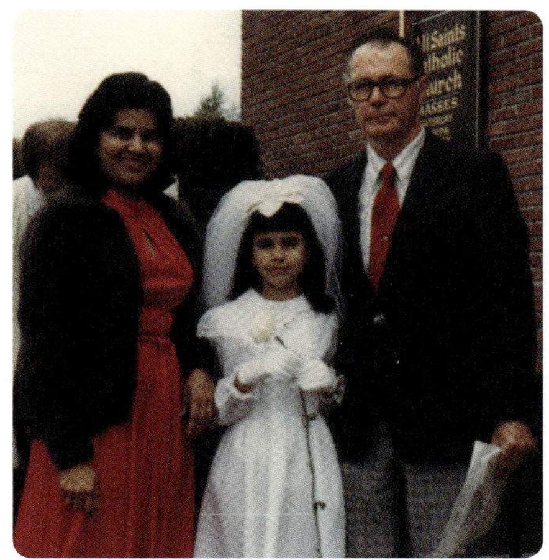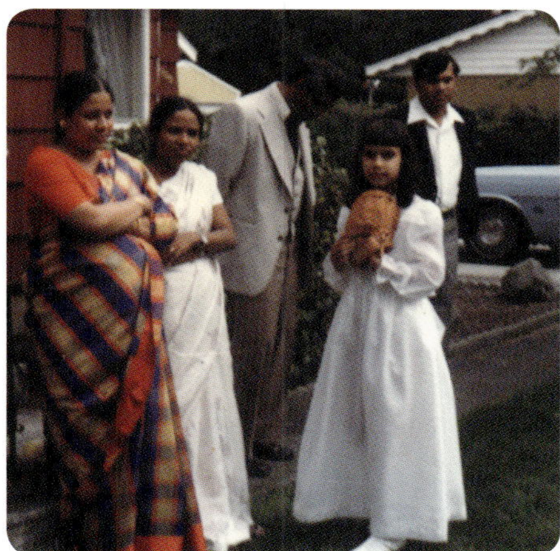

indigenous, Portuguese, and Dutch heritage that existed throughout parts of India and Burma for over five hundred years. I learned later in life of her double-refugee experience, first as a child escaping from Burma to India during World War II, and then leaving Burma again after the military coup there in 1962 to come to the States. She is a survivor of formidable strength with whom I have often clashed, inadvertently when I was younger, and with resignation as an adult. I know I have inherited a thin rod of her iron will. I resist it, longing for the tragic poet in me to triumph sometimes, but it is there, pulling me vertical more often than not.

Mom interpreted my childhood discomfort with people questioning my "look" as insecurity, and pointed out that when people asked her where she was from, she simply answered the question. I could never adequately convey to her that it was different for me; I was not *from* anywhere else. She spoke very little about her own childhood or culture, preferring to assimilate into her new homeland, which didn't give me much to draw on to connect some parts of what I looked like to who she was. I began to use terms like "mixed" or "half-breed," to explain an identity I neither questioned nor fully understood.

My father was a little more aware of issues of race and social class in America. An only child born into an Irish American family in Iowa (some of the Dunns shifted from desperate to wealthy to desperate within three generations), he was shuffled between relatives and boarding schools for his first ten years. During the Depression, his father coped by drinking. His mother, an immigrant from Ireland, worked as a nurse hundreds of miles away to try and earn enough money to save their farm. Like my mother, he too had a tough beginning to life.

My parents met at a Catholic mixer in Seattle and, after a brief courtship, married in 1966 (when anti-miscegenation laws still existed in thirteen states, though Washington was not one of them). With a broad circle of friends, they formed a multi-generational,

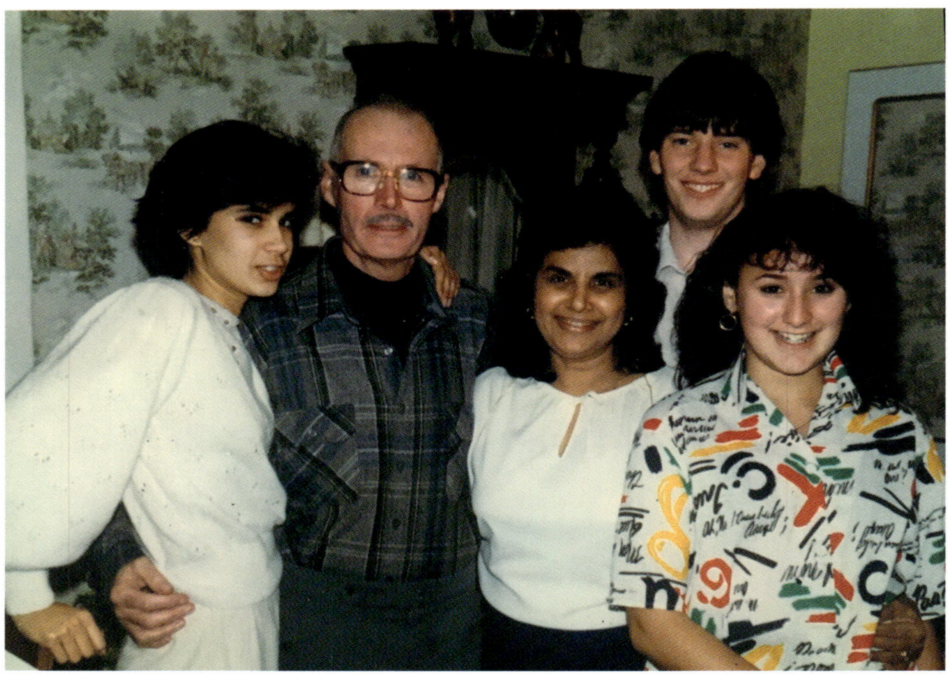

multi-ethnic bubble for my siblings and me to reside within and reinforced in us those most
American of values: work hard, take pride in what you do, invest in your communities,
and stand up for what is right. Dad also kept his own version of "My Creed" by Dean
Alfange (the essence of which is sometimes attributed to Thomas Paine) on his desk. It
begins with words I have long held close: "I do not choose to be a common man. It is my
right to be uncommon." Independence—financially, in thought, and in spirit—was also a
value they instilled and nurtured in all three of us.

Music was important in our household, prioritized after "God" and "Family,"
and equal to "Education." My sister took up the violin, and I followed suit. My brother
played piano. Dad took us to Ted Brown's in Tacoma to choose whatever sheet music
we wanted, then we signed an agreement to perform it within a set period of time. I can
only imagine how hard my parents worked to keep straight faces as we enthusiastically
performed Michael Jackson's "Billie Jean" as a piano and two-violin trio. In high school
I switched to singing in a capella and jazz choirs. Though I was not naturally gifted as a
vocalist, I understood phrasing from my years playing a stringed instrument and appreciated what lyrics could add to musical expression.

My father reiterated throughout our childhood that we could be anything we wanted
if we were willing to work hard. When I asked why I could not be a Catholic priest, he
paused for a moment, asked why I didn't want to be a nun (I pointed out they had duller
outfits), then made an appointment with Father Jack, our local priest, to explore the matter

    St. Patrick's Day, and our last family photograph with Dad, March 17, 1987

further. Poor Father Jack had to field my questions and counterpoints, so Dad could continue to reassure me that indeed, anything was possible.

The twenty cars in various states of decline awaiting my father's hobby of restoration all held his optimism. While my siblings contemplated the five to six functioning vehicles that they might one day drive, at nine years old I asked for one of the strangest dinosaurs in the barn, a 1950 Studebaker. It was a choice my father tried to talk me out of, pointing to options he considered stylish, or at least likely to start, but I was unmoved, and he finally gave in.

I liked misfits and things that were a little bit broken. Sometimes it was about the joy of seeing its potential. But often, as with the Studebaker, I offered my love and acceptance to an object I feared might not receive it otherwise. My favorite apple tree was the one that never produced edible fruit. I named one of my beloved stuffed animals "Mr. Nobody." It turns out my choice of car, however, was prescient. It was designed by the Swiss American provocateur of the mid-twentieth century, Raymond Loewy, so while it is odd, its design was at least *intentional*. We got it started after only three weeks of effort, though its restoration ultimately took me another two decades.

When my father died of cancer in 1987, I was fourteen—old enough to have had many significant interactions with him, yet still young and naïve enough to be in denial of death as a possible result of his nine months of treatment and decline. Without him physically present, I cultivated memories and metaphysical connections. Though I did not have many photographs of him, his letters to me became time travel devices—he held a pen

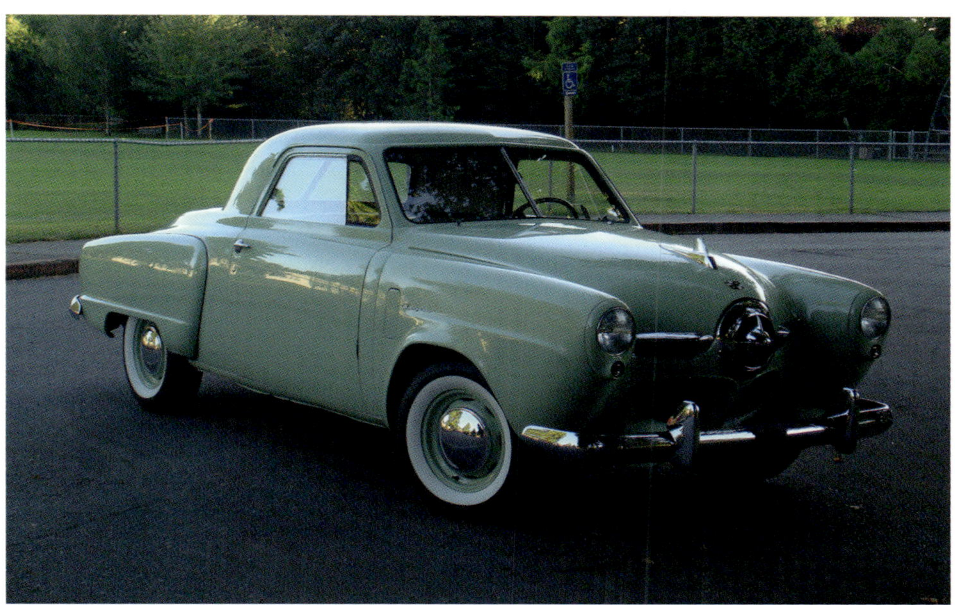

My 1950 Studebaker after restoration, Seattle, 2008

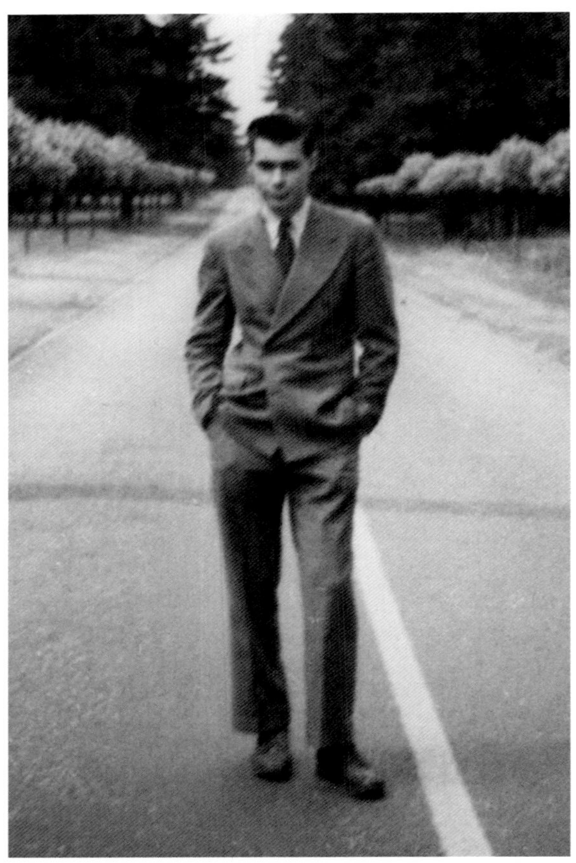

My father, Richard J. Dunn, likely Lakewood, Washington, photographer and date unknown

Location portrait of me in my father's tuxedo jacket, Tacoma, Washington, 1990 or 1991, by photographer Robert Quick

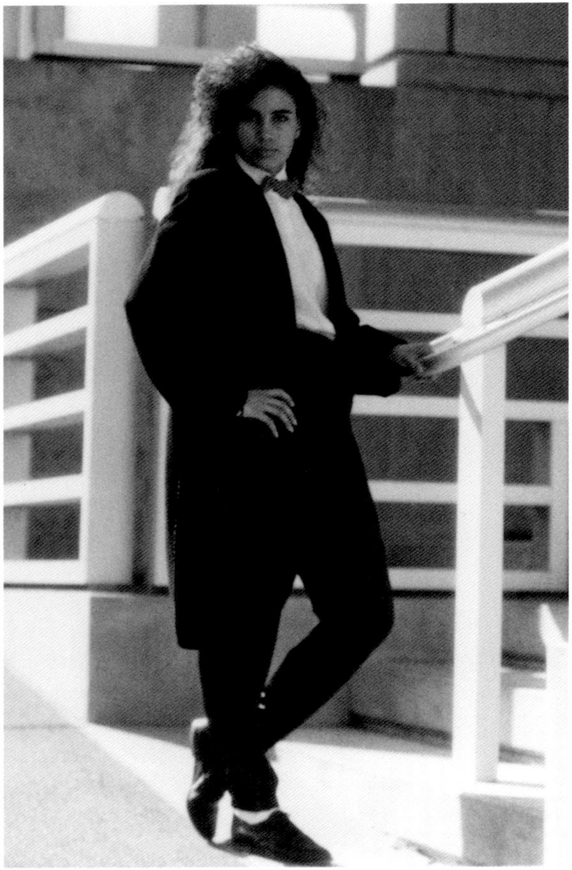

to *this* paper and wrote *these* words, so when I hold those letters I am entering that past, when he was present. His trace is there.

My conscious desire to make physical contact with what marks he had left on the planet made space for what I later learned to be an element of indexicality in photography. In simple terms, indexicality posits that the moment of time when a shutter opens and closes, including the environment and whatever is in it, leaves a trace in the "writing" of that light onto the film emulsion. It is suspending time and everything within that moment, rather than documenting or replicating it. This term has been and will continue to be debated by theorists and academics, particularly as the materiality of the medium has changed from its chemical and physical origins. It is an interpretation I love in the photographs I live with, and fear in the photographs taken of me. Once I absorbed the meaning of the indexical in photography, I became much more sensitive to who was capturing and holding my energy in that manner.

From my earliest years of nightmare management, poetry emerged as an essential form of expression, and I turned to it again in navigating the loss of my dad. When I took my first journalism class in junior high school, I assumed my interests in creative writing would expand into reportage. Instead, I became enamored with the physicality of bringing words and images to the printed page.

Using an Apple IIe as a glorified typewriter, I counted characters to determine the number of words that could fit in the space allocated in the layout, and marked up type specifications on the pages feeding out of the dot-matrix printer. We received waxed galleys for paste up from the local high school's graphics department. Although I don't recall photography being included in the art curriculum, journalism students were taught to develop film and print photographs to scale for designed layouts. That was my first experience in a darkroom, watching an image appear from a blank sheet of paper gently floating in the "soup." I loved all of it.

My junior-high yearbook advisor Jeanne Anderson put in a good word for me at Puyallup High School, and I was able to join the yearbook staff early, during my sophomore year. Through my chemistry teacher, Scott Brittain, who was also interested in computer sciences, I was introduced to a largely unused lab of Macintosh computers. I sometimes served as his assistant when he taught introductory courses to faculty in the evenings, and through that gained familiarity with what could be done through those chunky gray boxes.

From attendance at a summer yearbook camp in 1990 put on by Jostens—one of the largest yearbook printers in the United States—I learned about the burgeoning field of "desktop publishing." I did not know then that the term was coined by the Seattle-based founders of Aldus Corporation—named after one of my college heroes, sixteenth-century publisher Aldus Manutius—whose PageMaker software would soon take over my life.

Longtime English teacher and yearbook advisor June Colman was supportive of a dramatic leap forward in how we produced the yearbook, and the new educational outcomes it offered. She was also transparent in noting that she was unlikely to master the technology necessary to do so. She had quietly maintained a rainy-day fund for the yearbook (not an easy feat in a public school) and was prepared to empty most of it to purchase two computers and a laser printer—provided I, a junior in high school, would commit to learning the software, and teaching it to the class the following year.

I still can't quite believe the risk she took on this venture. Over the summer we completely restructured the yearbook class, and to the teams of writers and photographers we added a layout production team, which Mr. Brittain agreed to advise using the Macintosh lab. A few of us had two class periods per semester to navigate content creation, oversee workflow, and teach layout and print production. It was a wild ride between the summer of 1990 and 1991, but we delivered a 232-page yearbook entirely laid out in PageMaker, on time and on budget.

I almost didn't graduate from high school, though, because in doubling up on additional yearbook and music classes I'd neglected to fulfill a state-required vocational course. When the embarrassed school counselor discovered this oversight during my final semester of senior year, and suggested I drop one of my choir classes to take typing, I rallied previous and current teachers to assist with a solution. With their support, as well as my mother's, I petitioned the state of Washington to consider my four consecutive years of yearbook journalism courses as career skill building within creative fields.

To that high-stakes battle, I added one of personal significance. Ours was a sports-focused community with many decades of state-ranked champions. The letterman's jacket was the visible marker of athletic achievement, and a talisman of the quintessential American high schooler. Though I was clumsy, weak, and demonstrated no outstanding physical ability, I wanted a letterman's jacket. The only option readily available to girls like me was to date a guy who had one. I found this unacceptable (and also unlikely). I think it was my brother who pointed out that marching band members who traveled with the sports teams were eligible to receive athletic letters, though members of the school's debate team were not. I competed in debate tournaments, so I asked the school's administration to change this policy, and award letters for non-athletic competitive activities.

When it came right down to it, jocks were cool and nerds (outside of band nerds) were not, and never the twain would meet under the hallowed symbol of the letterman's jacket. The end compromise was "separate, but equal": athletic letters remained the same, and the new activities letters were approved—in a different color. So there could be *no confusion*. Even though it took me up to the last days of my senior year in 1991 to secure the deal, I did, and my brother made good on his promise to pay for my jacket. I still love wearing it. A lifetime later, I can see that obtaining a jacket of my own was one way of connecting to systems that tended to prioritize things that some of us were not. I wanted our differences to be valued, not for the purposes of standing out, but so we, too, could fit in.

Puyallup had its share of racism and homophobia. Yet, in my experience at least, locals maintained an "us" and "them" mentality. A student I'd grown up with who made offensive racial comments about someone he didn't know would pummel any outsider who dared make those same kinds of comments about me. As the youngest of three, I

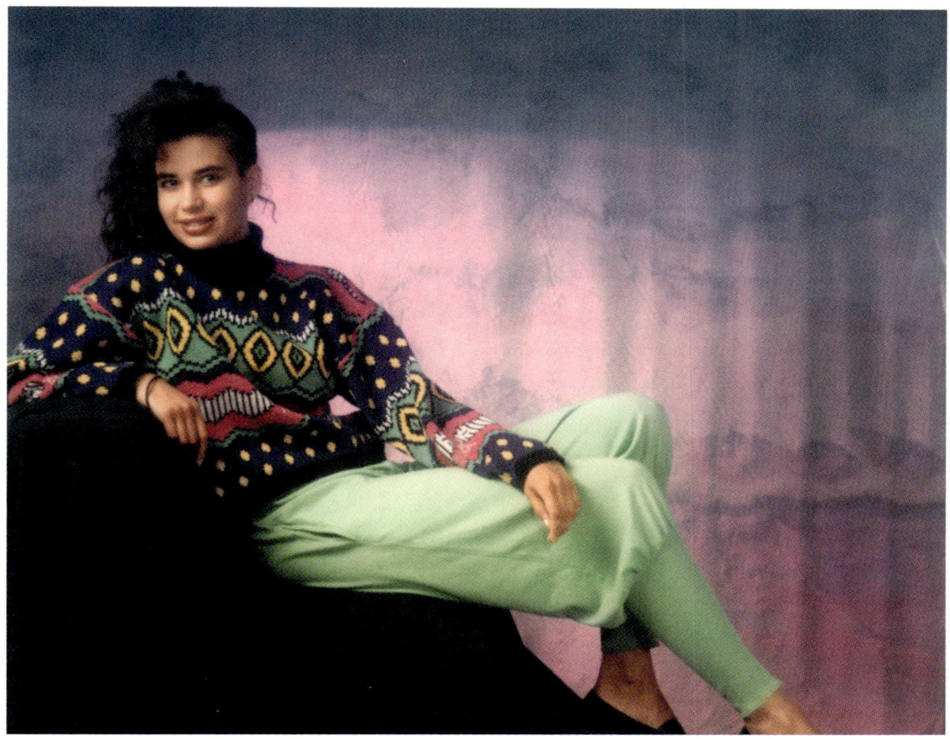

also had the advantage of popular siblings. I might be weird, but I was the little sister of Dunns who were normal, and that bought some tolerance in a small town.

Like a letterman's jacket, senior pictures were a rite of passage I wanted to take part in. It was an expense my mother found extravagant, and neither of my siblings had them done. I have no idea where I met photographer Robert Quick, but I agreed to be a student ambassador for his studio (in the rival town of Auburn; there were two studios in Puyallup who held the lion's share of the local business), resulting in a portfolio of images to show others the range of studio and exterior environments he worked within, and a stack of the all-important wallet pictures to trade with my friends. While I suppose this was my introduction to one professional aspect of photography, I did not then—and do not now—connect it to the personal expressions of the medium I later encountered.

Sometime after I'd taken a practice test to determine my collegiate worthiness, a promotional brochure arrived from Bard College, located in the quaint-sounding hamlet of Annandale-on-Hudson, New York. It contained large photographs of people sitting under trees, and reading. Bard's tagline then, "a place to think," said everything I needed to know. My mother was a little unsure. Then I was awarded an unusual scholarship that made all costs to attend Bard the same as we would have paid at the only other school I applied to, an in-state university in Washington. It also included a plane ticket home annually. Though I had never been to the region, or the college, I headed east.

One of my favorite 1980s outfits, Auburn, Washington, 1990 or 1991, by Robert Quick 19

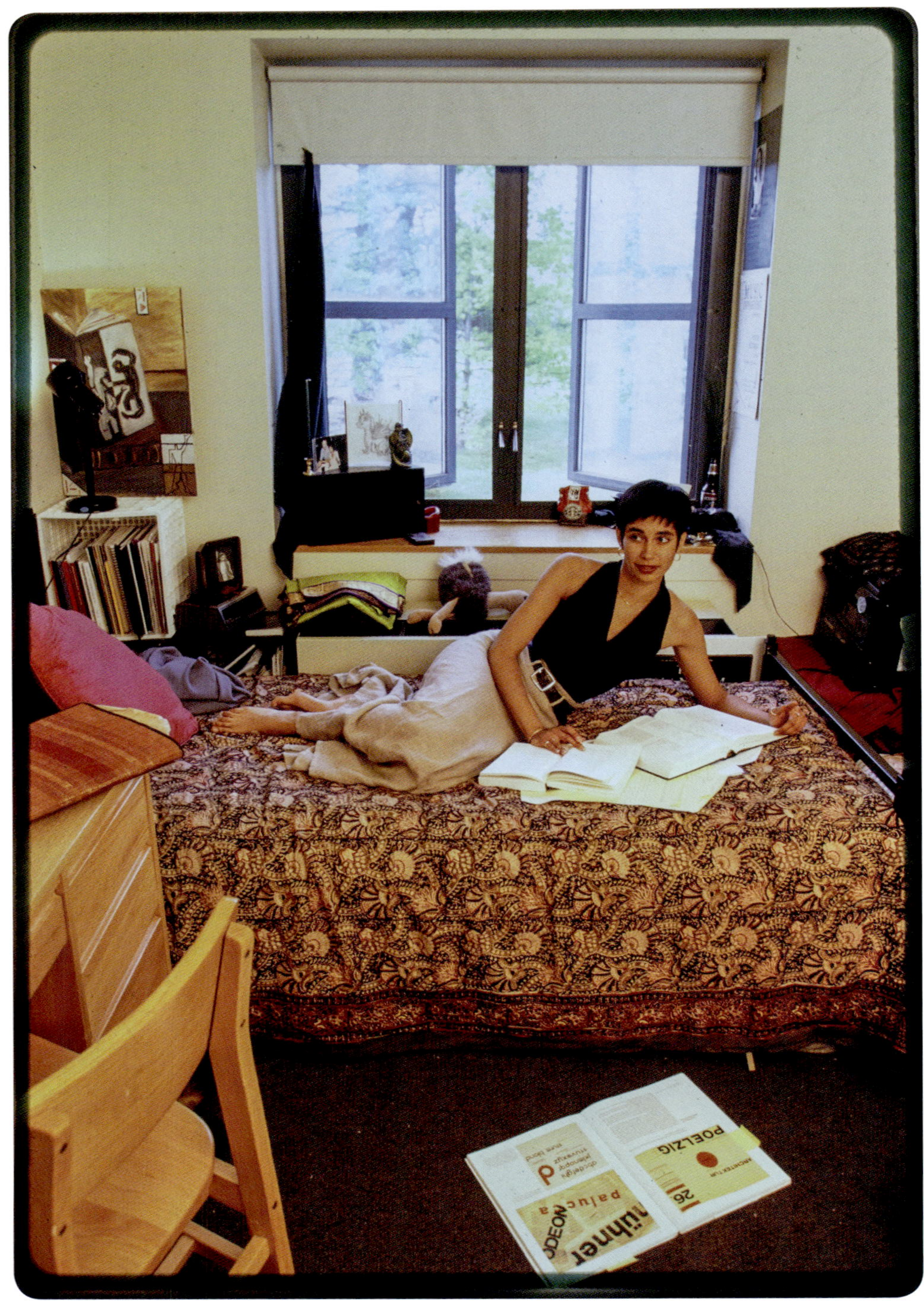

Bard's campus in the Hudson Valley is about ninety miles north of New York City. My first dorm, an architectural experiment on stilts, was designed for twelve students, but in August of 1991, when I moved into it, housed twenty-four. Officially known as the Ravines, the students called them the "Treehouses," and they swayed gently from loud music, sex, laughter, and pretty much any other movement occurring within them.

Nearly everyone at school seemed cooler, more experienced, and more philosophical than I was. Considered smart in high school, I was stunned into silence more than once as we discussed texts I struggled through, which classmates, yawning, said they'd read years earlier. Foreign students from the Indian subcontinent eyed me with friendly confusion; emerging activists of color, and other culturally based student factions greeted me in coded words or altogether different languages. I couldn't respond—most of the time I didn't even understand what they were referencing. Pretty soon "Where are you *really* from?" shifted once again to *"What are you?"*

My social consciousness, birthed at home, definitely matured in college. The simple task of choosing where to sit and eat in the cafeteria's colloquial sections of "Africa," "Europe," and "The Paranoids" (the student smoking section) carried consequences. Where were you intruding? Who were you avoiding? Where were you welcome? I settled into sitting in a zone of Europe closest to Africa, and accepted invitations to join people in other areas when they were offered. The array of student clubs that existed or could be formed for every imaginable fan base, from classics to debate to S&M, pushed me daily to ask myself who I was, and what I stood for. I rarely had an answer.

With professor Drew Keller (who called me "the voice of the church," as I often had my Bible in his class for the religion course following) I discussed the *Lysistrata*, Ibsen, and the pain of watching a loved one waste away—my father from cancer, his uncle from AIDS.

With Terry Dewsnap, Irish verse, and the concept of "both/and" inherent in Irish language and culture. With Fernando González de León, why history was in his mind the freest of all liberal arts. Nancy Leonard dissected Shakespeare's sonnets. Physics professor Peter Skiff taught Light & Color, also known as "science for lit majors." I first took for credit, and then audited, both classes the acclaimed Nigerian author Chinua Achebe taught on modern African fiction, just to spend more time listening to his spare and lucid observations on literature and life.

Sunday services at the school's exquisitely restored Chapel of the Holy Innocents (Bard was once St. Stephen's College, an Episcopalian seminary) were grounding, though for many weeks running it was just Bruce Chilton, the chaplain and religion professor, and me. At one point he said, "Would you like me to Catholicize it up? I don't mind since it's just the two of us." An expanded spiritual identity emerged through adapting familiar rituals and implementing new ones. Informed by friends and dormmates raised in Islam, Judaism, Siddha Yoga, Buddhism, and other philosophies, I began to form the tenets of my own unorthodox belief system. Spiritual, rooted in the tradition with which I was raised, yet embracing the similarities or improvements I found in other practices. My later devotion to photography was partially motivated by the peace I found working on photographic books that were both socially conscious and embodied transcendence.

My churchy affiliations at Bard created some suspicion for my fellow Gen X students (particularly those who'd attended Catholic school), so that, combined with the fact that I rarely consumed alcohol and studiously avoided all other available substances, made social engagement in a very uninhibited environment challenging. Part of my impetus in starting a yearbook at Bard was to participate in collaboration that was familiar when so much else seemed impenetrable.

Fifteen or twenty students and I navigated the logistics of setting up a yearbook—working with the dean of students to secure permissions and funding, organizing portrait sessions for students willing to be pictured in the book (not many), and soliciting or creating text and artwork that reflected, in our minds, the authentic student experience. We had discovered in the school library intermittent editions of a student annual throughout Bard's 125-year history, and decided to use the same name, the *Sketchbook*, to align ourselves. I was ultimately engaged in the production of two volumes.

During my second semester at school, I was typesetting a book for Bruce Chilton (who from chaplain and professor became my spiritual and academic guide) when he suggested that I talk to "the women in publications." Bard produced beautiful posters, journals, and an alumni magazine, and he thought I could learn more about design in a hands-on manner there, since it was not formally a part of the college's curriculum.

After numerous attempts to get in the door, I was eventually accepted on a "trial basis." My position was unlikely to continue when their steady work-study student, Hugh Garvey (who went on to a career with the *Village Voice*) returned to campus after the school holidays. But my willingness to work for free and my improving skill set in the latest

Issues of Bard College's alumni magazine *Annandale*. Top: Vol. 132/1, Dec. 1992. Cover photograph by William Wegman. Bottom: Vol. 133/3, May 1994. Cover photograph by Cindy Sherman.

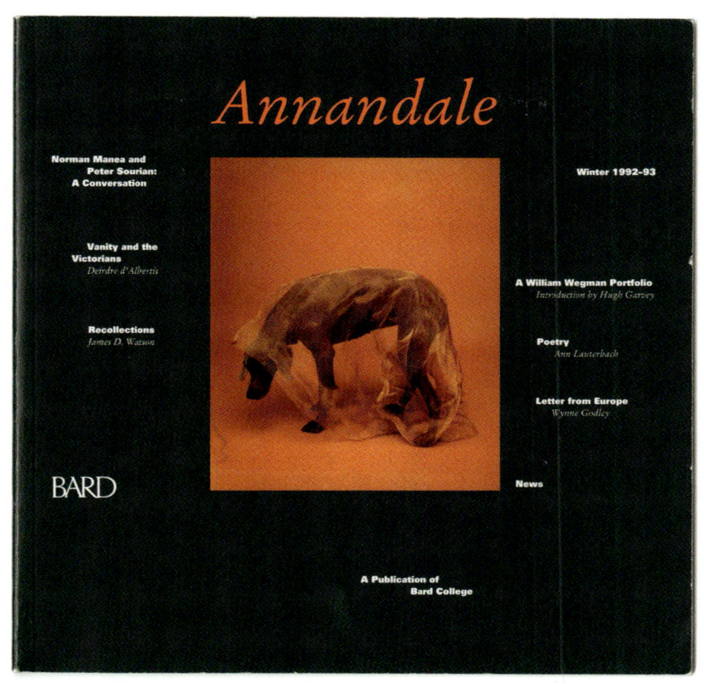

Annandale

Norman Manea and
Peter Sourian:
A Conversation

Winter 1992–93

Vanity and the
Victorians
Deirdre d'Albertis

A William Wegman Portfolio
Introduction by Hugh Garvey

Recollections
James D. Watson

Poetry
Ann Lauterbach

Letter from Europe
Wynne Godley

BARD

News

A Publication of
Bard College

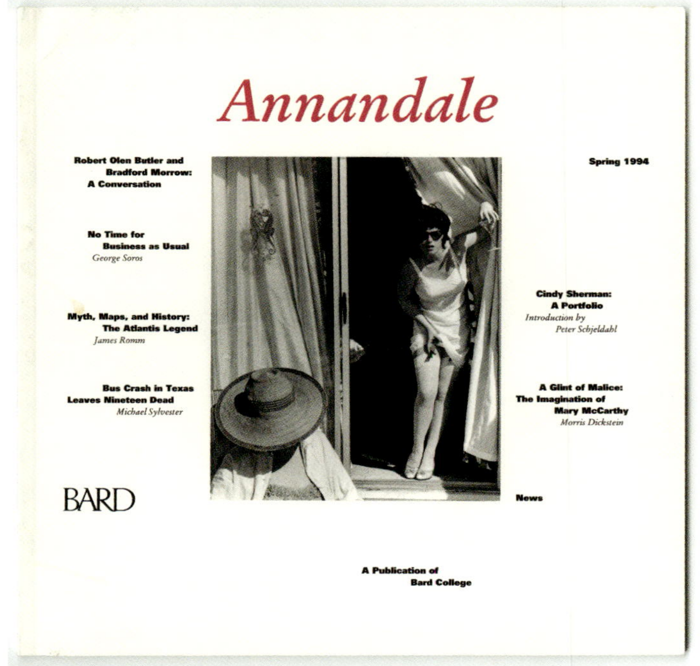

Annandale

Robert Olen Butler and
Bradford Morrow:
A Conversation

Spring 1994

No Time for
Business as Usual
George Soros

Myth, Maps, and History:
The Atlantis Legend
James Romm

Cindy Sherman:
A Portfolio
Introduction by
Peter Schjeldahl

Bus Crash in Texas
Leaves Nineteen Dead
Michael Sylvester

A Glint of Malice:
The Imagination of
Mary McCarthy
Morris Dickstein

BARD

News

A Publication of
Bard College

layout software, QuarkXPress, eventually secured me a consistent shift in the bagel-and-coffee-fetching intern rotation.

During my delivery of the requisite breakfast fuel one morning, I walked in on a cover discussion for a forthcoming issue of the alumni magazine. Questions were posed in response to the prototype hanging on the wall: should the title of the magazine be brighter, the same tonality, or darker than the hues within the cover photograph by William Wegman (p. 23)?

Is the title of the magazine more important, or the photograph on its cover? Should they be given equal visual weight? While I don't recall the standpoints exactly, my guess is the director of publications, Ginger Shore, was calling for the photograph to dominate, while art director Elena Erber and designer Juliet Bell were advocating for equal balance or giving prominence to the title. That this single point was debated for what felt like eternity, but was likely an hour, riveted me. I didn't know what *this* was called, but I knew I wanted to be a part of it.

My introduction to art photography began there, in Bard's Publications Office. Wegman, Wynn Bullock, Cindy Sherman, Thomas Struth, and others were featured in any and every print environment, though as far as I am aware most had no association to the college. Bard's photography professors Larry Fink and Stephen Shore, photography legend and part-time Hudson Valley local Charles Harbutt (see p. 101), and numerous photographers from New York City (including Don Hamerman, p. 20) were also pulled in to photograph from time to time.

Ginger's integration of art photography to the overall presentation of the college in those years stands out now as a decision that elevated both the institution and the art form. Bard's materials went to alumni, donors, and parents of prospective students, an audience engaged in culture. I'd chosen to study literature at Bard primarily because of a photograph in its brochure. How many bright young minds chose to study photography under Ginger's husband, Stephen Shore, subconsciously inspired by a portfolio of images she published? How many people, like me, saw photography as art, not solely a form of commercial illustration, because Ginger and Elena chose to present it as such to a broad audience?

Through working in the office while continuing classes toward my literature major, I deepened my awareness of the marriage of content and form. An awakening that spaces were intentionally designed, that typefaces, margins, and paper surfaces were chosen to elicit specific responses, was electrifying. I had a voracious appetite for this new sphere, which was not well received by some of my literature professors.

I thought about transferring to a school where I could pursue studies in graphic design. Those programs, however, required portfolios of drawing and painting, skills I did not possess. When I met with faculty at the University of Washington on a visit home, they told me I would essentially have to start over, given that they were on a quarter system, and Bard was on semesters. Most of the credits from my first year would not transfer, even *if* I was accepted to study design, which was unlikely without a portfolio. They suggested I consider the program at Seattle Central Community College as a supplement once I completed my undergraduate degree; that school had a high percentage of job placement in the industry. The prospect of spending five to six years completing my undergraduate degree, even if I could muster the family or government financial support for it, was not appealing.

Ginger encouraged me to stay the course at Bard, and develop good research skills so I would have an array of associations to draw upon for design concepts. All four women in the office—Ginger and Elena, along with Juliet and editor Kate Norment—went from mentors and colleagues to de facto faculty. They were patient with me as I peppered them with questions going about my mundane tasks that, when I completed them well, led to new opportunities within the office.

Even when Kate knew answers to editorial questions off the top of her head (such as why 'cello included an apostrophe) she would sometimes say, "Well, let's look it up," demonstrating how, and why, resources like the *Chicago Manual of Style* were important tools. In assisting Elena or Juliet on changes to pieces they were designing, I observed both the conceptual and technical considerations of how various projects were constructed. I was given some smaller projects—a poster here, a program flyer there—to tackle on my own. As I implemented hundreds of Kate's type corrections to the voluminous course catalog, I found what became my ticket to graduate school—an obscure paragraph about a self-created, 3–2 "Professional Option," resulting in both an undergraduate and graduate degree in five years.

To qualify for the "Professional Option," and begin graduate school early, I had to identify a field of interest that I could not formally study through Bard's liberal arts curriculum and obtain acceptance into a graduate program in that field. The description was literally one paragraph, with no examples, and no further information. I began researching programs related to design or publications that might be receptive to this arrangement. After sending inquiry letters to fifteen schools in the spring semester of my sophomore year, I heard back from nearly all of them saying no, I could not apply to their graduate program without having first earned an undergraduate degree.

But two schools were willing to talk: the Gallatin division of New York University, itself an experimental "choose your own adventure" model of graduate school, and the MS in Publishing program at Pace University. Both schools agreed to receive an application and negotiate possibilities if I was accepted. I then had to get Bard on board, and *no one* at Bard, except my allies in publications, seemed enthusiastic. Dean Stuart Levine searched for any background information on this "Professional Option," and could find no record that it had ever been used. The only equivalent was the existing 3-2 program in physics and engineering between Bard and Columbia University.

The dean kicked the decision down to Peter Sourian, the chair of Bard's Languages and Literature division where I was pursuing "moderation," a formal review whereby students are accepted (or not) into a major. I hadn't studied with Peter but knew him from his occasional visits to the publications office. By some stroke of luck, Peter quickly approved the "Professional Option" as my course of action. Of course I still had to be accepted into a graduate program. It also meant that, if I *did* get in, I would not be completing a year-long senior project, one of the hallmarks of a Bard degree.

One of the professors on my moderation board was not pleased that a decision had been made prior to my acceptance as a candidate in the literature program. Since he could not reverse it, he eviscerated the paper I presented, questioned my serious love of language, and derided my "capitulation" to commercial interests of publishing and design. (I later learned he'd worked briefly as an editor at Penguin Books. Apparently that wasn't a good fit for him.) In the end, though, I passed the board and was accepted as a literature major, with a heavy elective dose of art history. In some ways the next year was my most enjoyable at college. For a brief period, I experienced Bard as what it originally promised to be—a place to think.

The "publications women" weighed in on what classes would further my development as a designer, including history of photography, basic painting, and a tutorial on the origins of Italian typography. There were also seminars on the Bauhaus and the rise of modernism from a visual perspective, a movement I had previously studied through its impact on literature, philosophy, and history. In between typesetting and compositions, there were softball games, dinners, office parties (the most memorable was when we filled the watercooler with vodka without telling anyone), and my absorption of communications styles from the two very different personalities of Ginger and Elena.

Ginger, her cigarette hovering perilously close to whatever design ideas I was presenting, only ever offered one of two succinct responses: "It looks good," or "It looks like shit." Elena would then explain to me why what I'd created had possibly provoked the latter reaction, and how I could change it. Ginger doesn't like this kind of cropping—it turns the photograph into an illustration. Ginger doesn't like type running over the image that way. That typeface is too trendy. The layout is trying too hard; I'm *seeing* the design. It was a fortuitous beginning. Elena was a great designer and art director, and a patient and collaborative mentor who encouraged my continuation when I felt down or incapable of addressing the visual problem at hand. Ginger's predilection for choosing powerful photographs and designing to their maximum strength and visibility was similar to what Michael Hoffman, executive director at Aperture Foundation, would desire when I encountered him a few years down the road.

Bard's publications staff involved me in photo shoots, press checks, and every imaginable aspect of the editorial, design, and printing process—I absorbed so much from them. Through their conversations with each other and with me, I also learned about the importance of well-made shoes, how basic black attire transitioned easily from professional to social settings, the essential elegance of pearls, and the refreshing flavors of sushi (complemented by the gentle sting of wasabi, or in my case the overpowering headrush as I experienced it for the first time over lunch with them, while they all laughed).

Everything I'd learned at Bard came to fruition through my involvement with a legendary student-initiated party, the Ménage à Trois. Co-founded by Noah Colman and my friend Ephen Glenn Colter in 1991 to foster AIDS awareness and promote safer sex practices, each iteration of the Ménage had extravagantly exceeded the preceding one.

From drag competitions to an S&M chamber, screenings of student-produced porn films and a pitch-black, padded room that was "only for touching," the student organizers celebrated sensual stimulation in every manner they could think of, while promoting the use of condoms and other safety measures to minimize sexually-transmitted illnesses. The few Ménages I had attended I found a little terrifying. Yet the tenor of open discourse on the campus was such that I could ask my dormmate, who was part of the S&M club, what he found pleasing in experiencing pain and he told me, demystifying and humanizing practices I could not otherwise relate to. Heated discussions were common among students, but people listened to one another, and usually remained friendly, even when conversations concluded with parties agreeing to disagree.

Spring 1994, the end of my junior year and my final semester on campus, marked the fifth Ménage. Multiple student groups joined forces to have a series of events that culminated in the party itself, and Ephen asked me to develop a graphics campaign. Though many of the students involved saw me as far too straight and conservative to accurately convey the general flavor and feeling of the party, we all had to withhold judgment, and let our guards down a little. We drew in larger and broader audiences to many of the ancillary activities through the elegant posters and invitations distributed, while t-shirts and signage for the main event were more edgy and in keeping with its energy. It was a formative experience and one I later drew upon as I tumbled into the fullness of humanity that comprised the New York City art world.

I was accepted into both graduate programs that had been willing to receive my applications; I chose the MS in Publishing program at Pace University. None of the arrangements of the "Professional Option" had been formally noted in my student records, so I pleaded for a letter from Bard's president, Leon Botstein, indicating that I would actually receive my diploma from Bard after completing my first year of graduate school.

I had encountered Leon with some frequency—requesting funds to start the yearbook, pushing, with other students, for greater ethnic diversity in curriculum and faculty, and then negotiating implementation of the "Professional Option" (which was later removed from the catalog). Student access to him reinforced our assumption that we had the right to be heard, and that leaders had a responsibility to listen. Leon provided the letter I requested.

Decades later, I still pay attention to the culture of Bard College, to support it and also to question whether it is living up to its stated ideals. That is Bard's legacy in many of its alumni; it taught us to excel, and it taught us to participate as citizens of our culture, leading change when necessary. I feel a responsibility to remind the college of the best it can be, because when it mattered, the institution, and its president, did that for me.

In early September 1994, Elena Erber, who had absorbed me into her family over the two years I'd worked with her, drove me from Bard's campus to New York City. After moving my belongings into yet another dorm room, the two of us explored the neighborhoods of lower Manhattan where the downtown campus of Pace is located, and pored over subway maps to determine the best commute to my classes in midtown. After waving goodbye to Elena that evening, I returned to my new home quietly singing "New York, New York" to the large rats on the otherwise empty blocks of Fulton Street.

"God is in the details." Modernist architect Mies van der Rohe's quote and my correct attribution of it was my introduction to Stevan A. Baron—one of my first professors in the MS in Publishing program at Pace University. Baron was responsible for book manufacturing for a few publishers, including the photography-focused Aperture Foundation. He had printed Bard professors Stephen Shore and Larry Fink's first books; the fact that I knew them, and he knew them, seemed to me a fortuitous connection. New York City was a lot to absorb at first, and I clung to any familiarities I could find. I was *that* student in the book class with Baron, sitting at the front of the room, lingering after to ask just one more question while my classmates, ready for Italian food and a bottle of wine on a Friday night, impatiently waited for me.

Pace's masters program, the first of its kind in the United States, explored all aspects of publishing, from the editorial development of projects through contracts and accounting. About a third of my fellow students were already in the industry, pursuing their masters degrees to move more quickly up the long ladder to senior positions, or pivot into different departments. The presence of working professionals in the classroom, in addition to those teaching us, fostered a rich exchange of questions and answers, immersing students new to the field in both theory and on-the-job practicalities. It was a different kind of dialogue from what I'd experienced at Bard. I found courses like accounting tedious, yet some of the most mundane business information I gained through Pace's publishing program has ended up being useful in nearly every role I've occupied.

Nothing was boring about Steve Baron's course on book production. We had field trips to the Metropolitan Museum of Art, and to the basement locations of offset printers. He gave us seemingly simple assignments (study your shadow at three different times of day; develop a tactile résumé) to heighten our sensory awareness. He tore apart a hardcover book to show us how each element of its manufacturing was relevant to the structural end result.

I became anxious about all my outstanding questions for him as the semester drew to a close. Nearly all the faculty in the program were adjunct, so our access was generally limited to class time. At the end of our last session, Baron (I struggled at Bard and at Pace with calling professors by their first names, so used their surnames instead) called me forward and said, "I know you have more questions. I'm going to make you a deal. Put together a list of them, and I will take you to lunch to answer as many as I can. And then, just so you're clear, that will be that." It was both generous and direct.

I knew that I ultimately had to deliver my master's thesis both to Pace and to Bard. Just one advisor managed all the thesis students in Pace's publishing program, and I sensed that he did not have the time nor the specific expertise I needed to guide my analysis. When I asked him if I could have a second advisor to work with me on content before he evaluated my paper for form, he shrugged and said "sure." My long list of questions for Baron had just narrowed.

Baron and I met for lunch at the Morgan Library's café, an elegant and quiet spot he had chosen near his office. After we ordered, he sort of sighed and said, "Let's hear your questions." When I said I had only one, he raised an eyebrow. Then I asked if he would work with me for the next year on my thesis. He sighed again, then laughed, and said he would have to think about the time commitment. When he wrote me to say that he would do it, but that I would have to be prepared to work, I knew I'd made the right choice. Before he left on multi-week press checks he'd ask for whatever I'd written. His typed notes were sometimes as long as the chapters I'd sent him. Lunch at the Morgan was the first of many meals we shared over the next fifteen years. Pasta dinners at his home with his wife, Caryl, kept me well-fed as I juggled full-time work with graduate school. Lunch at Live Bait, his favorite spot on 23rd Street, always included one refreshing beer.

Baron, or "Maestro," as I later called him, was my first point of contact with Minor White. Baron had extended his own education through a live-in internship with White in Rochester in 1963, and was deeply tied to the man, his work, his philosophies, and to the journal White co-founded that became a major entity and influence in the world of photography—*Aperture*. Baron's work with the company—which would expand to become one of the world's great publishers of photography books, in addition to its quarterly magazine—spanned forty years, from 1963 to 2003, when he formally retired. Over those four decades he was intermittently employed and inconsistently paid by Aperture, but quietly committed to its ideals and to its continuation. I had been exposed to some of Aperture's publications in the Bard bookstore and loved the wholeness of them—the photographs, but also the weight of the paper, the elegance of the typography, the timeless design. Learning more about the organization, first in Baron's book production class and then personally from him, drew me closer and closer to its flame.

He suggested I apply for Aperture's Work Scholar internship program while writing my thesis, though he acknowledged that it was unlikely to result in a job right away. I was already working full-time at an experience design firm as a receptionist, and had applied for a salaried administrative position there. When I was offered that position,

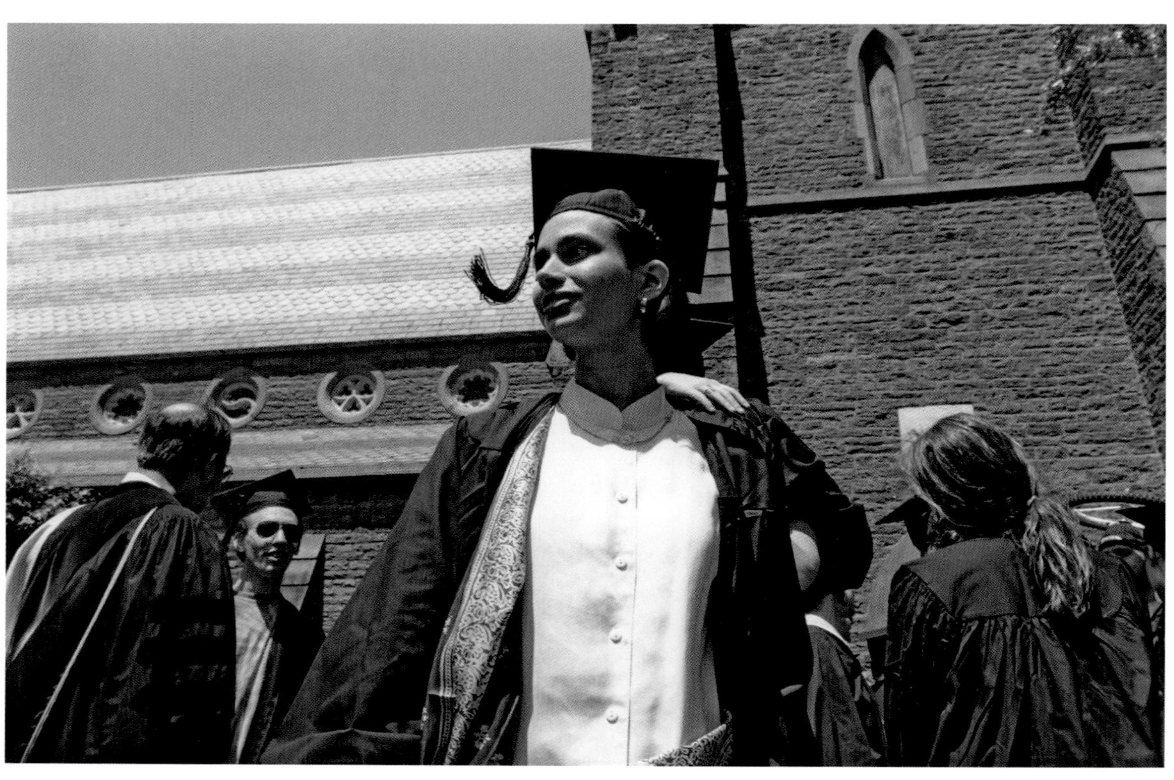

he advised me to take it and earn some money while I could, promising to keep me engaged with Aperture as opportunities arose.

I graduated from Bard College in May of 1995, after my first year in the publishing program (as Leon promised). Ginger Shore kindly sent me this photograph as a memento; it languished in a manila folder for nearly a decade. I had a vague memory that perhaps her husband Stephen had taken it. While at Bard, I knew Stephen Shore as a poetry-reciting, flower-bearing partner to his formidable wife. I had heard he was as daunting in the classroom as Ginger was in the office, but, not having studied photography, I never saw that side of him. My interactions with him while babysitting their son, or visiting with him briefly at social gatherings, were always pleasant. He was fairly quiet, and spoke more of baseball than photography. I was so unaware of his reputation as an artist that when I saw an image of his included in my history of photography textbook, I showed him, thinking perhaps he did not know. He thanked me, and said he'd seen it a few times before—a gentle response to my naïveté.

In 2004 I showed the photograph to Stephen, and asked if he remembered it. He confirmed he had taken it, then asked if I wanted him to sign the print. When I said, "Absolutely not! First, it will confuse the art historians, and second, I'll have to take it proper care of it," he laughed and pulled out a pen. It is now properly framed. In 2017 I saw his retrospective at the Museum of Modern Art, and the vast range of visual imagery he had created over his fifty-plus years of photography at that point. I realized that this photograph is in keeping with the formality of his seeing after all.

STEPHEN SHORE, **Graduation, Bard College, Annandale-on-Hudson, New York, 1995**. Gelatin silver RC print, signed later, 6 ¹/₁₆ x 9 ³/₈ inches. Unique. Gift of Ginger and Stephen Shore, 1995.

In 1996, two years after I met him (and for me three jobs later), Baron had finally obtained a Macintosh computer at Aperture, and began offering me small hourly projects—typesetting the captions for a book designer, placing images in a sales catalog—and those small tasks began to increase in number. From the fall of 1996 through spring of 1997, I worked the equivalent of two full-time jobs—on weekdays as an in-house designer for a trade magazine publisher in the audio industry, and then every night and on weekends for Aperture. The day job was paying the rent, but I took little joy in looking at what I'd created. The night job made me happy and every word I typeset took me back to the quiet satisfaction I'd felt counting characters and doing paste up in junior high school. I didn't know how to choose between them.

After six months of this schedule and a near-collapse, I sat down with Baron, in tears, to say I that I couldn't keep up with the work he was offering, but I didn't want to stop. Unbeknownst to me, he was already working on a solution and, in May 1997, I began my fourth full-time job—and the first of three phases at Aperture.

In the late 1940s, while Minor White was settling into San Francisco and his new teaching position in the country's first academic program in creative photography at the California School of Fine Arts, my father was earning a living through manual work: in a gold mine in Nevada, as a brakeman for the railroad, and driving a logging truck up and down the west coast. He and Minor would have both been a few years out of their military service post–World War II. My dad, in his early twenties, could have been on the streets of San Francisco passing by as Minor made this photograph of a laborer. I feel a little jolt of the universal current when I imagine even the possibility of their interaction. Minor had converted to Catholicism while in the service; they might have discussed that. Hearing Baron's stories from over a decade of his interactions with Minor, I was compelled by Minor's spiritual curiosity, and how that influenced not only his photographs, but also his creation of sequences—image groupings, sometimes with language intersections.

Sandblaster, however, is a universe unto itself. What equation might this hooded being solve in my subconscious? Heaven and hell, the destruction that often occurs in the act of creation—this photograph suspends me in those thoughts for a moment before I dive or ascend. I've woken up to it nearly every day over the last two years, and it presents a constant choice of attitude.

I was encouraged by my father to envision a life of fulfillment, and I have done so believing I was entitled to it. It's hard for me to process how much can change between some generations. My parents shared the traumas of war with their parents, a result of the proximities of World Wars I and II. My childhood was so different in comparison. Almost unrelatable. I feel the remnants of two generations of success and of struggle within me, an acceleration of energies I cannot entirely explain. But I see what results from it.

MINOR WHITE, *Sandblaster*, San Francisco, 1949 / 1971. Gelatin silver print, 8 1/4 x 10 1/16 in. from incomplete sets of *The Jupiter Portfolio (Twelve Photographs)*, planned edition of 100. Acquired through work trade, 2002.

Minor was nearly forty when he began teaching in San Francisco, and a few years later was editing the first issue of *Aperture*. My dad was forty when he took on a sales position in reference publishing that became the longest professional relationship of his life. I started my dream job at twenty-three.

Founded in San Francisco in 1952 as a small journal, *Aperture* had expanded over the years, and by the time I arrived in 1997, it was a foundation producing a quarterly magazine, limited-edition prints and portfolios, and ten to twenty books a year, all with the mission to "communicate with photographers, and creative people everywhere." Through this small nonprofit publishing house, books—a technology humanity had been utilizing for nearly a thousand years—were issuing forth from the evolving medium of photography, using mid-twentieth century practices of offset printing, which bumped up against the latest advancements of the desktop computer. It was a swirl of the past and future coming together in the present to create objects that, if we did our jobs well, would long outlive us. It was exhilarating. Baron told me early on that I would probably never make very much money, but I would have an interesting life. He was right on both counts.

Aperture's townhouse at 20 East 23rd Street, with Madison Avenue concluding at its orange door, was a long block east of the Flatiron Building. It was familiar territory

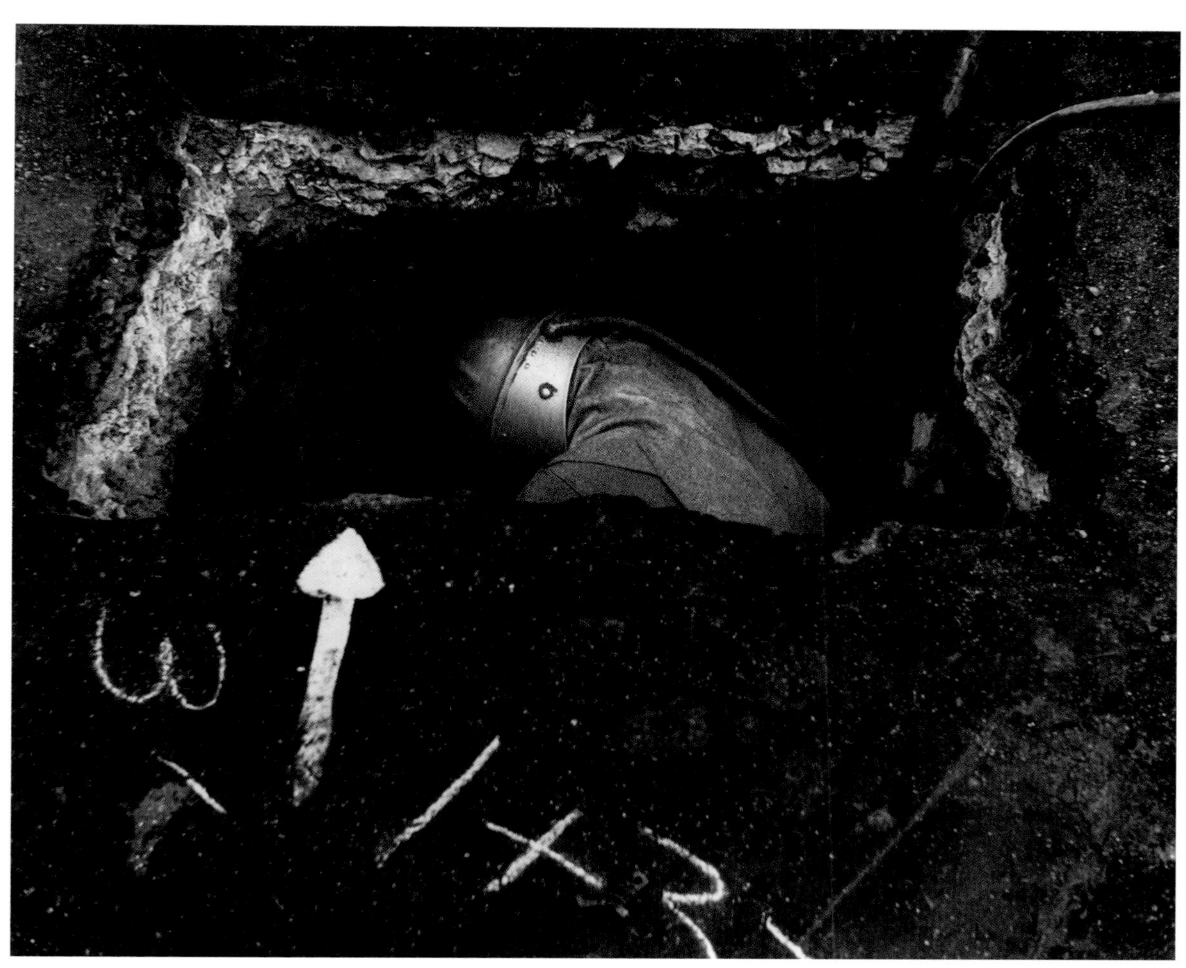

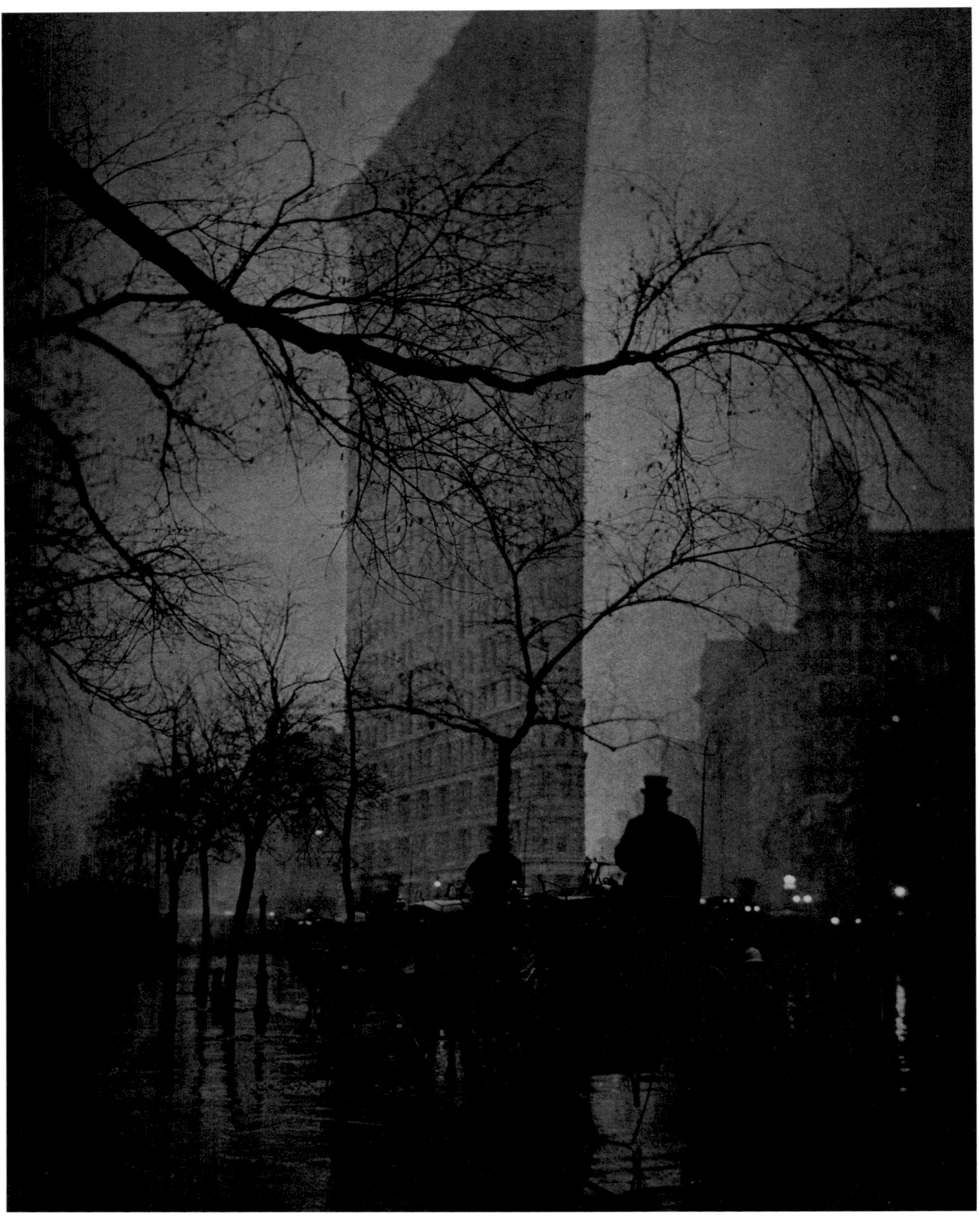

to me; the Flatiron had been a part of my commute to my very first job in Manhattan. From its base I could look north to see the Empire State Building, or south to the Twin Towers. To borrow a title from Minor White, the Flatiron was my first "navigation marker" in New York City.

Like the mountain of my childhood, the Flatiron shifted scale depending on the light and the location from which I approached it. I was delighted that, in the winter, I could walk south on Fifth Avenue from 29th Street and enter into the frame of Edward Steichen's famous gravure.

Though at first overwhelmed by the pace and the crush of humanity in the city, I found after a year or two that New York is really a series of small communities, and most of them were ready to embrace me. From feeling an outsider in the city where I was born, I was now a potential insider to everyone. "Where are you from?" was asked with a hope of similarity, not an accusation of difference. I'd found my rhythm, and my dance partner, in this place that was always ready for *more*.

Aperture owned its five-floor walkup, which had once been a mortuary. The first-floor bookstore and receiving area was governed by LaVerne Johnson, the fiercest of gatekeepers when she wanted to be. No visitor made it upstairs without her buzzer. She was also the staff member with the largest collection of signed books, since she encountered *everyone*. Behind the bookstore and first-floor offices was a large walk-in vault with long shelves (where cadavers had presumably once rested), and a discreet stairway that led up to the second floor. What was once the funerary viewing room was Aperture's primary meeting area, attached to a long, narrow room that was used for exhibitions, and for sequencing books. Editorial, design, production, and their attendant interns occupied the third floor; the fourth floor housed another three departments. We all bumped into each other at staff meetings or waiting in line on the fifth floor outside Michael Hoffman's office.

EDWARD STEICHEN, *The Flatiron*, New York, 1905 / 1973. Hand-pulled dust-grain gravure by Jon Goodman, 12 7/8 x 9 5/16 in; Portfolio edition of 1,000; 400 available individually. Produced by Aperture Foundation. Acquired through work trade, 2002.

Michael had been Aperture's executive director since the mid-1960s, and if you remained with the institution for any length of time, at some point you experienced his mercurial personality. Michael retained final approval on every visual element Aperture presented publicly, from postcards to the sequence and typographic treatment of each book, so from the beginning I often interacted with him. Design, the process of visual problem solving, is both alchemical and iterative. Some scenarios inspire immediate ideas, resulting in successful solutions. Others are elusive and require days or weeks of experimentation to land on the right combination of image, color, and type. Michael would invariably weigh in, no matter the process.

Wendy Byrne, a freelance designer who had worked at Aperture for more than twenty years at that point, was in the office frequently, and her quiet observations taught me volumes. She would compliment a color choice in passing or suggest a book to look at to show how margins changed the spatial sense of the photograph. I had completed two interior book layouts that in retrospect felt like the images were sliding off the page before she showed me, in her own layout files, how she set up guides to establish each image's optical center instead of its actual center. Transformative.

What is now often referred to as the "photobook" is related to but distinct from the tradition of artists' books in other media. They are authored not by an art historian, curator, or gallerist, but usually by the photographer. The text complements the visuals, not the other way around. Photographers as authors increased in frequency from the late 1940s onward, when photographers began asserting their ownership of and legal right to the images they created (as opposed to the images belonging to the publication or newswire that commissioned them). Books were a way to expand upon, or tell a completely different narrative from, the few images a magazine or newspaper might select for publication.

Through a box of photographs or a portfolio, photographers proposed books to Aperture just as writers presented manuscripts to be considered for publication. Sometimes the photographer included ideas for writers; at other times an editor interested in the work would develop a book concept with the photographer. Editors at Aperture also initiated thematic books and issues of the magazine, selecting images by multiple photographers to be presented together.

Book teams generally began with the editor, the shepherd of the project (that person may or may not have presented the project to the publisher for acquisition). Editors were assigned to see books through from concept to completion, on schedule and within the determined budget (editorial assignments were for "life of title," through every reprint or revised edition of the book). At Aperture, editors were also involved in supporting fundraising for the book. The editor was the primary contact for the photographer. The production manager was responsible for cost estimates and manufacturing, and worked closely with the editor, designer, and printer on the physical size of the book, the page count, the choice of paper that was best for reproduction of the photographs, and the binding elements. One or two designers (sometimes jackets were designed by different people than the interiors) determined typefaces, how text appeared, positioned images on the page, and were sometimes engaged in the sequencing of the photographs. Most of the books were printed then in Europe, or in China.

It was not easy to view photographs in person throughout much of the United States, even by the late 1990s. It was our responsibility to get inside the photographer's intentions, and then create the best possible translation of those intentions in the form of the book. We agonized over every choice and detail to honor visual fidelity to the original photographs, and relate the *energy* of the work, as what the public saw in the book might be the only relationship they ever had to those images. Engaging the expertise of the photographer, the editor, the designer, and the production manager led to occasional feats of magic.

Though desktop technology made some typographic elements of the process WYSIWYG (what you see is what you get), photographs were still separated manually into film that was stripped into place along with the type. Reviewing advance copies of a book was a nail-biting experience to see if all the elements had landed as we envisioned.

Creating books with beauty and precision was made more precious for me by my previous positions with Edwin Schlossberg, Inc., an experience design firm (1994–1995), then with the nascent interactive arm of advertising giant Ogilvy & Mather (1996). Both companies were on the forefront of exploring how screen-based technologies were expanding human communication. I learned a great deal from the very different roles I occupied in those environments, but my work did not result in something tactile, in an object I could hold. I had never considered this detail relevant to my choice of occupation, yet I felt the difference viscerally when I began designing art books. It was not just that they were physical; I had worked on magazines that were physical. These books were weighty. Serious. *Beautiful.* It was one of those rare and important realizations connecting labor to an essential and not easily definable sense of personal fulfillment.

My ultimate transition from screen to book initially involved going back to the screen for a while: Aperture had no web presence, and Steve Baron was determined to change that. So one of my first tasks when I joined the staff in 1997 was to solicit my colleague and grad-school roommate, Paula Freedman, to work with me on launching the foundation's first website. As a side project to her full-time work at Ogilvy & Mather Interactive (Paula brought me in there, and stayed on after I left) she took on the massive lift with me of determining the navigation, and setting up a strategy for digitizing and asset management of forty-plus years of book covers, magazine issues, and the briefest of text descriptions. I designed and she coded the entire site. Aperture.org went live in December 1997, and it has been online and evolving ever since.

As we were doing a logistical dive through the past to leap into the future of online communication, Michael Hoffman, Aperture's executive director, asked the staff to create a PowerPoint document that tied the philosophies of the photographers, curators, and writers who had signed Aperture's original manifesto in 1952 to books and thematic magazine issues published during its first forty years. Defining characteristics of each of the founders—Ansel Adams, Melton Ferris, Dorothea Lange, Ernest Louie, Barbara Morgan, Beaumont and Nancy Newhall, Dody Warren, and the magazine's first editor, Minor White—was a thorough way to explore the breadth of the institution's contributions to the history and contemporary practice of significant photography.

From that rapid-fire group effort, I worked my way through the entire library of Aperture's books over the next year. Some projects fit easily into Ansel Adams's environmental or Dorothea Lange's social justice interests or reflected the editorial and curatorial minds of the Newhalls and Minor White. Of the "famous" photographer founders, I knew the least about the work of Barbara Morgan, but was drawn to her sometimes subtle, sometimes wildly fantastic photomontages, and from there to some of her earliest work with dancer and choreographer Martha Graham. I'd worked on a small book about Barbara Morgan in 1999, when she was added to Aperture's "Masters of Photography" series. When a colleague brought in two vintage prints by Morgan—$150 for both, their owner wanted to sell them together—and asked if I was interested, I knew I should say no. That dollar figure covered my food and transportation for two months. And the prints were far from pristine (Baron would definitely have rejected them for reproduction). Yet they appealed to me, despite the fact that the paper had yellowed and the surfaces were cracked. They were artifacts of a previous time, a little bit broken, but still in existence. They had *survived.* I connected with that.

I did the math, and figured that six months of living exclusively on Top Ramen was worth it to own them. I kept the more damaged print, which had the stamp of Morgan's studio on it and was a photograph reproduced in the "Masters of Photography" book, and gave the better print (also from the "Lamentation" series) to my sister. She eventually had hers repaired and conserved. I saw it recently, and it is stunning. Mine remains imperfect, of little value to anyone but me. I've grown to love it even more because of that. It is a reminder that survival is a necessary and valid goal in times of duress, and that in life there are going to be factors, including time and weather, that are outside my control.

Those were the first two photographs I purchased. I'd been on the job for nearly two years by then, and had learned to distinguish original photographs from copy prints, to note how a small white dust spot in a print could loom large if it ended up in reproduction. We typically held or saw the photographer's prints or chromes for a book project only twice—at the beginning and again at the end of the bookmaking journey. In between, the art was stored in Aperture's vault, and we worked with copy-stand prints, duplicate slides, or photocopies to create the edit, sequence, and design. The editors usually reviewed the reproduction artwork with the production staff when a project was first initiated in case production had concerns ("Garbage in, garbage out," was one of Baron's blunt sayings), or the photographs required some particular printing technique for accurate reproduction. At the end of the design and editorial process, once the editor, the photographer, and Michael Hoffman had approved everything, hours were spent methodically sizing and preparing the prints to go to the separators or to the printers.

BARBARA MORGAN, *Lamentation* (oblique), 1935 / 1946. Gelatin silver print dry-mounted on board with studio stamp, 12 3/4 x 10 1/8 in. Edition unknown. Private purchase, 1999.

Prints are rarely perfectly "square," so we measured top and bottom, left and right, to $1/32$ or $1/64$ of an inch, choosing the smallest of those dimensions so the image would not appear askew on the page, while checking to see if that could cause noticeable cropping to an essential element at the edges of the frame (in which case, the photographer was notified and we brainstormed solutions). If a print had rough borders that were to be included in the reproduction, then we measured to the outside of the widest border. The percentage of reduction or enlargement to the original to achieve the size intended in the design, along with the page number, and any other notes, were marked on acetate sleeves. It was a time-consuming task, but I found it meditative.

After those photographs went to the printer they would, when all systems functioned correctly, end up back with the photographer. I would know those photographs only through their reproductions. So for me, living with a mounted, gelatin silver print by Barbara Morgan, one of the photographers who co-founded Aperture—a print that in its

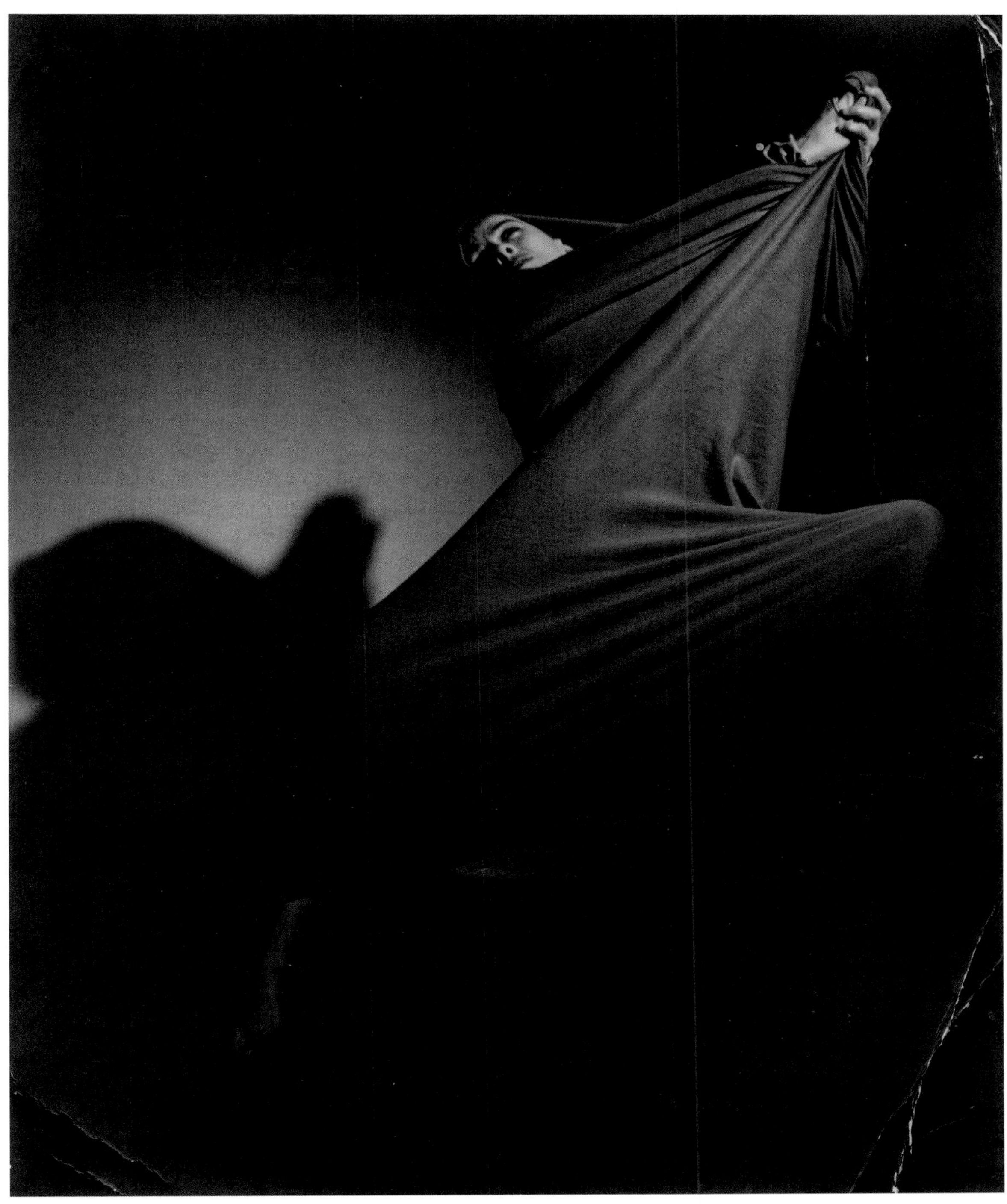

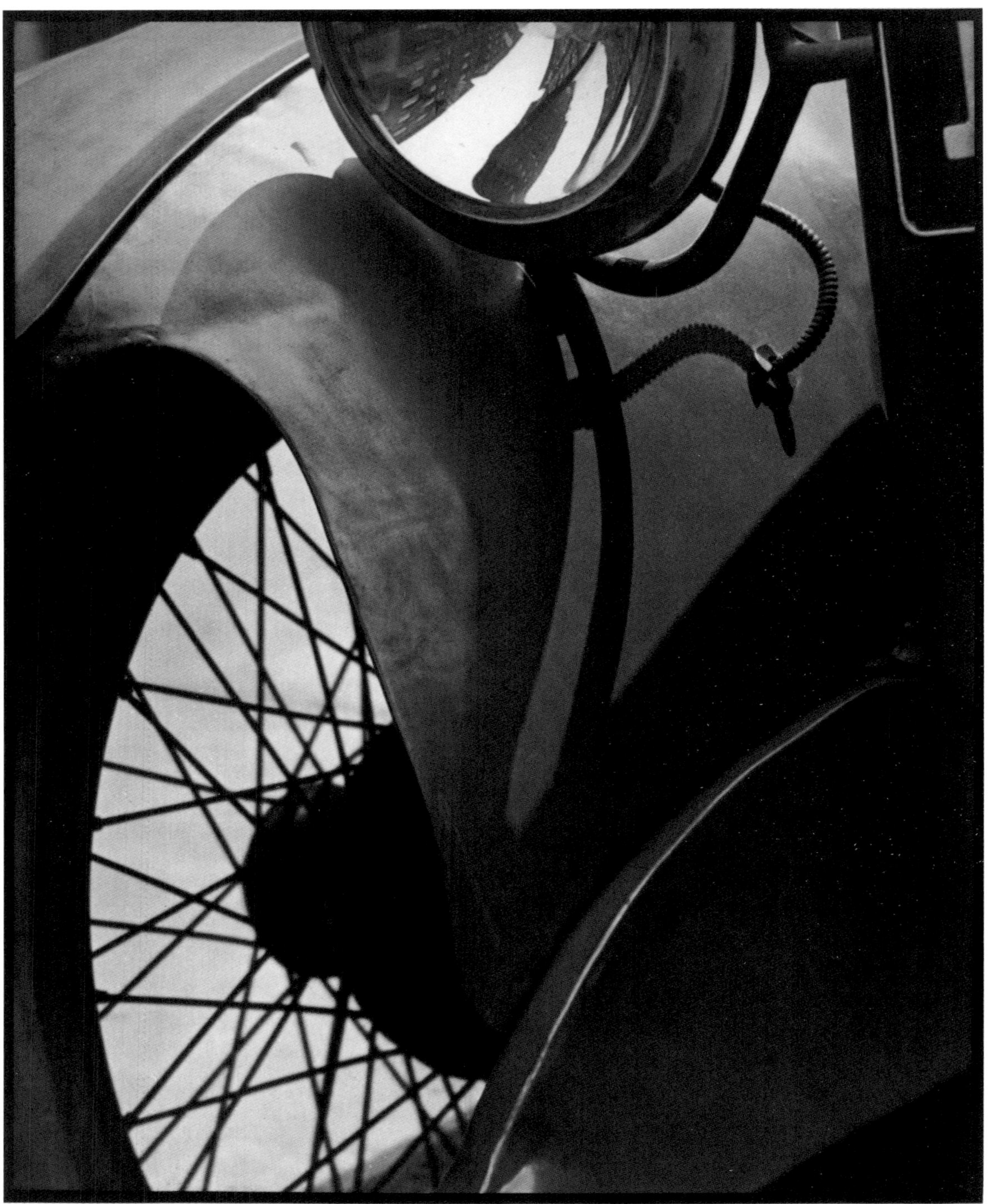

bedraggled condition still vibrated with an energy that the image in reproduction could only strive toward—was contact with the divine. A bit like receiving daily communion.

Twelve-hour days in the office were normal. That gave me time to meet with colleagues, and time alone to research, generate visual ideas, and mock them up using whatever I could render from a black-and-white laser printer, scraps of Pantone paper, hand lettering, and leftover press type. I preferred measuring prints and setting type in the quiet evening hours when I didn't have to think so much as *concentrate*. I inhaled all the history and the images I could, learning not only about photography, but the photographers, and cultural mores within the projects they had undertaken. From the beauty of Paris to fighting in Algeria, the metaphysical experience of fly-fishing to the Chinese occupation of Tibet, I dropped into worlds entirely new to me, and lived in many of them simultaneously for the duration of each book. It led to some very strange dreams.

Michael Hoffman encouraged living with photographs, not only through the development of Aperture's limited-edition print program beginning in the late 1970s, but in more direct ways as well. Aperture's Work Scholar internship had never paid much for the full-time, six-month commitment it required, but during the course of its first thirty years work scholars were given a print at the conclusion of their service. It was considered acceptable for photographers to give prints to staff who had worked with them. Senior staff were sometimes given prints by the foundation as an act of recognition, or in lieu of a bonus, and all staff were entitled to discounts on most limited editions, and the option of an interest-free payment plan.

PAUL STRAND, *Wire Wheel*, New York, NY 1920 / 1976. Platinum palladium print from 5 x 7 negative by Richard Benson, under the direction of Paul Strand, 12 ³/₄ x 10 ¹/₈ in. Number 36/100 and ten artist proofs. Produced by Aperture Foundation. Acquired through work trade, 1999.

Paula Freedman and I were each given a Paul Strand gravure upon the successful launch of Aperture's website; *Wire Wheel* was the first print I negotiated in trade, with the insistence and guidance of Baron. A freelance designer had been hired for, then fired from, a small project, and Michael asked me to complete it. Baron knew that a fee had been approved, with some of it paid out to the previous designer. He suggested that doing the project for trade was not costing the institution any extra money, and it would establish with Michael that I understood the value of my time.

When it came to collecting my compensation, I asked the project manager to present Michael with two options: one was *Wire Wheel*, which was, at retail, more than the dollar figure we'd agreed on. The other option was six gravures adding up to just under the agreed amount. Having spent a little bit of time around Michael, and knowing his affinity for Strand, I believed he would appreciate my choosing this platinum print. If I was wrong, I'd have multiple photographs to enjoy myself or to use as gifts. In typical Michael fashion, he did what I'd hoped and approved *Wire Wheel*—with the caveat that I owed him an additional $500 in "extra work." We both knew I worked far more than the hours on which my salary was based; he never formally collected on the debt.

I initially perceived abstraction in this image, which resolved into the form given away by the print's title. As one of the first photographs I chose for myself, I see in it a balance of peace and chaos that exists in many of the photographs I live with. Photographs I encounter every day must have both dimensions—buoyant on some days, weighty on others—to ebb and flow through life with me. Prints by Barbara Morgan and Paul Strand established a duality of simplicity and complexity that resonates with me and has informed every other print I have had a hand in choosing.

Direct and indirect interactions with master photographers filled me with awe. Speaking by phone to Harry Callahan, or with Edward Weston's son Cole, made my heart race. Hearing that Richard Avedon approved my layout for a spread of his photographs in the magazine, I considered going by his studio to finally meet him, as Baron had suggested years earlier when I was working on my thesis (I never did; I was still too shy). Henri Cartier-Bresson was so surprised that I used scissors and Photoshop to manipulate a fax he sent, and "write" different words in his handwriting for a jacket proposal, that he refused to pen it himself for the final version. Photographers' approvals of ideas I'd developed felt like blessings from celestial beings, particularly as they were one big step toward achieving Michael's approval. It was hard for me to absorb that photographers were also human. My first major book design project brought me back to earth.

My working relationship with photographer Jeff Dunas in 1997–98 was far from amiable. His book proposal, *State of the Blues*, included gold-toned silver prints of musicians, environmental portraits and landscapes, interviews, and multiple essays that had to be woven together with a sensibility suited to blues music. The book's editor, Michael Sand, was smart and easy to work with. Jeff, drawing from his years as a magazine publisher, had very strong opinions on how the book should look. Jeff and I had a 10:1 ratio for "no" to "yes," but through phone calls, faxes,

JEFF DUNAS, David "Honeyboy" Edwards, 1994–1997 / 1999. Hand-toned gelatin silver print, 8 x 9 ³/₄ in. Edition unknown. Gift of Jeff Dunas and Aperture Foundation, 1999.

and email, we very slowly progressed on the book's structure and design. Our final disagreement was over a photograph leading into the first text section of the book. Sand threw up his hands at the stubbornness Jeff and I were both displaying, and the matter went to Michael Hoffman to make the determination so the book could go to press.

I showed Michael both versions, and he said, "Oh, yes dear, the photograph you've chosen is definitely stronger." Affirmation was rare from him, so I felt triumphant as he picked up the phone and called Jeff in Los Angeles. The phone was on speaker as Jeff made his case, and to my astonishment, Michael said "Yes, of course," we'd use the image he wanted. The line had barely disconnected when I blurted out, "But you just said the photograph I picked was better!" In his next words, I learned a very valuable lesson: don't lose sight of whose work this is. "Yes, the one you chose is better. But using the one he wants is not going to hurt the book. And it's going to make him happy." I still put my

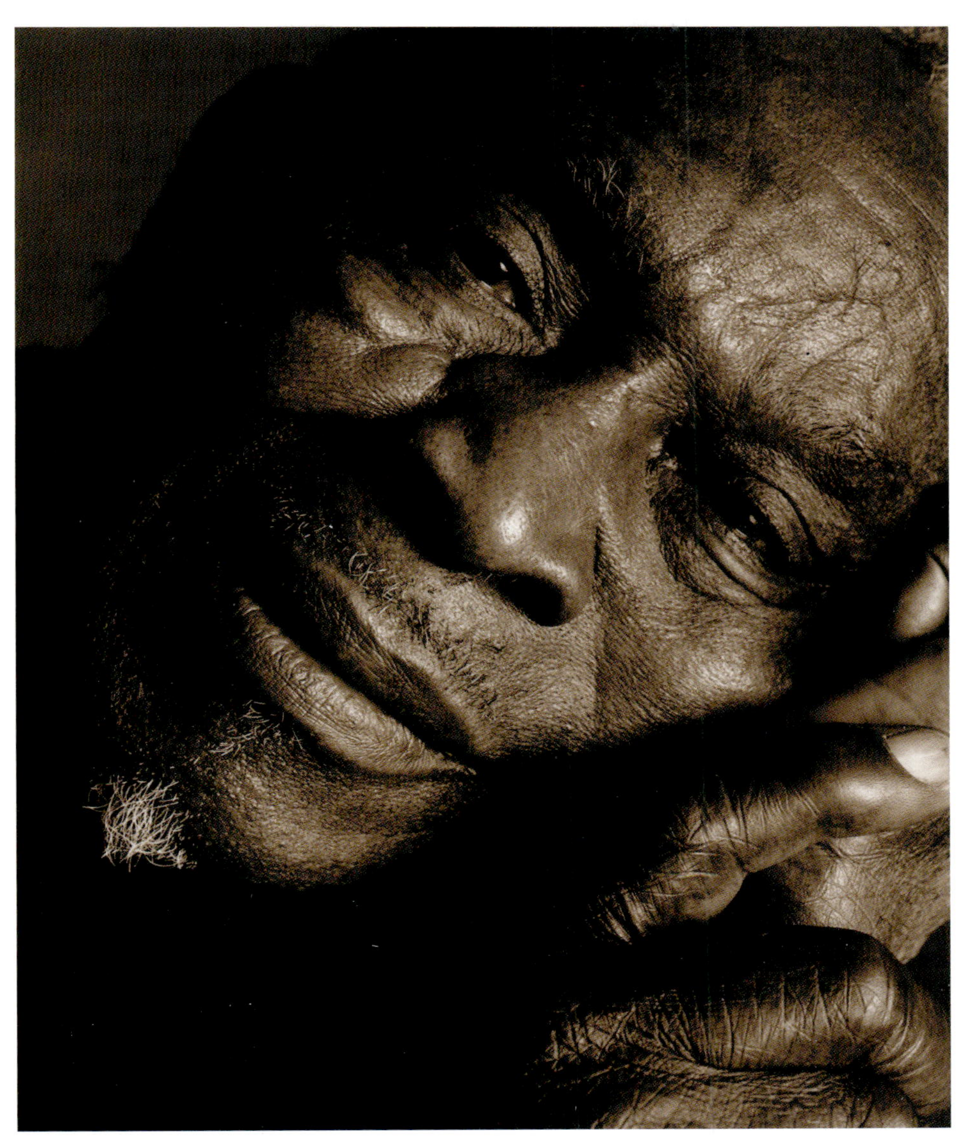

preferred resolutions on the table, with conviction, on every book I am a part of. I see that
as my professional responsibility to the author, and to the project. And because of Jeff
Dunas, many books I've worked on include an image I don't agree with that remains in the
publication because it is important to the author.

Jeff negotiated that every musician depicted in *State of the Blues* receive a personalized copy of the book. For the next year or two many of the musicians would call the office
when they were performing in New York and offer comp tickets to staff who might be free
to attend their show that night. Jeff's commitment to and respect for the musicians softened
some of the antagonism I felt toward him, and the combative nature of the book's process.
In time we recognized our likenesses, and we have developed a deep friendship made
stronger from our mutual desire to put forward the best we can deliver.

State of the Blues became a popular traveling exhibition. It opened at the Delta Blues
Museum in Clarksdale, Mississippi, and was seen throughout the United States. The book
served as the theme of Aperture's annual fundraiser in 1999, and blues guitarist and
vocalist Honeyboy Edwards (p. 43) was invited to perform there. I had the privilege of
escorting him from his hotel to the event. At eighty nine, he was spry and charming, inviting me throughout the evening to visit him in Chicago so he could drive me around town in
his Cadillac.

After the dinner and auction had concluded Honeyboy quietly ascended a small
platform, and his raw, soulful voice filled the hall, with the slap of his hand on the guitar
as occasional percussion. New York's elite shuffled uncomfortably, and I was horrified
to see nearly half of the attendees leave during his performance. Moments later, though,
those who remained moved their chairs closer to him, swaying to the sound of his voice.

Steve Baron started out as a photographer. When he realized that he might not achieve
in his own photographs the perfection he saw in Paul Strand's or Minor White's work,
he chose to become expert in the reproduction of photographs in print. This kept him in
contact with the people, and the medium, that moved him. He nurtured in me a sense of
discipleship to the masters of his generation he deeply admired.

Whenever Baron started a new Strand project, he requested that vintage prints
and previous editions be brought in from the Strand archive, which Aperture managed.
He would summon me to his office or into the better lighting of the gallery, where he
explained what he was looking at, and how it would inform his production decisions.
Comparing gelatin silver or platinum prints to gravures from 1945 and 1965, he discussed the aging of the paper and the patina of Strand's experimental (and ultimately
problematic) lacquer on the surface of his prints, which ignited memories of his own
conversations with Strand. I was a willing recipient of his stories about the people and
the printing intricacies he recalled from past projects.

Michael Hoffman also had close relationships with Minor White and Paul Strand.
Like Baron, he understood and presented photography as an art form and a metaphysical
vehicle through which to experience the world—a cause constantly in need of a champion.
I joined their ranks as a solider for photography, and a novitiate to a spiritual order.

Michael's extreme mood swings would likely be attributed to chemical imbalances now. But then, people in the office just quietly told each other when to "look out." He could be breathtaking in his cruelty to staff members, and many feared him. Though his public admonitions usually stemmed from something related to a project, they sometimes spiraled out into personal attacks. It created a moral quandary: should I defend someone who was being treated unfairly, and become the recipient of his derision myself, or sit quietly while they suffer, hoping it will pass? Occasionally one of us attempted to disrupt him, but in many instances we did nothing. Recipients of his ire sometimes yelled back, or stormed out of the room, or quit—or some combination of the three.

The first time he yelled at me (about the type being too small in a sales catalog, the design of which he'd approved before it went to print) I was almost relieved—facing his temper was a twisted rite of passage to continued employment. Still, when it happened it was shocking. Though I told myself not to react, a basic survival instinct compelled me to say, "People don't talk to me that way," before walking out of the room. We didn't speak for two weeks. He once told me that through his military service he'd learned that abuse could be motivational and he sought to use it in the same manner. That statement is the closest I ever heard to an admission of his actions, let alone an apology.

When he was his best self, he was brilliant—pushing us to think bigger and find the optimal solution, extending deadlines and stretching dollars to find some way to deliver on it. I learned focus from him, and a willingness to do any task that needed to be done to move the project forward. Perhaps most influential was his sense of sequence, an instinctual flow of photographs speaking to each other with an awareness of the afterimage the mind retains from what it has previously seen. That was the language I most needed to understand to present photographs well in book form. It was not communicated verbally, but visually, as I observed him reversing images from left to right, or rearranging a particular grouping. The change of a few key images amplified the structure of the whole.

Michael sought elegance and refinement in the way images were presented, and would suggest surprising colors for endpapers or binding cloth to accentuate the energy of the photographs. He was often inspired by nature. I'd been struggling with a jacket treatment for a few weeks and had pushed to get his feedback on the latest set of options before he headed out for the weekend. He was noncommittal. The following Monday morning, he came straight to my desk and handed me a single, multi-shaded petal of a dahlia, saying, "The jacket should feel like this." Then he walked away. Those were indelible moments.

Book by book, I matured in my understanding of collaboration, staying flexible to the changing dynamics inherent to creative people and projects. That was put to the test on a complex multi-institution project in 2000. Williams College Museum of Art and Hampton University Museum jointly commissioned new work by Carrie Mae Weems that would be exhibited at both institutions, and elsewhere. Aperture was contracted to produce a book that would serve as the exhibition catalog, and I was assigned to design it.

An editor I worked with frequently and well, Phyllis Thompson, and I were both thrilled at the opportunity not only to be working with a woman, but to be working with

Carrie. It was the first time I had been assigned to a book by someone whose work I was familiar with. The education I had been giving myself through studying past publications was paying off, but more relevant was the impact Carrie's work had already made on contemporary visual culture.

Her "Kitchen Table" series pierced my consciousness when it went into the world in the early 1990s. Seeing her centered at the table—a site of meals and laughter, of conversations where I could enter and pull up a metaphorical chair—was only the second time I had any sense of self visually reflected back to me through contemporary art. I did not realize I desired that until I experienced it and, once I saw the series, I could not forget it.

Carrie's commission through Williams and Hampton in 2000 was intended as a response to Frances Benjamin Johnston's photographs made of students and activities at Hampton in 1900. The two institutions intentionally selected a female photographer who was not Caucasian. Carrie chose to use archival material from many sources in the diaphanous banners she created, and incorporated imagery of African American students as well as Native American students who resided at and attended Hampton. In an audio piece that runs as text throughout the book, she lists the names of some of the Native American students who not only attended Hampton, but were buried there. Powers that be at Hampton did not want Carrie to include Native Americans in the project, citing her "lack of understanding" of the "historic complexity" of the circumstances, and as a result chose not to exhibit the work. Hampton's museum director used her essay in the book to defend her position. It was a charged and a delicate situation that brought many rounds of editorial and visual changes. The 96-page book included essays by six different contributors, and an interview with Carrie. The greatest challenge was to keep the emphasis on the work first and foremost, without minimizing the dialogue around it.

CARRIE MAE WEEMS, Untitled, from the "Kitchen Table" series, 1990 / 2010. Gelatin silver print, 9 7/8 x 9 3/4 in. Number 46 / 100, signed and numbered by the artist. Produced by Lightwork and purchased from them, 2013.

As an artifact of history, *The Hampton Project* is a tremendous example of dissonance in discourse. The multiple perspectives presented within the texts represent the views held by the artist, and by various administrators and art historians, at the moment the work was created. It extends what future readers can bring to their own understanding of the work, and of that time period. In this case, it elucidates that in the late 1990s, the good intentions of "inclusion" still resulted in an attempt to exert control over an artist who was known for calling out unacknowledged layers of oppression.

When we met for the first time at Williams College in the spring of 2000, Carrie noticed the hue of my skin. My mixed ethnicity came up rarely, if at all, under professional circumstances. Her immediate recognition of an aspect of my identity that was so often overlooked was unusual for me and, at the time, uncomfortable. She quickly saw that I did not know how to respond. My melanin is, to use a printing term, metameric—it can shift depending on who is viewing me and who I am around. I had become used to "passing"

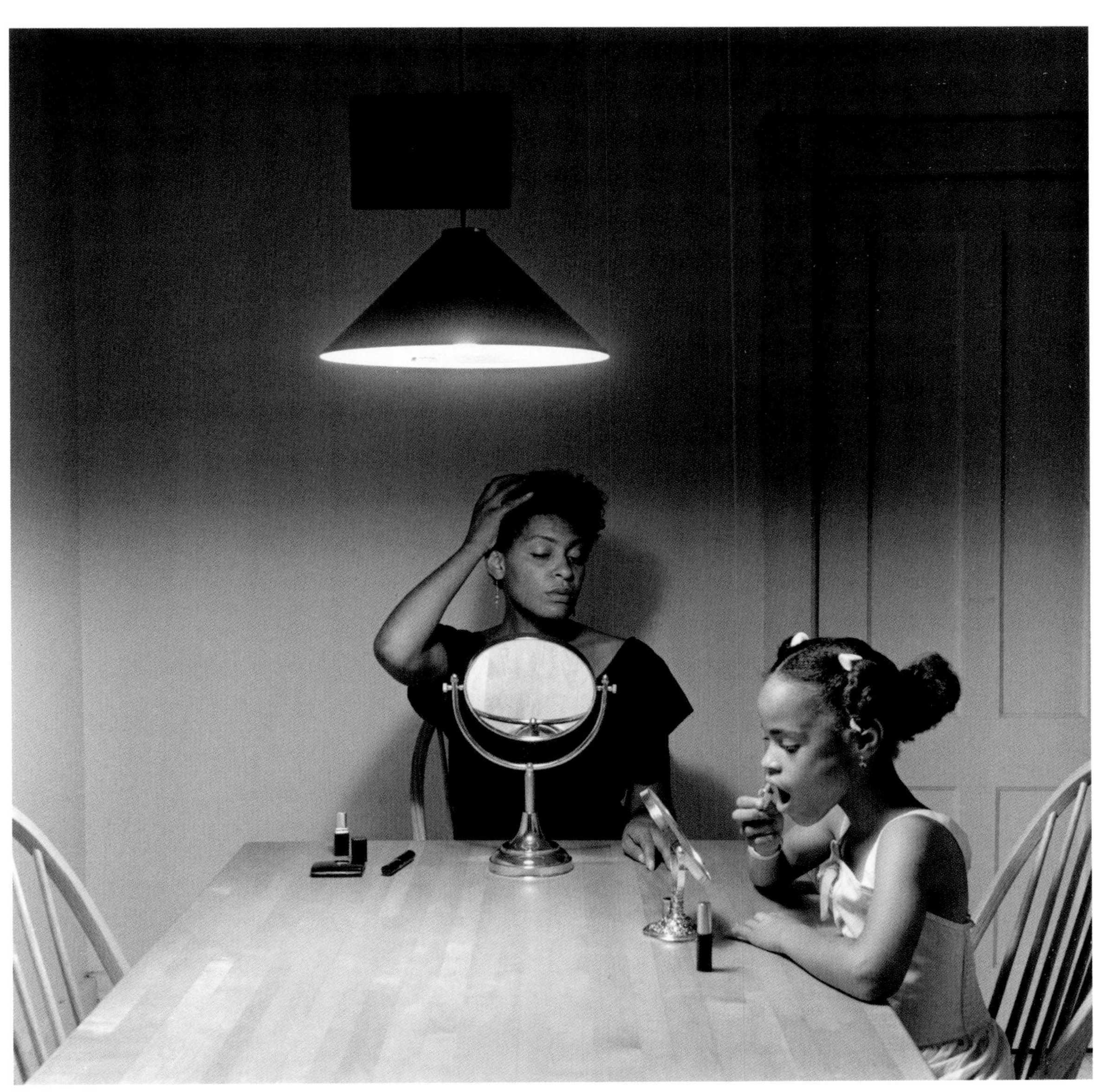

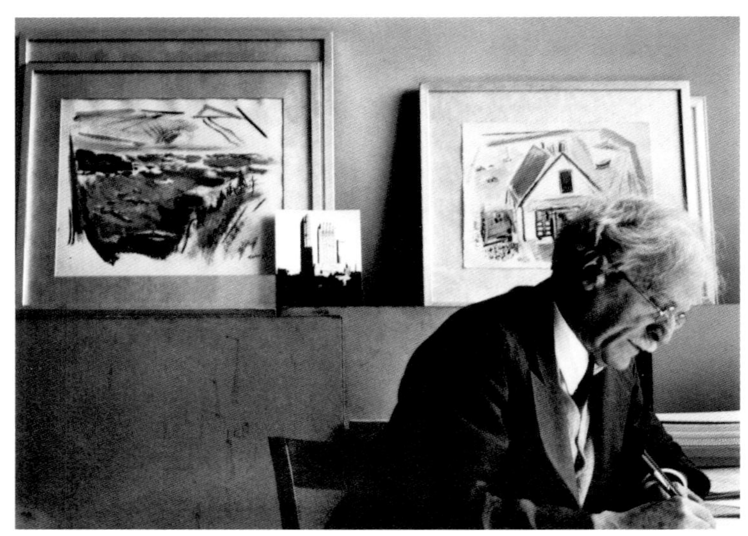

in the predominantly Caucasian photographic community I was working in. Many years went by before I had the occasion to speak with her privately about the significance of that moment for me. I was surprised that she even remembered it; she was not surprised that I did. Being seen by Carrie in that first meeting, and having the privilege of ongoing contact with her throughout the next twenty years, bolstered my confidence in how I moved through the world. Engagement with her and her work has supported my sense of agency in choosing language to describe myself that is complex and celebratory, rather than reductive. It took a long time.

Quality and fidelity in the reproduction of photographs was inherent to the formation of *Aperture*. Engravings to print photographs well were expensive in the 1950s, and Minor White erred on the side of quality, even if that meant including only a few images in each issue. By 1959 the modest subscriber base and Ansel Adams's negotiation of an "advertising" relationship with Polaroid (this consisted of a back cover photograph with a discreet caption indicating the image was shot on Polaroid film, or on a Land camera) provided enough stability to shift from the vertical format of 9 $^3/_{16}$ x 6 $^3/_8$ inches to the more accommodating horizontal format of 8 x 9 $^3/_{16}$ inches. A greater number of images also began to appear in *Aperture*'s pages.

DOROTHY NORMAN, *Alfred Stieglitz Spotting Portrait of Dorothy Norman (with Marin Paintings and Stieglitz in Background)*, **An American Place, New York 1930s / printed before 1993.** Gelatin silver contact print, 2 $^3/_4$ x 3 $^7/_8$ in. Edition unknown. Produced by Aperture Foundation and purchased from them, 2002.

Alfred Stieglitz's publication *Camera Work*, in circulation from 1903 until 1917, served as an inspiration and ideal, though the hand-tinted gravures tipped into its pages (now considered worth collecting in their own right) far exceeded what the modest pages of *Aperture* conveyed. Still, Stieglitz was a friendly spirit permeating much of what happened at 20 East 23rd Street. This photograph of Stieglitz hung in Michael's office, on a wall to the right as one sat facing his desk. Stieglitz's posture here, hunched, focused, is the view I often held of Michael through the door to his office, as I waited to be summoned in. A mandala painting from India hung behind Michael's desk, and though it contained a universe worthy of contemplation, staring at it meant staring directly at Michael as he punched away at his typewriter, or engaged in some other task before he turned his formidable gaze upon me and whatever design iteration I was trying to get approved.

So I often gazed off to the right, at Stieglitz, absorbing the petite scale of the print and the energy that nonetheless reverberated from it. I felt him almost manifesting the future with the posture of his body (Leon Botstein often strode across the Bard campus at a similar angle, shoulders first, as if he couldn't move forward fast enough). I have a sense of solitude from this photograph, though Stieglitz is in the company of one of his own photographs, and of paintings by his friend John Marin. But of course, Stieglitz is not alone here. A woman who respects and loves him is present behind the camera. I see many other layers in this photograph when I consider the viewpoint of Dorothy Norman.

Michael said he sometimes channeled Stieglitz, and once, when he was in a good mood, asked if I thought he could he get away with wearing a cape, like Stieglitz did? More often he looked up, surprised, as if after twenty minutes he'd just realized I had been sitting in front of him. Sighing, he'd glare over the edge of his glasses, and say, "Michelle, dear, do you see what we're trying to do here?" Some days, I could honestly reply, "yes."

Tailor's Apprentice was given to me in 1999, when I made a panicked move back to the Northwest. My mother decided to downsize, and I wanted to move into the house I'd grown up in. I did not want to leave my job, my boyfriend, or the studio apartment on Manhattan's Upper West Side where I'd finally obtained a legal lease. Yet I was also not ready to let go of "home," a place by which I still somewhat defined myself. My Studebaker awaiting restoration sat in the barn there. My apple tree was nearby, holding vestiges of the quieter version of me. I still dreamt of a spouse, children, writing a little poetry—the life I imagined before I discovered Bard or moved to New York City, before Aperture. All I'd experienced felt like a marvelous dream that I could not quite believe was my reality. So I woke up, and went back to Puyallup.

Michael initially refused my request to work remotely in some capacity for Aperture. Ever my mentor and guide, Baron told me just to be patient, and give it time. *Tailor's Apprentice* reinforced my hope that there would somehow still be a role for me at Aperture. The print was a reminder of the many lessons I'd absorbed through my years there, including my unforgettable trip to Italy to observe Baron on press. The blazing gaze of this young woman demands my attention regardless of how many times I have seen it; I have to take her down periodically, and give us both a break. In his choice of print, I trusted that Michael still saw me as an apprentice to the craft of bookmaking, and through it to the dissemination of photography's metaphysical energy. My gift to Michael, a small *murti* of Shiva Nataraja embodying energies of creation, destruction, and the perpetual cycle of time, felt equally apt.

PAUL STRAND, *Tailor's Apprentice*, Luzzara, Italy 1953 / 1997. Platinum print by Sal Lopes. 8 3/16 x 6 1/2 in. Edition of 150 and fifteen artist proofs. Produced by Aperture Foundation and gifted by them, 1999.

My universe erupted over the next twenty-four months. My mother did not sell the family home to me. I began, then quit after thirty days—and one phone call from Michael Hoffman—a job with a book packager in the Seattle area. I returned to New York for a month, initiating a bicoastal existence that continued for the next twenty years. I began the new millennium by eloping with a handsome man I'd known intermittently since childhood while he was vacationing in the United States. A few weeks after our heady leap, he continued on the rest of his global trip alone. I put everything I owned in storage and moved into a furnished rental in Seattle, wondering if he would return, and what exactly I'd done to my life.

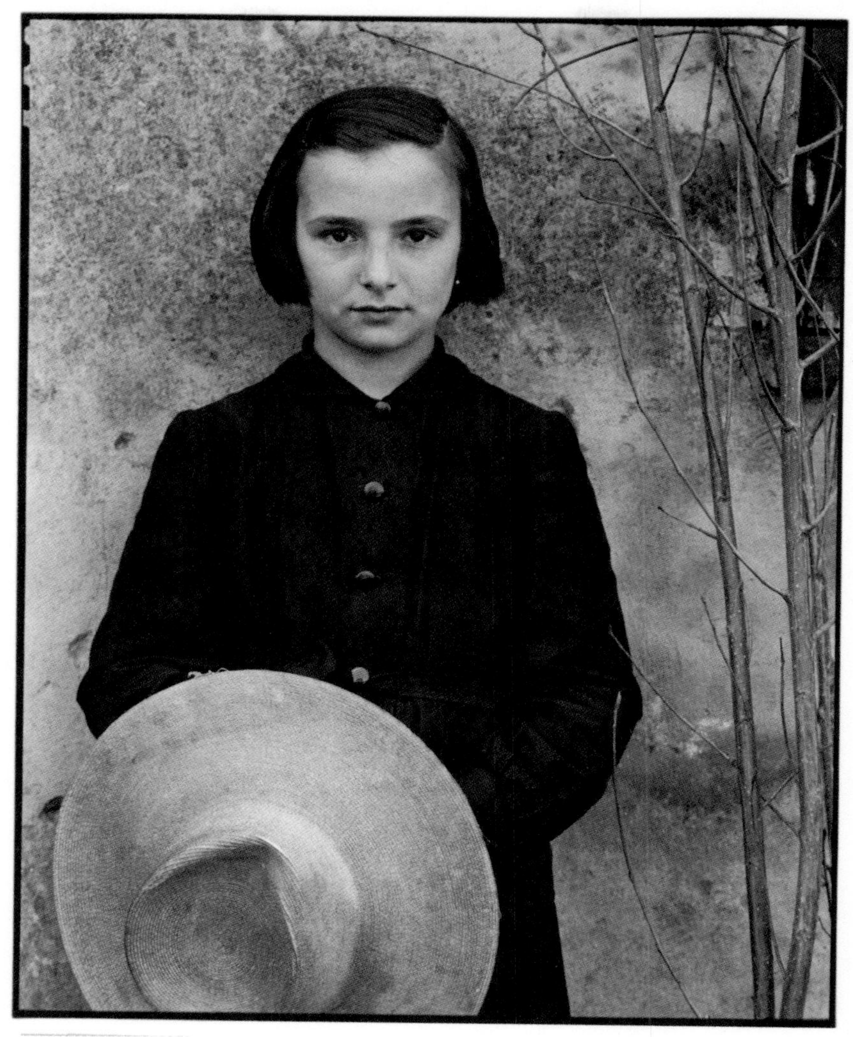

The man I married relocated from Australia (with a few cases of wine and his two Harley Davidsons) to Seattle, his preferred of the two cities I was torn between. With Michael Hoffman's assurance that I would be assigned books if I agreed to work from New York during the summers, I accepted a tenure track teaching position in graphic design at Seattle Central Community College (the institution I once considered attending).

When its academic year ended in June 2001, I returned to New York for the summer as promised, while the man I married settled into his full-time job in Seattle. A long-distance scenario seemed advisable at that point as, nearly a year into living together, we were discovering how little we really knew each other. He visited New York in July. We rode his Harley from Seattle to Carmel, California, in early August (seeing Edward Weston's mailbox, and a glimpse of Clint Eastwood, clinched the choice of destination). I returned to New York to wind down my routine there, and prepare for a third fall in Seattle.

Except that when I returned to New York, Michael Hoffman was in the hospital. What began for him as back pain progressed quickly, and mysteriously. As the days passed and he continued to decline, there was fear, and uncertainty. We were planning for the magazine's fiftieth anniversary the following year, and working on the catalog for forthcoming books. Should we keep moving forward? Wait on everything? I would soon have to extricate myself and return to Seattle to teach. I felt like I was abandoning the team.

The morning of September 11, 2001, was sunny and clear after a rainstorm the night before. I was scheduled to leave New York in just two days, and every hour felt precious. I started my day at the hospital to say hello to Michael, and then walked from there to the office, about eleven or twelve blocks away. The smoke from lower Manhattan was not in my line of sight, and I reached 23rd Street not yet knowing what had happened. I will probably always be haunted by what next unfolded. Going into the office and learning that the plane crashes were not accidental. Going back outside to get as much cash as I could before the banks closed. Buying water, and trying to think of what else we might need to exist for an indefinite period of time at the office. The shocking implosion of the North Tower as I stood on Fifth Avenue and 23rd Street was a line of demarcation. Suddenly there was life *before*. And the immediate present. I could not trust the continuation of a single second after that.

On the evening of September 12, I learned my friend Bella Bhukhan was missing, and turned my energies to helping her family make flyers and inquire about her at makeshift triage centers around lower Manhattan. Doctors and nurses stood at the ready, waiting for patients who never appeared. It took weeks to absorb that the majority of the missing, including Bella, would never return. I continued to visit Michael in the hospital, and his condition worsened without explanation.

I eventually made it back to Seattle and began the fall quarter. A week after I'd returned, I was standing on a corner in downtown Seattle waiting to cross the street when

Pages 54–55: EUGENE RICHARDS, *A Firefighter Sits Alone in the Rubble*, World Trade Center site, New York, from "Stepping Through the Ashes," 2001 / 2011. Gelatin silver print, 15 x 22 ³/₄ in. Open edition, signed. Gift of Eugene Richards and Janine Altongy, 2016.

a man in a truck slowed down and yelled, "Go back to your own country!" The racial vitriol expressed in Seattle, on behalf of what had occurred in New York, was yet another layer to process. Anyone with features that could be construed as Middle Eastern was a target for harassment from the federal government, the local police, and some of the general public. I continued to wear my Indian shawls in defiance, on the days when I wasn't wearing my letterman's jacket and a baseball cap out of fear.

I obsessively watched the news and cried. My husband came home from work each night, cooked my favorite foods, put on a comedy or a western, and gently encouraged me to be in the present.

Trauma presents itself in unpredictable ways. For a few years I couldn't enter the primary stairwell near me during routine fire drills at the college, or drive over certain bridges. It took me fifteen years to even begin to associate with the depth of grief I feel from that period in my life. I have been claustrophobic ever since, and sometimes have to determine my exit routes when in new environments. I am conscious that Bella's family, and so many others, have far worse experiences than what I manage. In 2018, through the September 11th birth of a child in my immediate family, I formed a new and positive association with that date, and his arrival brought some healing.

Michael Hoffman died at the age of 59 in November 2001. Aperture lost its leader of thirty-five years; his wife lost her partner; Baron lost his compatriot of three decades; and photography lost one of its visionary champions. I lost a professional compass, and the boss I'd intended to argue with for the rest of my career, a sparring partner who always pushed me toward more and better.

When a few months later an acquaintance in Seattle asked me what photography I'd seen recently that I liked, I burst into tears. I'd never had to form an opinion. I just had to learn from what Aperture presented. If I didn't understand the subject, or the photographs, or I couldn't figure out why they were important, then I just had to keep looking more. There were people I admired, but I didn't know what I "liked" in photography. I had never even asked myself that question.

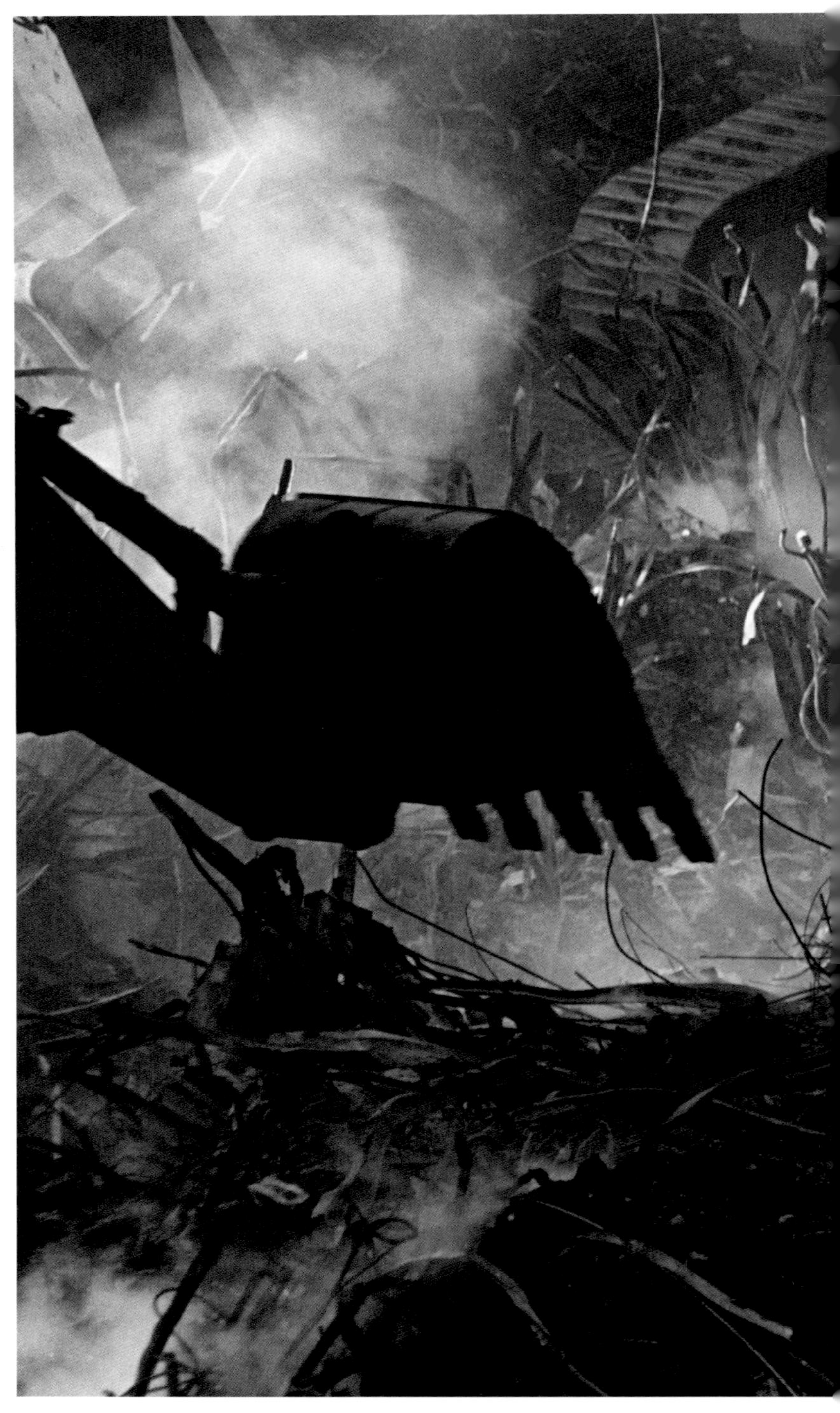

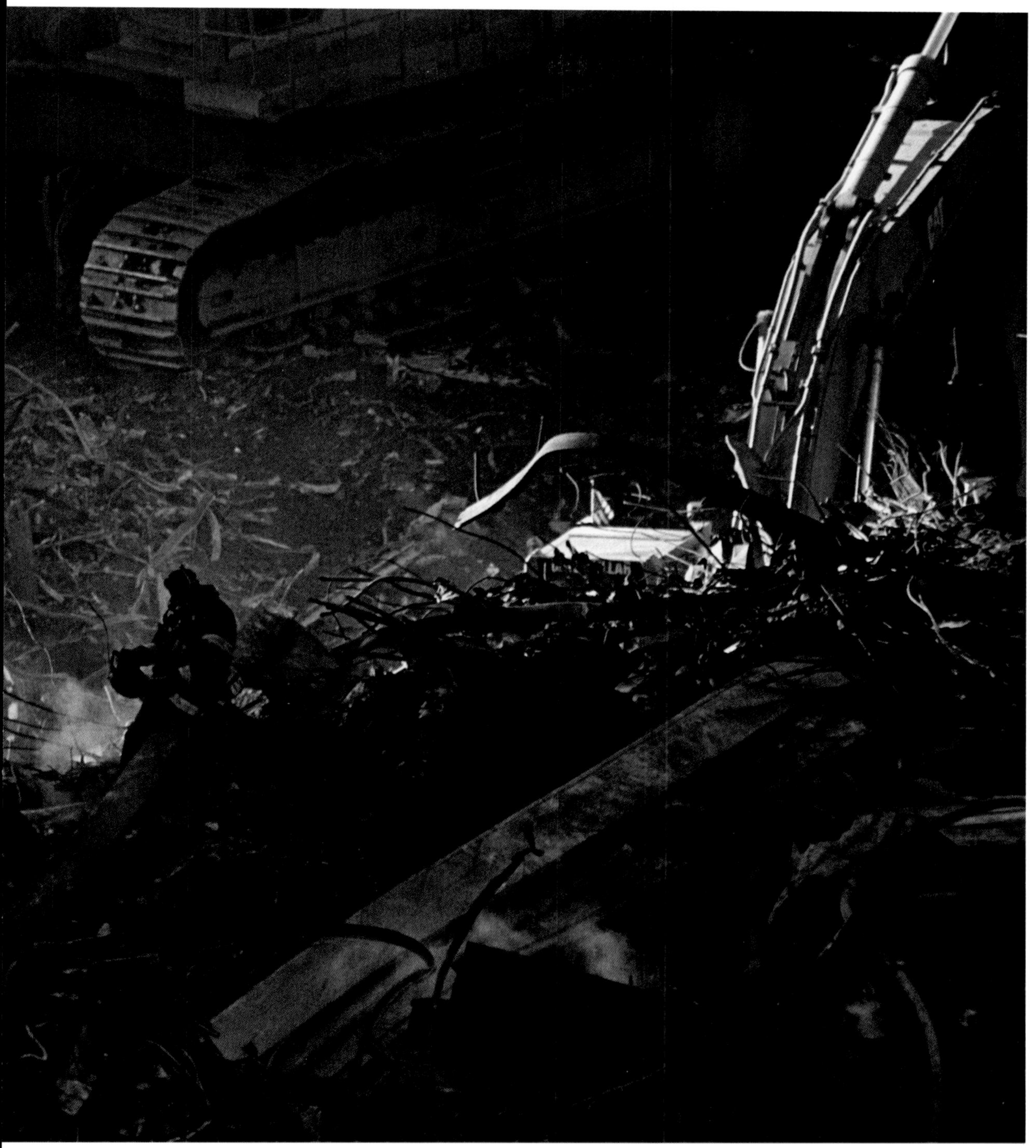

Being Seen

Michael Hoffman's death on the eve of Aperture's fiftieth anniversary left the foundation in crisis. Board members were asking me to return to New York to assist in the formation of the institution's next phase. It was the only time I was interviewed to be Aperture's executive director. I was surprised even to be considered; I did not want Michael's job. Few did.

At some past point I had typeset business cards for consultants working on a nascent regional concept, Aperture West, and suggested engagement with that instead. The board agreed. My first tasks were to review an existing position paper, meet the five-member advisory board, and formulate a program and a plan for execution. Though my graduate degree was business focused, I had no direct experience or models to draw on for the position I'd accepted. Atlanta-based trustee and healthcare executive Bob Yellowlees, one of the foundation's only board members outside of New York, mentored me through the development of a strategic plan with three investment levels. Though everything was in flux with the search for a new director, the board chose to move forward with a small financial commitment, covering a retainer for my time and some travel expenses. I had to figure out what Aperture had to offer to the communities where it was seeking increased visibility, while demonstrating to the board that investment in the west would yield direct and quantifiable, though not necessarily immediately financial, results.

After a year of diplomatic visits to San Francisco and Los Angeles, where I heard the full range of how brilliant and how terrible Aperture was ("terrible" largely from people we had not published, as well as devotees to black-and-white landscape photography who wished we published nothing else), I had a two-part plan to present to the board. First, find host institutions on the west coast for Aperture's upcoming fiftieth-anniversary exhibition, which would, through exhibition fees, raise money, and could attract press, and additional public programming. Second—an idea that came from potential partners in the west—initiate a lecture series bringing high-profile photographers to the west coast in collaboration with those institutions. I hoped profits from the first might support the second.

Placing exhibitions was a combination of knowledge, relationships, patience, and persistence. When I started outreach in 2002, I had only the last. Figuring out the right person to contact, and then wrangling a face-to-face meeting, was difficult. My desperation in that effort knew no bounds. At a Bard College holiday party in New York, I mentioned how challenging the process was to physics professor Burt Brody, who then casually asked if Sandy Phillips was still at the San Francisco Museum of Modern Art. I was surprised he knew of a curator of photography so renowned in the field, and said yes, she was on the list of near-impossibles to reach. He smiled and said, "Tell her you know me." I couldn't imagine how kindly Burt Brody was going to get me to the esteemed Sandra Phillips, but in planning my next visit to San Francisco I made reference to him in my inquiry to her and, sure enough, got a meeting. I had no idea she'd completed her undergraduate degree at Bard. Her willingness to meet with me led others to do the same.

In the early years of the millennium, photography was still fighting for serious consideration in many cultural spaces. From a steady progression of interest and visibility beginning in the late 1970s, it seemed there was a plateau, or even waning, of attention by the early 2000s. Academic departments of photography were folded into interdisciplinary practices. Curators of photography were still non-existent at many major institutions or not replaced after retirement (which directly affected the ability to place photography exhibitions within those institutions). Venerable organizations such as Friends of Photography dissolved; other photo-based institutions struggled to hold onto rental spaces as real estate costs in major cities escalated.

The preservation of Aperture during this time felt imperative. Though Michael Hoffman and other institutional leaders of his era made some ethically questionable decisions that would likely not pass conflict-of-interest standards today, they certainly embodied the ethos of "we must continue at all costs." After one of my particularly passionate explanations for why I was taking on yet another arduous task for no additional pay to shore up the regional outreach program, my sister said, "I get the feeling from you that the continuation of this art form is never guaranteed."

When it came to placing exhibitions, a frequent response from many larger museums then, particularly those without photography curators, was "We just did a photography show, we probably won't do another one for a few years." I had to fight my first response—"I'll bet you just did a painting show, too, but that isn't going to rule out that entire medium!" Which of course, I could not say, because I had to try and keep connected to those decision makers, at those institutions, to convince them to give photography another chance in two to three years' time.

Monumental changes to the materials and processes of the medium reinforced an urgency to preserve what was before, while digesting what was to come. Traditional darkroom papers were disappearing quickly, film became scarce and processing ceased, and darkrooms were dismantled. All the while digital sensors increased in sensitivity, drum scanning and other forms of digitizing transparencies and prints opened more achievable and affordable opportunities of scale, ink pigments stabilized, and different paper surfaces compatible for use with inkjet printers emerged.

There was a desire to protect the fragile foothold photography had formed in the collecting sector, simultaneous with fear around who was laying claim to the medium. Why were those artists "using" photography getting more attention, and obtaining higher prices, than the "traditional" photographers? There was jealousy, fear, and heady excitement at the new possibilities rapidly unfolding if the makers, the custodians, the publishers, the educators, the sellers, and the loving viewers survived it all. That swirling energy, combined with trauma from my personal life upheavals, 9/11, and Michael's death, propelled me forth. I couldn't afford to be shy anymore. I was an advocate with a world to transform and save. Through photography.

By offering flexibility with exhibition duration and loan fees, and coordinating shipping in a geographically efficient manner, I placed *Past / Forward: Aperture at 50*, a multi-photographer show curated by the magazine's editor-in-chief Melissa Harris, at institutions in Seattle, Portland, Monterey, and Los Angeles. I worked with local curators at each venue to ensure that the work was presented as Melissa intended, gently pushing against any inclinations to group work chronologically, and confirming that difficult or controversial pieces were not omitted or relegated to positions of obscurity.

Overseeing installations of the same objects in different environments taught me about sightlines, and a translation of visual relationships from the page to the wall. Each space presented its own challenges and opportunities to draw attention to individual prints as well as sequences. My engagement with the installations, and occasional public speaking at opening events, was a sign of trust from Melissa, who as the show's curator would typically have taken on those responsibilities. I understood the importance of accurately presenting what I had learned of Aperture's approach to photography.

In my first five years at Aperture I had been assigned projects—books and occasional issues of the magazine, seasonal sales catalogs, gala invitations, and exhibition graphics. The Aperture West program gave me the opportunity, for the first time, to *choose* photographers or institutions to partner with. I began forming my own views on artists whose work I found distinctive. The longest-running program I originated, a multi-city lecture series, was produced in collaboration with the Hammer Museum at UCLA, San Francisco PhotoAlliance, and Photographic Center Northwest in Seattle. Each photographer lectured in three cities over five days, with a networking dinner, and visits to galleries or museums, according to the photographer's interests. I often traveled with the featured speaker from Los Angeles up to Seattle, to make the logistics as easy as possible, and create visibility for the foundation.

After a pilot event with Mary Ellen Mark at the Hammer Museum in 2003 (more on that shortly), we presented thirteen more photographers—Stephen Shore, Eugene Richards, Lorna Simpson, Gary Schneider, Sylvia Plachy, William Christenberry, An-My Lê, Nicholas Kahn and Richard Selesnick, Bruce Davidson, Larry Fink, Pieter Hugo, and Hank Willis Thomas—in each city over five years. Each regional institution managed local promotion. Aperture paid for the photographer's travel expenses, and a modest honorarium (two years in, we secured sponsorship through one of *Aperture* magazine's west-coast advertisers, Freestyle Photographic), and had its name on events in the west a few times a year. It was a program of synergy and mutual benefit.

This card (opposite, top), from Mary Ellen Mark's "Indian Circus" series, shows up in pictures of my first dorm room in 1991, and is tucked in a folder next to my computer today. I don't remember where I got it, but acquiring it and bringing it home was a subliminal extension of a practice my siblings and I participated in with our mother. Seeing anyone who looked like her in our hometown was an occasion, so when we saw a lady with brown skin in the grocery store, we immediately pointed her out to Mom (who usually invited the lady over for tea). I felt the same need to embrace likeness when I saw this card; it was the first time I saw someone who physically resembled my mother, and by extension, me, in art. It was years after meeting Mary Ellen that I finally connected it to her.

My conscious association with Mary Ellen was from *Streetwise*—a renowned book, and a documentary of the same name filmed by her husband Martin Bell, made in Seattle. I had met her a few times in New York and was thrilled and a little intimidated when she agreed to headline Aperture's first foray into the Los Angeles art scene. We had a capacity crowd for her conversation with Getty photography curator Weston Naef at the

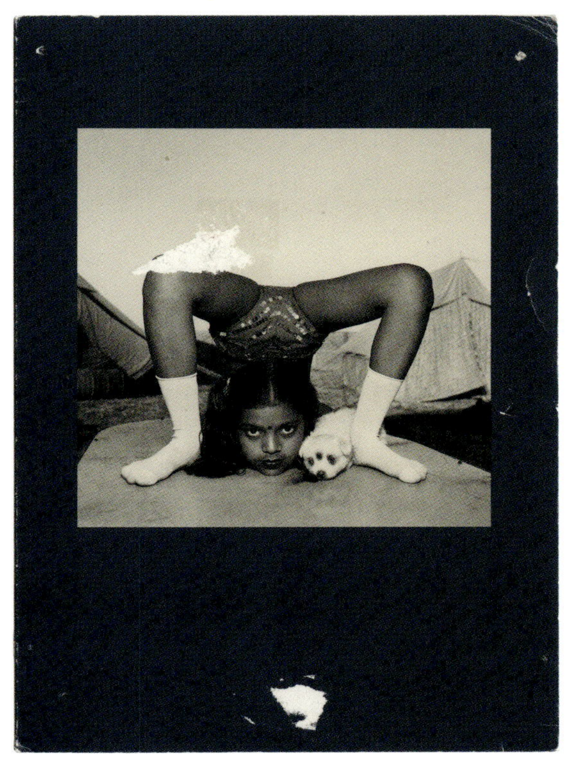

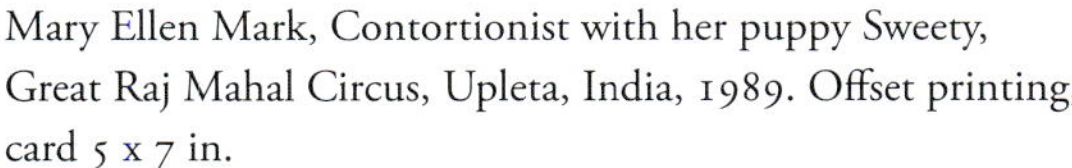

Mary Ellen Mark, Contortionist with her puppy Sweety,
Great Raj Mahal Circus, Upleta, India, 1989. Offset printing,
card 5 x 7 in.

Mary Ellen Mark and Michelle Dunn Marsh, Seattle, 2006.
Polaroid, 4 x 5 in. Unique. Purchased at a PCNW fundraiser,
2006.

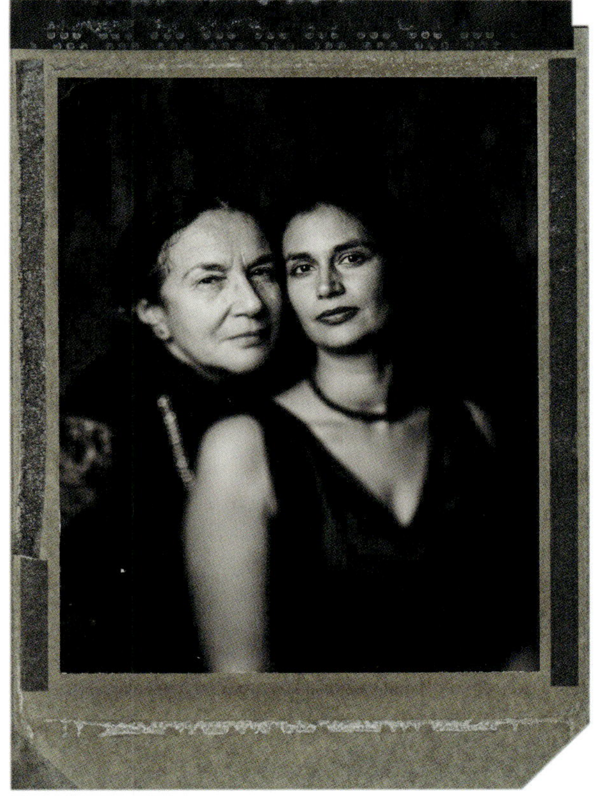

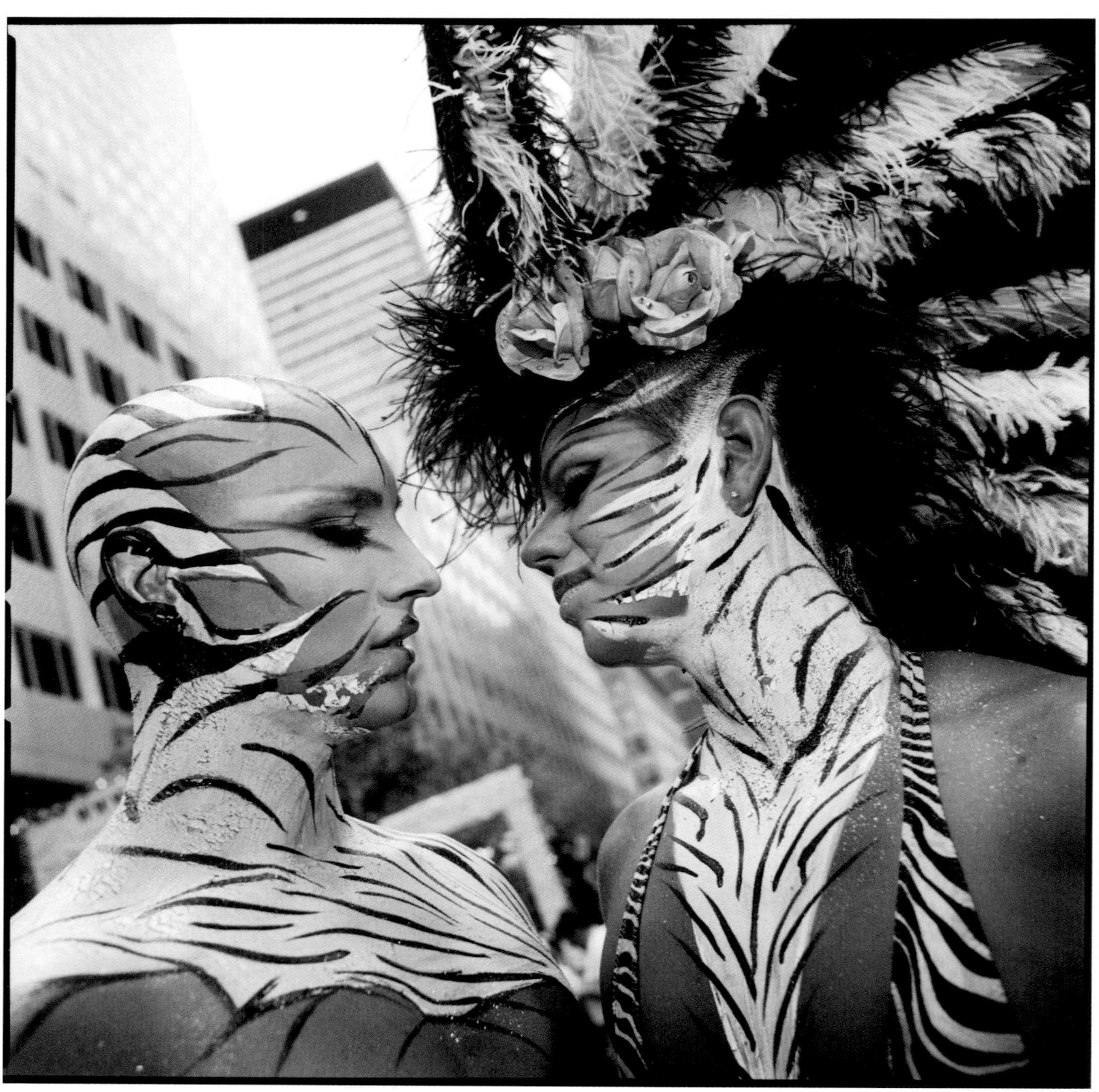

Hammer Museum, and the patron dinner following, both made more glamorous by the attendance of Mary Ellen's friend, the actor Jeff Bridges. The success of her lecture and a book signing in Los Angeles was an auspicious beginning for the program. I was glad the Aperture West advisory board was happy, but considered it equally important that Mary Ellen felt good about it. She possessed a fierceness and tenderness, with unpredictable fluctuations between them, that was disarming. She reminded me of Michael Hoffman.

Mary Ellen stood up for people she believed in. She readily championed her students from annual workshops in Mexico, India, and other locations, and would have Julia Bezgin, her studio manager, or Meredith Lue, her librarian and a former Aperturian, get me on the phone so she could recommend a recent student. During times of my own professional transitions, she called me just to check in, and see how I was doing.

She was a tough negotiator and had clear guidelines for travel (business class) and lecture fees (significant). Mary Ellen knew what her time was worth. Working with her was on her terms, which were sometimes expensive, but more often priceless. Just a week after the Los Angeles event that had taken months to plan, she agreed (with no fee) to a film screening, tucked in around her planned shoots, while she was in Seattle. It took 48 hours of phone calls and favors, led by fellow Seattle Central faculty Sandy Cioffi, to pull it off, but the fans showed up, and the event led to a *Seattle Times* feature on Mary Ellen.

I associate pageantry, heat, and possibility with summer in New York City, and this photograph has them all. It was made in 2008, when Mary Ellen did a series on parades and festivals as part of a project that Aperture sales manager Kellie McLaughlin and I developed with the USA television network. Eleven photographers (including Jeff Dunas and Sylvia Plachy) were selected to make photographs related to the character of America; it became a book and traveling exhibition, and each photographer was featured in short TV spots. Mary Ellen

MARY ELLEN MARK, Alex Londono and Chayanne Yate, NYC Pride March, New York, 2008. Gelatin silver print, 14 ¹¹/₁₆ x 14 ¹¹/₁₆ in. Edition of 25. Gift of Mary Ellen Mark, 2009.

schooled me many times as we settled on the final images and her sequence in the multi-photographer book *American Character: A Photographic Journey* (Chronicle, 2009), and I was glad to be engaging with her editorially. When she invited me to choose a print for myself from the series as a thank you, I selected three and asked her to make a decision from there, so the photograph would represent our mutual tastes. I have sometimes followed that model of selection when given the opportunity, so no one feels pressure. I always enjoy the ultimate surprise of seeing which image the photographer determines.

Having asked for Mary Ellen's permission to do so, I used this series many times to teach students about editing and sequencing photographs. When workshop attendees are asked to remove a few photographs from the series, then form a sequence, this one is routinely cut. Many viewers begin edits by seeking similarities in composition or content among the photographs. This is the only image Mary Ellen chose to include from the Pride March, and it doesn't immediately "fit in" with the others—one more reason why I love it.

Many of Mary Ellen's iconic photographs possess formality and intimacy. In some of her husband Martin's short films complementing her "Twins" or "Proms" series, you can occasionally hear her interacting with subjects, guiding their posture or the positioning of their hands. I had this split-second experience when she agreed to be photographed with me at a fundraiser in Seattle, where she was the guest of honor (p. 61). Positioned behind me, she moved in close, then quietly instructed me to raise my head but tilt my chin down for optimal angularity. I am very aware that this version of me only exists in the photograph, and because of her. In is even more precious to me now that she is no longer here.

Photographer Will Steacy edited a fantastic book called *Photographs Not Taken* (Daylight, 2012). Witnessing a "photograph not taken" once with Mary Ellen was a gift from her I will never forget. I was leaving the World Trade Center site with my friend Bella Bhukhan's family after an annual 9/11 memorial service when I saw Mary Ellen and her husband Martin Bell just outside the perimeter. There were sometimes contentious encounters between family members desiring privacy, and

MARY ELLEN MARK, Elise Collins, Union, South Carolina, 1995. Gelatin silver print, 7 $^{11}/_{16}$ x 9 $^{7}/_{8}$ in. Edition of 50. Gift of Mary Ellen Mark, 2008.

photographers choosing or commissioned to witness, and each year I feared running into photographers I knew. I whispered to Bella's sisters that I was going to say hello to Mary Ellen on the way out, and would find them after, but they decided to come with me so we could all exit together.

I approached with some trepidation—Mary Ellen and Martin were clearly working, and I was unsure if I should interrupt. Mary Ellen saw me and gave me a hug, asking why I was there. I saw her eyes as she took in my two friends, who share the beauty of their younger sister, and their matching t-shirts, bearing Bella's photograph. And just as I was struggling with how to say, "Photographers have been invasive toward the family . . . you're of course different, but please don't take their pictures?" and fearing her response, she took her hand off the camera, and began asking each of them about themselves and about Bella. My exhalation in that moment was likely audible.

My shift from working primarily as a behind-the-scenes book designer to leading event production and public programming dovetailed with the advancement of my teaching career. The curricular rigor of Seattle Central Community College's program in graphic design was enhanced by its portfolio review for incoming students, an unusual process for a community college. Students could submit as often as they chose, receiving feedback each time on how to improve their portfolios and achieve acceptance into the program.

I participated in my first review when I became a full-time faculty member in fall 2000, and saw a portfolio that was re-submitted by Yadesa Bojia. Yaddi's work was *raw*: full of passion and political messages. My colleagues felt he was still not demonstrating adequate drawing skills. While I don't recall that we knew the demographics of our applicants, I saw in the portfolio a visual approach that seemed outside of Western culture, and could be additive to our environment. We could teach him drawing skills; it would be much more

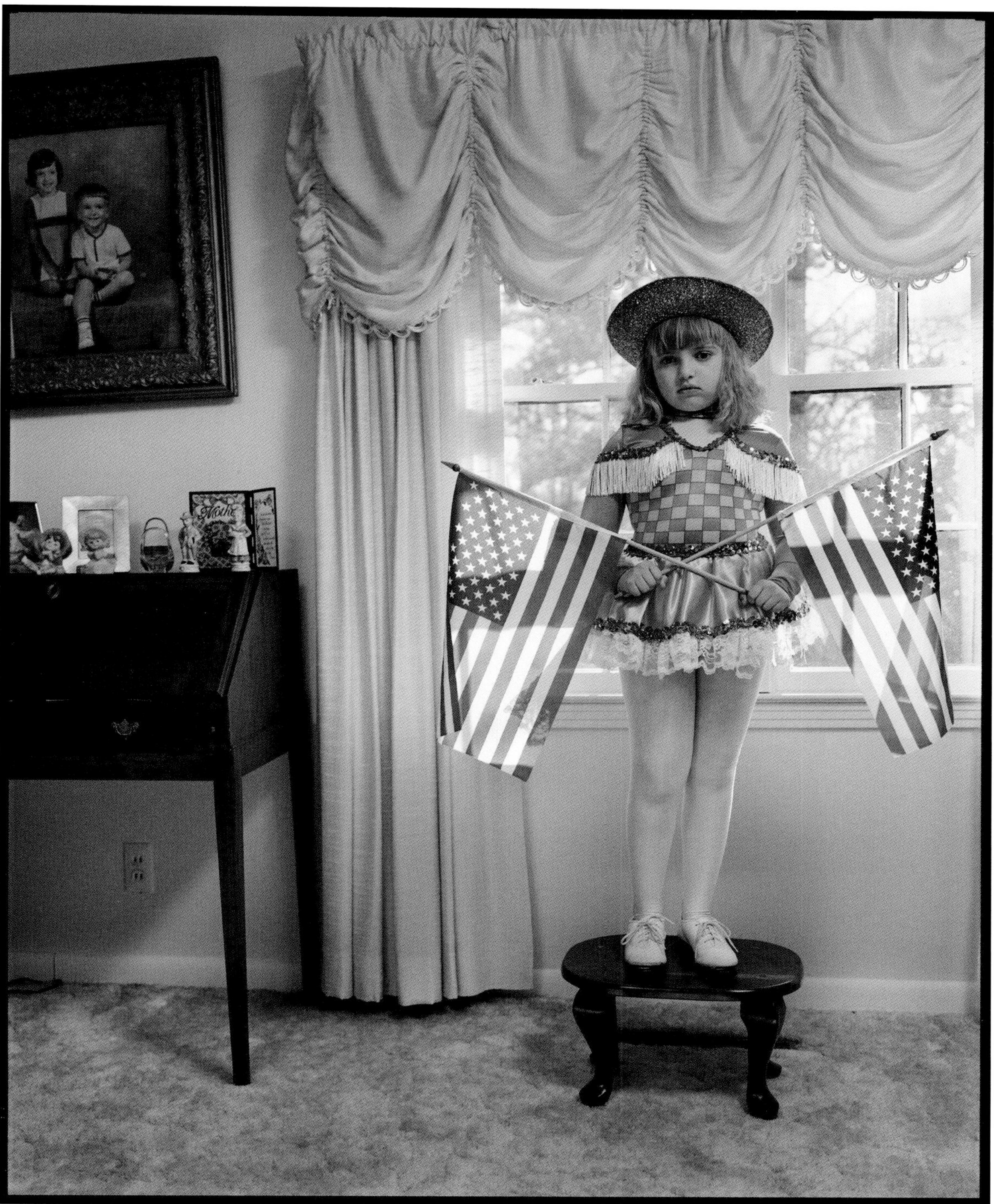

difficult to teach the depth of expression his work conveyed. He was granted admission. Seven years later, his design was selected to be on the new flag of the African Union, and he was flown to his birthplace of Ethiopia for an inaugural ceremony. He is one of many students from that program I continue to learn from.

I taught a range of courses, from the history of communications and color theory to advanced electives in experimental typography. In a course on professional practices, I asked students to envision their ideal life, being specific about what work schedule, perks, region, and income represented success for them. It was an assignment I created from the comment of one of my professors in graduate school, Berenice Hoffman, who said success was not simply about paying rent. Can you set your own schedule? Can you buy that pair of Gucci shoes you've always wanted? Can you risk time on developing manuscripts you believe in? I still sometimes hear from former students when they have achieved a milestone they envisioned from that assignment years ago. I still give it to myself occasionally, to check in with my own priorities. In doing so I often see through the forest that I am, in fact, hanging out in trees I have always wanted to climb.

My other favorite statement from Berenice cuts to the heart of every good pitch: "Don't tell me why this job, this project, is good for you. I don't care about it being good for you. *Tell me why it's good for me.*" Why should a photographer work with me on their book, how will they benefit? Why should a donor support the organization I am representing—how does its mission reflect positively on *their* interests? When I have mentored recent college graduates or junior employees, I have noticed they often lead with the strength of their ideas. I use Berenice's words to encourage them to reframe how they state their concepts and abilities, to present them as an answer to unspoken needs. Defining a project's problem is an essential skill set for a graphic designer; it's tough to render a solution otherwise. I've found that aspect of graphic design translates more than I ever imagined to many other business scenarios, as well as to my personal life, when I remember to utilize it.

The graphic design program at Seattle Central Community College was classed as "workforce education," and as a full-time faculty member I was expected to remain professionally active. Once I was within the systems of a state college, however, I learned quickly that what was said publicly and what happened internally were not always the same. My ongoing design work was encouraged by some of my colleagues, and was of interest to my students, but created resentment with others.

During my tenure process I noticed that, though the division's full-time faculty were evenly split between male and female, most women in our division carried heavier teaching loads than our male counterparts. After receiving tenure, I requested the same teaching load as my male colleague. The dean said no, without explanation for his decision. My colleague later confronted me, asking, "Why do you think the system should change just for you?" His question surprised me. I hadn't realized that he saw my request to have his teaching load as some sort of personal or systemic challenge.

I didn't think the system should change *for me.* The system was clearly broken if gender was influencing our assigned workloads. The strata of (male) administrators did not see it that way, despite the documentation I provided them for many female faculty in our division. At the recommendation of the teacher's union representative, I also presented the information to the Equal Employment Commission (EEC) of the city of Seattle. I was told by the EEC that it would be a stronger case if I accused the dean of racism, in addition to misogyny. I had no documented evidence of racism. Though racism may have been a factor, gender was the shared point of consistent discriminatory action.

I'd spent two years fighting to be heard by the college's administration, and then by the city, and was drained by the repeated message to just be quiet and do my job. It was not the first, but was one of my most painful realizations that factual documentation of wrongdoing, and speaking up about it, was not enough to achieve justice. That is an ongoing reality many people face throughout our legal system. I had already learned from a different circumstance that highly unethical behavior was not necessarily illegal. In this case we had proof that, division-wide, full-time female faculty spent more hours teaching than our male colleagues, but politics at every turn stood in the way of change. The dean was later moved from leading Communications and Design to oversight of the college's facilities; it was small acknowledgment that he had mishandled the situation.

I am not sure where I first learned of the world *polyvalent*. Its literal definition has to do with chemical bonding. Its secondary meaning is as something effective against, sensitive toward, or counteracting more than one toxin. Finally, I had a word to describe myself, recognizing that I had an innate ability to bond in different environments, and that I was both "effective against" and "sensitive toward" multiple social toxins. I was gaining comfort in my ability to connect in seemingly incongruous spaces, and learning to survive toxicities that sometimes surfaced there.

Aperture West's pilot event with Mary Ellen Mark in 2003 was considered a success. From that, we aimed to run a three-city lecture series the following year, and Stephen Shore's agreement to participate in the week-long version launched the initiative. His "yes," added to Mary Ellen's, gave me some credibility as I approached other invitees.

Stephen was the first photographer I traveled with, an experience made easier because I already knew him. I'd never actually heard him lecture, though, and just before he was introduced to a capacity crowd at the Hammer Museum, I realized I'd never asked him what he was presenting. What if he started talking about baseball or fly-fishing, subjects he favored in social settings? My panic in that moment was real—*in future, confirm that the photographer intends to talk about photography*—but unfounded.

Stephen was the perfect star for a "handler in training," letting me know what activities he was open to, and when he needed time alone. While in transit, he inquired about my life in the decade since I'd seen him on a near-daily basis at Bard, but he was also comfortable with periods of silence, which I appreciated. He provided invaluable feedback to some of my professional concerns involving the college where I'd received tenure, noting that a lifetime teaching position with an institution that doesn't respect you is not exactly a benefit. His words gave me the courage to give up my tenured position, and the stress from fighting for an equality the college chose not to grant, later that year.

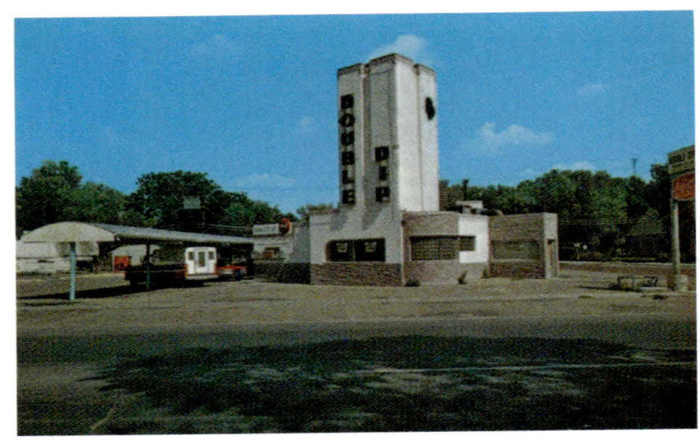

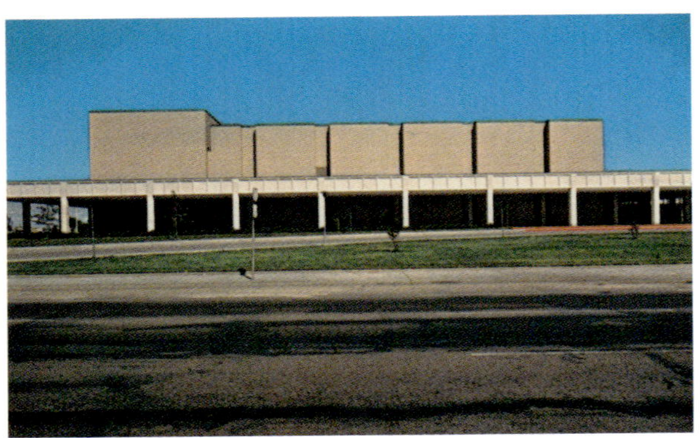

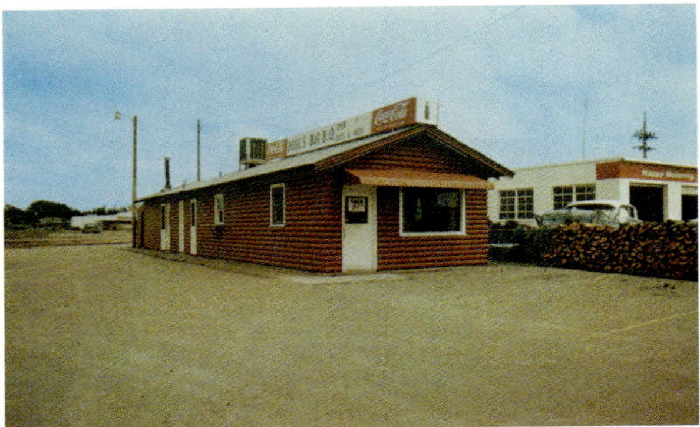

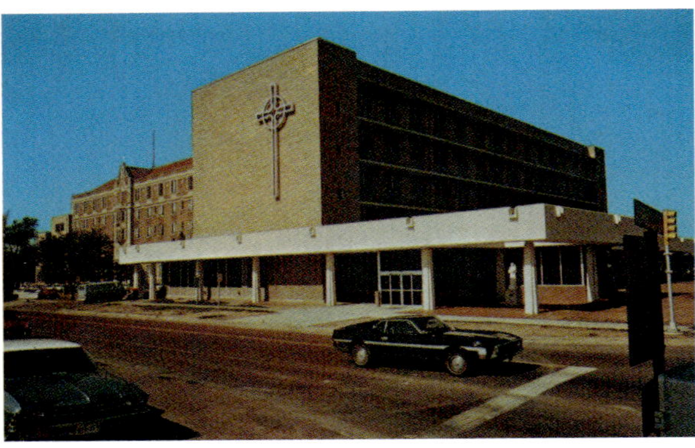

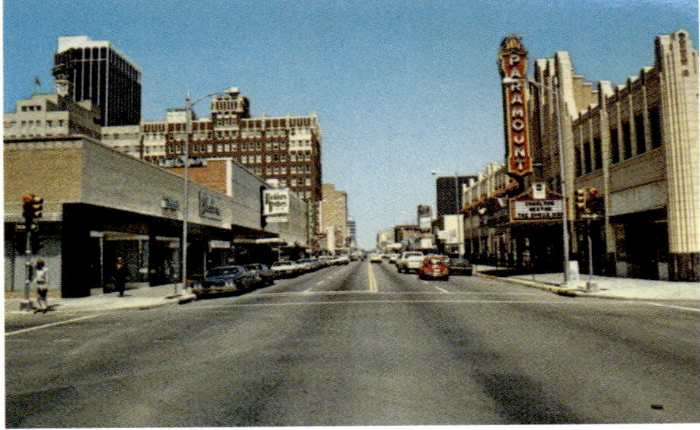

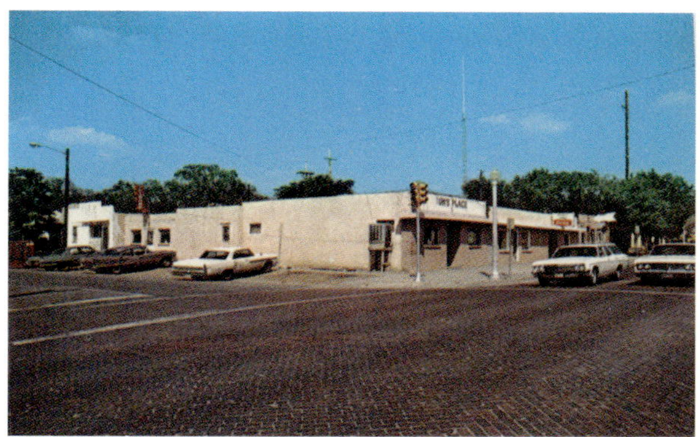
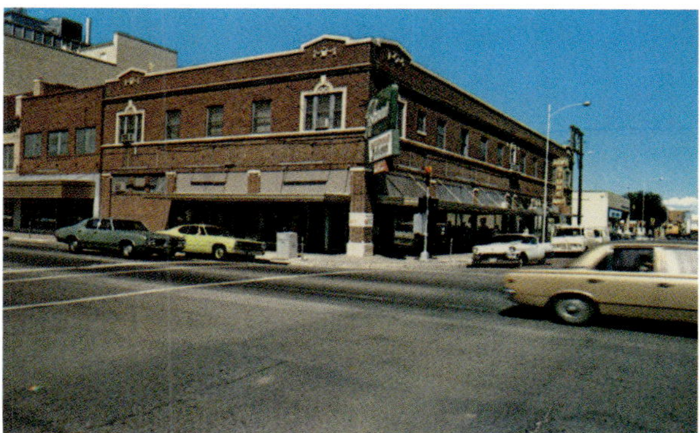
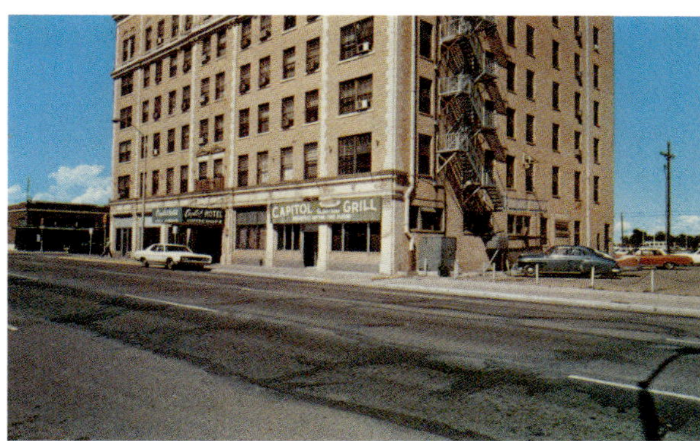
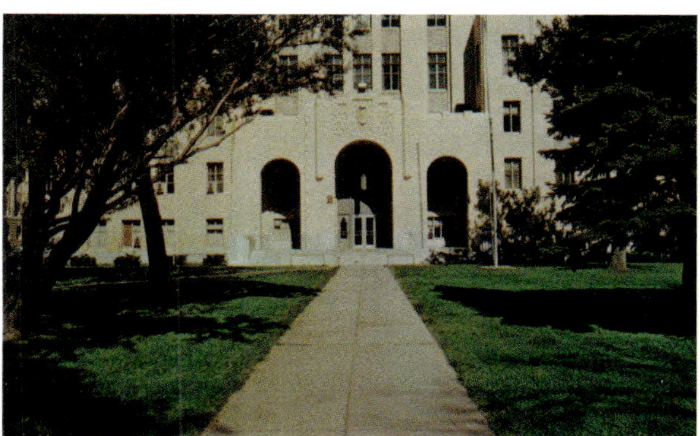
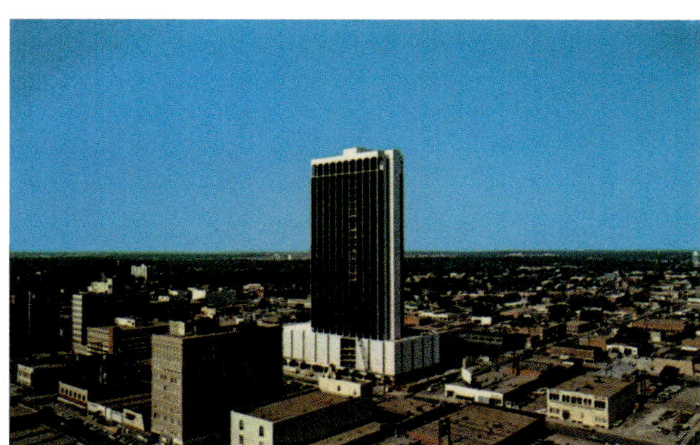

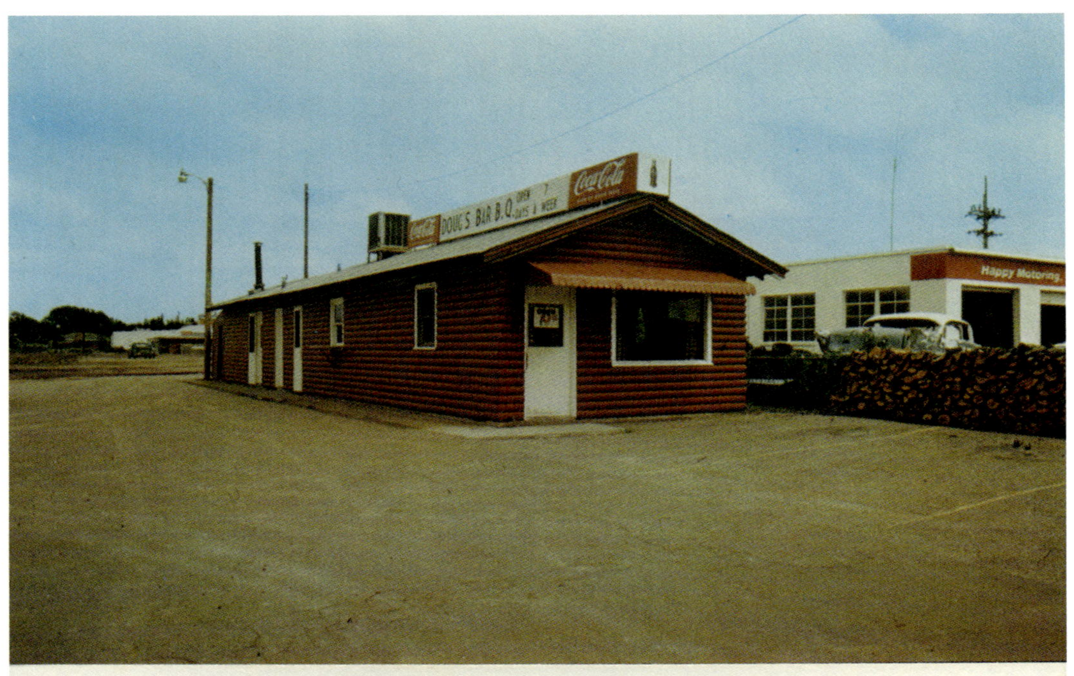

Doug's Bar B Q No. 1
3313 S. Georgia

Pub. by S. Shore - T. Wagner

Post Card

PLACE
STAMP
HERE

82810-C

dp MADE BY
DEXTER PRESS, INC.
WEST NYACK, NEW YORK

Much of Stephen's work requires a slowing of seeing, a receptivity to light and composition that took me many years to appreciate. I am grateful that I was raised with respect for my elders and wisers; that alone motivated me to spend more time with work I did not initially *feel*. With Stephen's photographs the lines and dimensionality of space unfolded for me only after sustained contemplation. I had to bring a meditative focus to spend a minute, or three, with his photographs. That said, he also appreciates that which others may find banal, and so in some photographs I don't try so hard to discover layers of meaning. I can accept a moment as he has seen it, and enjoy it. Had I stopped at my initial response to his work, or to that of Robert Adams, I would have missed out on an acuity of seeing that later made space for Charlie Rubin (p. 119), Isaac Layman (p. 145), and others.

In one of his public talks, Stephen mentioned that when he produced *Amarillo, "Tall in Texas"* as postcards in 1971, the printer had, without his agreement, added a tint of cyan blue to the skies of all the images in the series, even the cloudy-sky images, because "postcards should have blue skies." I loved this common-sense action by the printer. The cards are a cautionary tale for me: don't make assumptions on a photographer's behalf, even when it seems *obvious*.

Printing is always a matter of interpretation, an amalgam of the least noticeable decisions and compromises, and I am reminded of the individuality of perception every time I am on press. My most relevant contribution is to determine what the priorities are out of the six to eight pages we are reviewing simultaneously. Offset printing is a mind-boggling alignment of plates, blankets, paper, and ink traveling through heavy machinery that can produce 15,000 impressions in an hour. I try to ask questions rather than make statements, so I can engage the expertise of the men working these machines daily. They best understand how to achieve the exceptional result I am hoping for, and it helps to have them on my side. It is a very male environment, so that is not always easy (gifts of chocolate help).

Pages 68–70: STEPHEN SHORE, *Amarillo, "Tall in Texas,"* 1971. Set of ten color postcards, each 3 1/2 x 5 1/2 in. Offset printed by Dexter Press. Gift of Stephen Shore, 2006.

It took five visits to win the respect of one of the most senior pressmen at Oddi, a plant I worked with in Iceland. Ingjaldur and I just did not get along, to the extent that I would ask the production manager, Diana, to schedule my jobs avoiding his shifts. She always laughed at that, as he was the best and I wanted the best, but because of that we often clashed. In 2018, I learned that my next trip to Iceland would be my last. The plant was sold to new owners, who decided that binding books was not cost efficient.

Ingjaldur and I worked together on my projects—the last four books Oddi would ever print and bind. On each he went the extra mile, pointing out flaws I had missed, and teaching me things to look out for in the future. As I was leaving, I thanked him for giving the best of his years of expertise to those projects. He said that the books I brought them were challenging, but interesting, and as a client I was mostly reasonable. He would miss working on my books. It was a high compliment from a taciturn man.

William Christenberry was a sculptor and painter, a scavenger and collector, but most of all he was a gentleman. Tall, thin, with a soft drawl and twinkling eyes, in his white collared shirts he very much looked like the professor he was. He and his wife, Sandy, came to New York from their home in Washington, DC with some frequency, so I'd probably met them at an Aperture event once or twice before we all traveled together for the Aperture West lecture series in 2006.

His commitment to his home environs in Alabama, returning there to photograph annually though he made a life with his family elsewhere, felt familiar. I know the constant tug places can exert. I grew up on a property I loved. Electrified by New York City's current, I feel a little plugged into it no matter where I am. Through ancestry and family, far-flung locations in Western Australia, Ireland, Burma, and India have called to me.

Bill spoke lovingly of the various buildings he photographed year after year, the kudzu that could grow two to three feet in a day, and the rich soil of Alabama. When I referred to the red dirt of Australia seeming similar to what he was describing, he gently corrected me: "Dirt, Michelle, is what gets under your fingernails. We are talking now about *soil*. My grandfather taught me that distinction, and I am pleased to be able to share it with you."

The lecture series usually ended in Seattle. Though I would have welcomed all the photographers to our home there, they were usually pretty worn out after giving talks in three cities, and were ready to head straight back to their own lives. Books had been shipped to my house for Bill to sign, though, so he and Sandy stopped by on their way to the airport. On entering the living room, he looked around and drily remarked, "You're not a fan of color photography now, are you?" We had moved into the house a year earlier, and it was the first time there was ample wall space to hang some of the photographs I'd been gifted. I'd never noticed that all the prints were gelatin silver, gravure, or platinum until he mentioned it. He saw that I was embarrassed, and said, "My goodness, don't apologize! How nice to live with these." Looking to change the subject, I remembered that I had a Brownie camera—the Bullet-Nose edition that matched my Studebaker—and asked if he'd take a look. He inspected it and pronounced it light-tight.

Bill was right, I didn't often have a visceral response to color photographs. Yet when he projected *Green Warehouse* in the lecture he gave in Los Angeles, I wept. My reaction surprised me; I'd seen the image in books many times without being especially moved. But large, I suddenly saw on the screen the barn I'd grown up with, the barn I'd left New York to try and own. In the flurry of decisions I'd made in 1999, I'd lost both places I called home. If I could somehow live with that photograph, I could at least have my barn forever. It was a powerful realization, but one so fresh, so personal, that I don't recall even sharing it with Bill. A year later, that exact image was released as a limited edition. I took it as a sign, and bought the print.

WILLIAM CHRISTENBERRY, *Green Warehouse*, **Newbern, Alabama, 1997 / 2007.** Archival pigment print on Hanhemule paper, 10 3/4 x 13 3/4 in. Edition of 25. Produced by PhotoAlliance, San Francisco, and purchased from them, 2009.

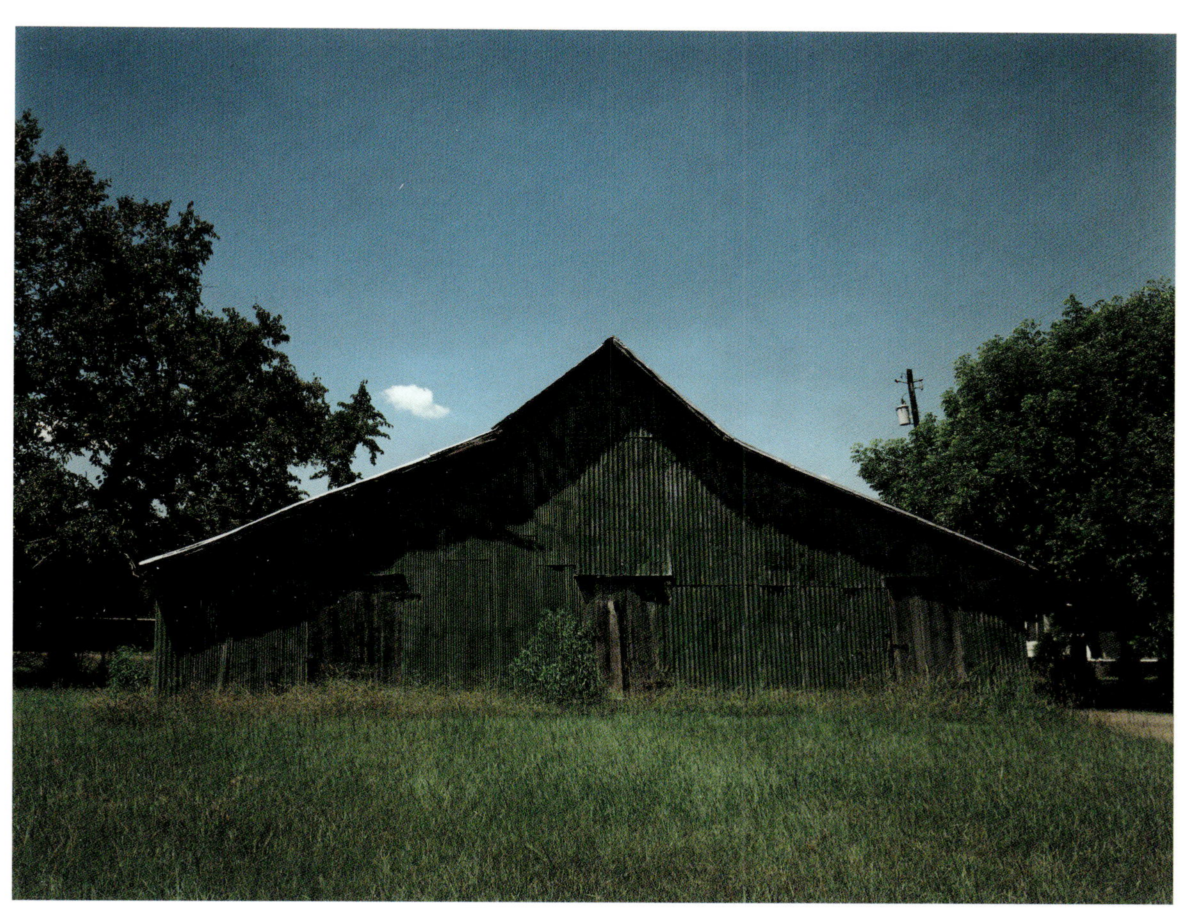

Bill and Sandy encouraged me to visit them in Washington, DC, and within the next year or so I did. It was delightful to be in their home and see much more of Bill's work than I'd yet experienced in person. I had located a used copy of Bill's rare first book, *Southern Photographs* (Aperture, 1983), albeit a pretty beat-up, musty smelling one. As I was leaving, I asked if he would sign it. Without commenting on its sad state, he took it into his studio, and returned the book in an acetate bag, protected with bubble wrap. "I found you a better jacket," he said, and smiled. When I later opened it, not only did it have a new jacket, but he'd wrapped that in acetate, as well. He signed it to me "with affection and best wishes," sentiments I will always hold him in.

If any contemporary photographer embodied the trust I felt in Michael Hoffman's vision, it was Robert Adams. By 1997, when I started full-time there, Aperture had published at least seven monographs and two collections of essays by him. His work was featured in many issues of the magazine. Yet of all the questions I had asked colleagues over the years, none were about his work. I just couldn't admit that I could not find a way into his photographs. I contented myself with his profound and moving writing, and though I owned many of his photographic books, I found myself frustrated by what I could not appreciate within them.

ROBERT ADAMS, *Pawnee National Grassland,* **Colorado, 1984 / 1988.** Gelatin silver print on Portriga Rapid paper, 8 3/16 x 6 1/2 in. Edition of 40. Produced by Aperture Foundation and purchased from them, 2005.

Baron, who deeply admired Bob, encouraged me to reach out to him since we both lived in the Northwest. I dutifully called to try and gain his endorsement, if not involvement, in the Aperture West initiative. Getting in touch with him was its own adventure as he did not then, and does not now use an answering machine, voicemail, or email. He politely declined participating in any public events, but was an active listener, asked thoughtful questions, and indicated he'd be open to further conversation if I found it useful.

Shortly thereafter I requested and Bob agreed to the donation of a print of his for a fundraising event. When it arrived, I unwrapped it in the presence of a colleague who had studied photography, confessing to her the wall I encountered when it came to his work. As I removed the protective tissue, I became distracted by the abrupt crop of the tree's trunk, and how it then drew my eye to the lower right of the frame. The ever so slight elevation behind the tree drew my eyes further into the undulations of the land, leading to the horizon. In that moment I discovered, again, that if I slowed my seeing a print would often meet me more than halfway.

It is no coincidence that I was having this epiphany around his work with a gelatin silver photograph, holding all the subtleties of his particular sense of light. That awakening broke down the blocks I had previously been unable to overcome, and I could appreciate his books on a new level. Yet the profound stirring I feel when I have the opportunity to stand before his prints and let the interaction of time and light and the thoughtful gaze of this man resolve into the quiet is irreplaceable.

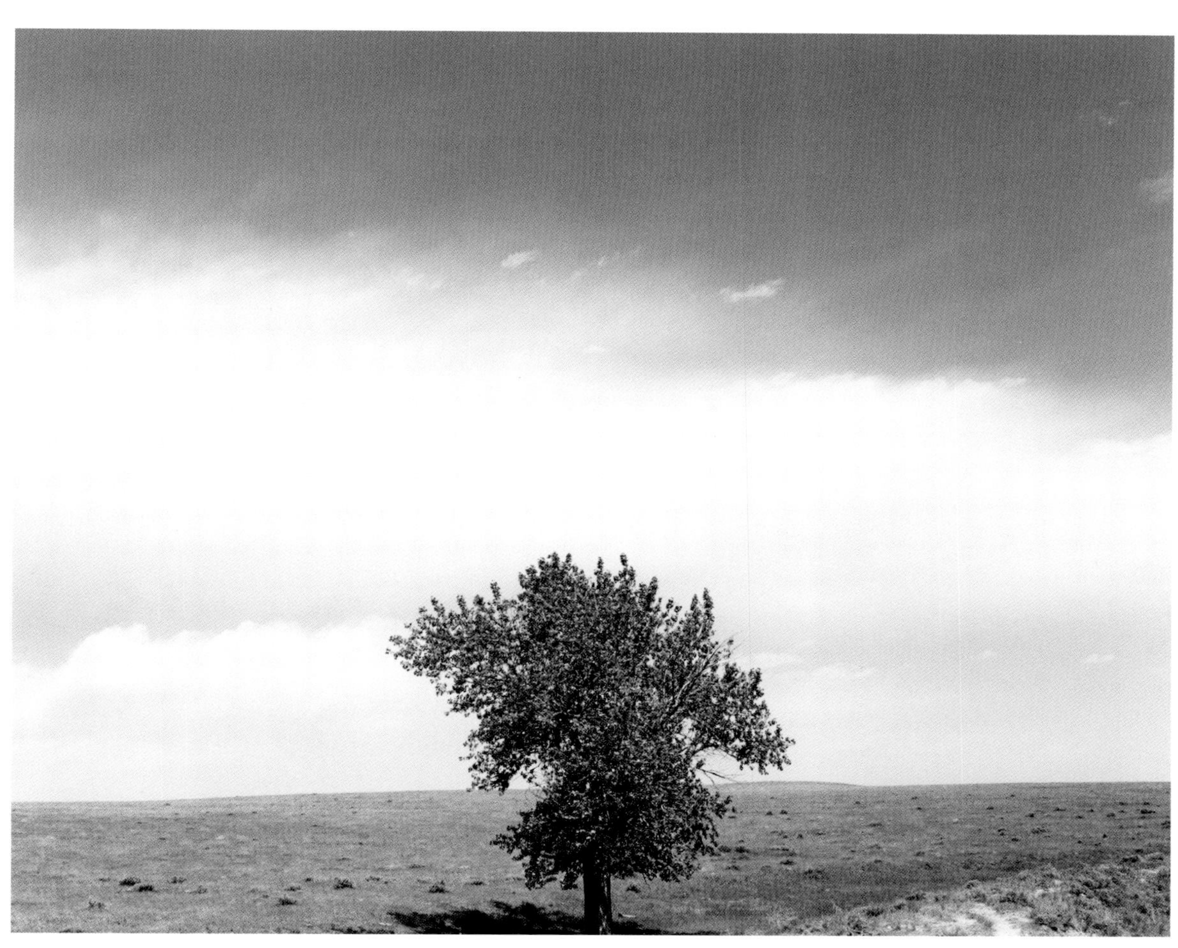

Through letters and phone conversations Bob has spoken to me honestly in dark times and in joyous ones, providing gentle critique and heartfelt encouragement. At my lowest moments, his words have kept me persevering in the work I am doing. I both did and did not arrive at an *a-ha!* moment through the experience of one photograph by Robert Adams. It came about through my struggling to see and not understanding (repeat, repeat), then finally understanding, then seeing anew (repeat, repeat). It is a journey I must continually commit to, because, as I grow and shift as a human, there are new details to delight in with many photographs, if I do the work to receive them. My exposure to Stephen Shore's work for a decade prior to attempting Robert Adams contributed to my ultimate awakening to Adams. That meant, once I had accessed Bob's work, I also had to return to Stephen's work with this new viewpoint and discover what other connections may reveal themselves there.

As I got to know more museums, art galleries, nonprofit organizations, publishers, and academic programs highlighting photography throughout the west, there was an abundance of proposed collaborations, but never enough funds to realize them. With new friends and like-minded colleagues at those institutions, I facilitated two fundraising events for Aperture West. The first, in 2004, was an unforgettable dinner and auction at the Space Needle in Seattle, co-produced with Bumbershoot and Photographic Center Northwest. We made our goal of over $75,000, splitting the net proceeds three ways. Aperture's portion covered the annual total of my retainer, which was welcome news to the board in New York, and daunting at the same time. The chemistry of a single evening could make or break a year's worth of planning; I would come to learn that was common for nonprofits.

Bob's print was solicited for the first event, but on the advice of his gallerist, I saved it for the second event in 2005. It was a simpler affair at the Los Angeles Public Library while Aperture's fiftieth anniversary exhibition was on view there. The Library graciously hosted us and the LA-based No Strings Foundation for a reception and silent auction, made special by the attendance of Aperture's last living founder, Dody Weston Thompson (née Dody Warren), along with nearly two hundred other guests. When halfway through the evening few prints in the silent auction had bids, I asked my sister to place one on Bob's photograph for me. It ended up the only bid on the piece, which speaks to the still-recent appreciation and escalation of contemporary photography. Only one of the ten prints in the auction garnered a "high" bid of $2,500 (Stephen Shore; an exhibition of his work was concurrently on view at the Hammer Museum). The $6,500 we gained from that event, while small, covered the participation of one photographer for the lecture series, with a little left over. Dollars gave me leverage in New York as I sought to extend cross-pollination between the photographic communities on either coast.

While we were traveling together for the lecture series in 2006, Bruce Davidson shared a great analogy about where you disperse your vitality. He said the problem with giving a talk is that it takes the same amount of energy as making a picture, except that at the end of it, you don't have a picture. I loved that, and could relate—I felt the same way about events. Organizing them sometimes took as much time as making a book, but at the end of the great experience, there was nothing to hold.

Bruce had learned to be efficient with the energy he expended through talks, and was unabashed about the consistency of his four-tray slide presentation. He reserved the majority of his focus for making photographs, not talking about them. I grew to love that the images, and their attendant stories, stayed the same, and as I heard him speak over many years would begin to anticipate the arrival of my favorite anecdotes, thinking "Ooh, the widow of Montmartre is coming up next!" The stories were new to most of the people in the audience, and the cadence of his delivery was always engaging, as if he were telling the story for the first time.

The spontaneity that occurs in public events does make them memorable, and distinct from the carefully considered publishing process. I recall one lecture with Michael "Nick" Nichols, who was at one time a member of the Magnum Photos cooperative. A young man started his question with a long description of his desire to make a life as a photographer, and then asked, "But how do you actually get started?" Before Nick could even respond, five or six other Magnum photographers in the audience, including Bruce, called out simultaneously: "you just *do it!*" I have observed that attitude of determination in every acclaimed creator I have worked with.

Bruce has been observing through his viewfinder for six decades. A titan in the field, he is in person somewhat short in stature, with an unassuming air, and bright blue eyes. It is often easy to forget who he is in the world of photography and simply enjoy his humanity. Bruce's wife Emily attended Bard, and their two daughters settled in Seattle, so with those additional points of connection I was treated as extended family. I visited them as often as mutual time permitted when in New York (food was always involved), just to be in their company. At times of transition, Bruce, like Mary Ellen, Sylvia Plachy, and others, checked in to see how I was. Bruce and Emily even let me know when a sublet became available in their apartment building (the New York photographers often encouraged my return there).

The Welsh Pony is a photograph I know Bruce is fond of —a large mural print of it hangs in his dining room. Although it has taken me a long time to get to know it, I tried because he chose to give it to me, and that matters to me. Just as Stephen Shore's postcards remind me not to make assumptions, this print reminds me not to ever dismiss a photograph by someone I respect. How do I need to adjust myself to enter into it? Am I willing to be flexible? Scale certainly affects my relationship with this image. In Bruce's home, I see the pony with a statuesque monumentality that does not necessarily translate in my 11 x 14-inch print. And yet, one of the great joys of living with photographs is how we change in relationship to them, and how they change in relationship to one another. It is an extension of the process of sequencing in creating a visual book. Finding what best serves each individual image, as well as the conversations with images before and after, results in a whole that stands equal to, if not transcending, each of its parts.

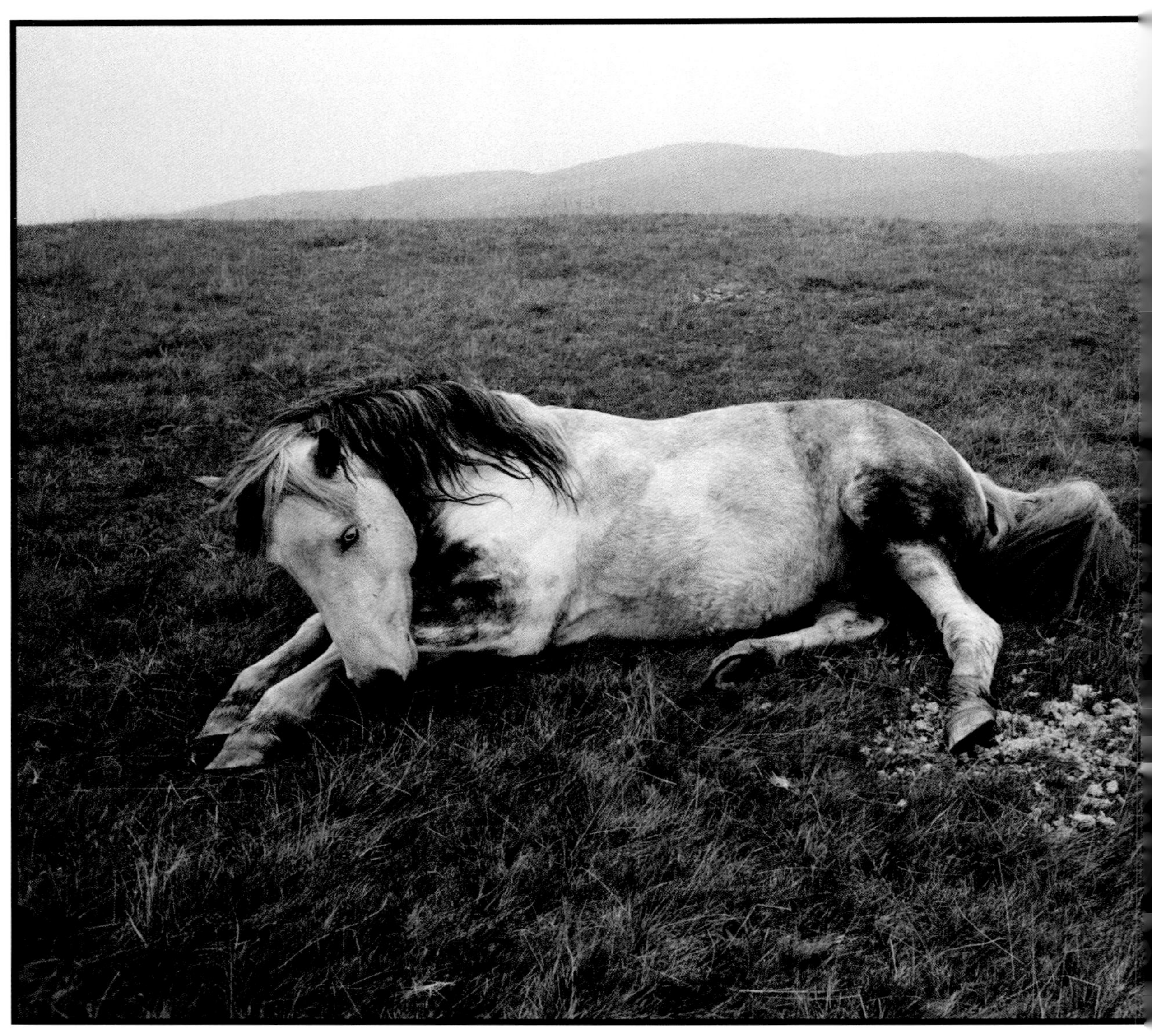

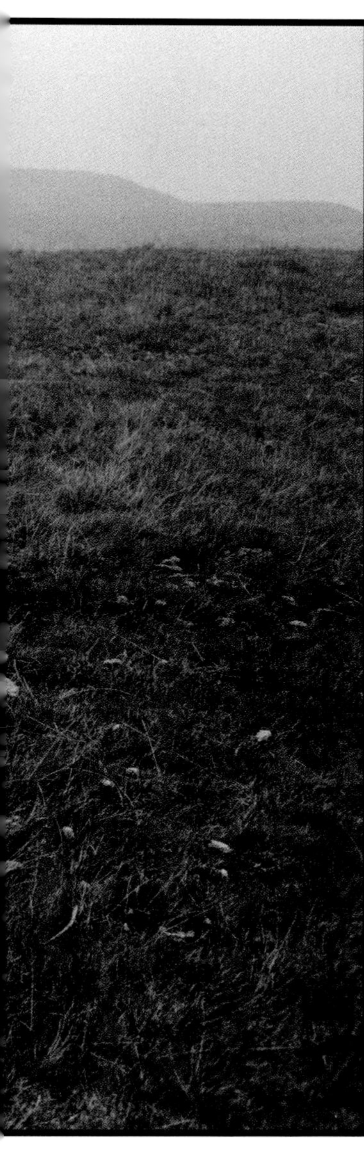

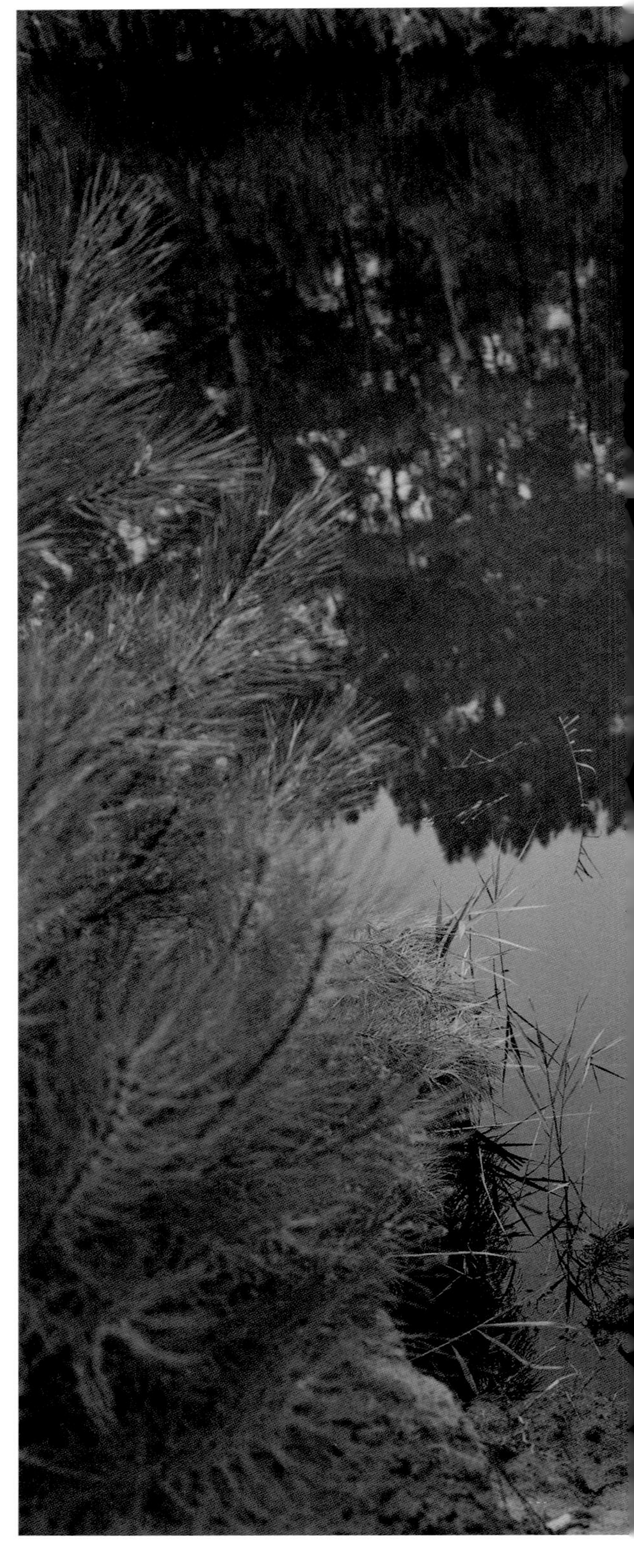

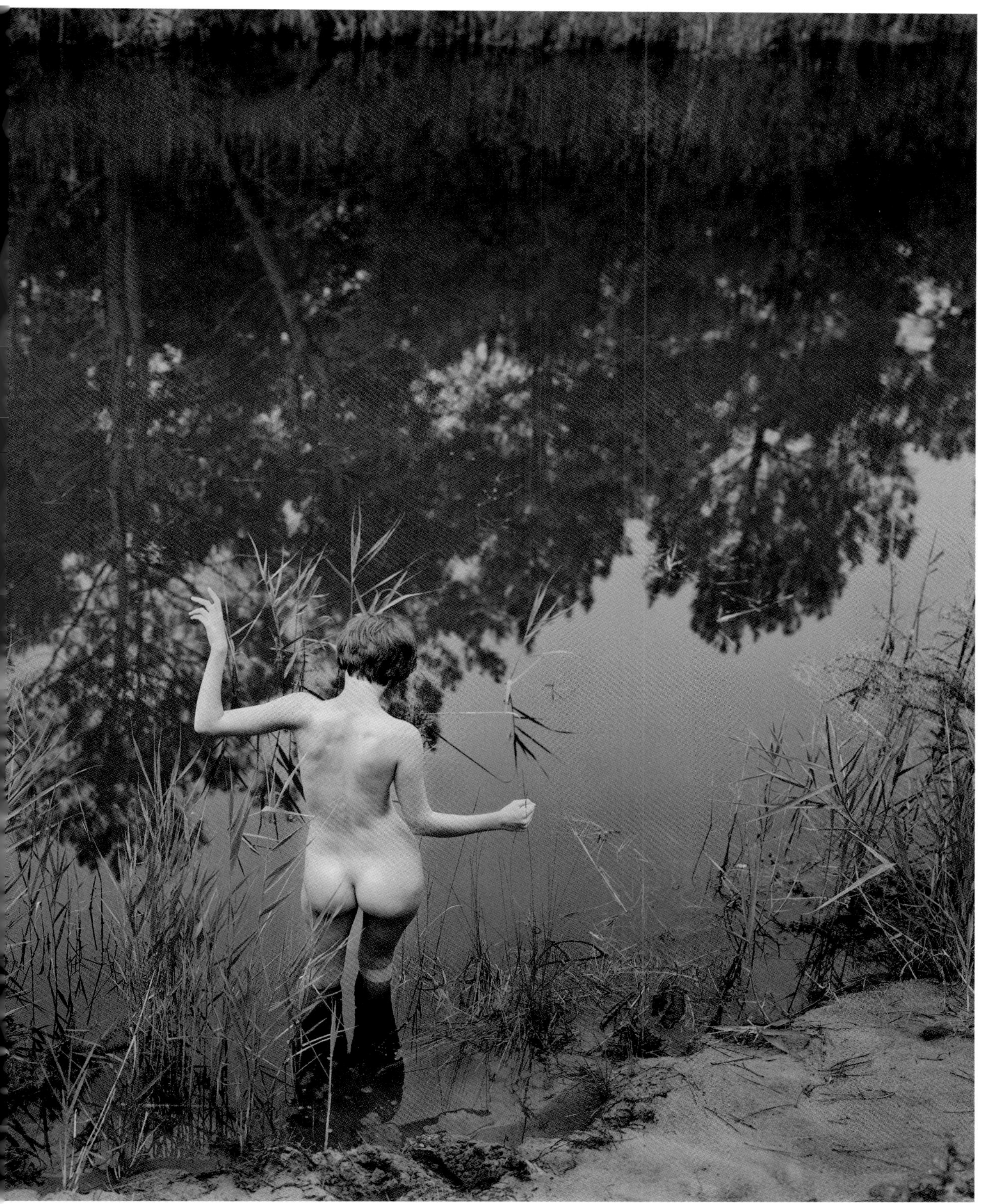

The Welsh Pony (pp. 78–79) spoke to me in a new way when it landed in this book in proximity to Jock Sturges's *Vanessa* (pp. 80–81). The prints are substantially different sizes but in the book, the progression from one to the other intrigues me enough that perhaps one day they will hang on a wall together. Robert Adams's *Pawnee Grassland* (p. 75), also nestled in my living room, and here, near *Welsh Pony*, awakened surprising connections I had never before seen in either. Adding even one photograph to a room causes me hours of delighted consternation as I sort out the visual relationships. It can sometimes be enjoyable; it can also disrupt my productivity on any other matter until the images are settled in harmonious dialogue. Because most of the prints I live with are by people I know, I cannot help but think of the photographers' personalities in addition to the images themselves. Have these three photographers sharing a wall ever even met in person? Would they like each other? It sometimes feels like seating guests at a perpetual dinner party, then stepping back to listen in on the conversations.

Photographs can be easily obstructed by the baggage we as viewers bring to their surfaces, baggage we drop unceremoniously, blaming the image for the heavy weight we've carried and have no intention of unpacking for ourselves.

When I arrived in New York City in 1994, the body and its representation was at the center of the culture wars. Nothing was more important, and nothing was more offensive, than the human form. Perfect or wracked with lesions, hooded in leather, or covered with honey, too young or too old (by society's standards) to be seen, or visualized through urine and blood, bodies represented gender, health, religion, and morals—humanity's complex expression of itself. I am not sure I will ever understand how so many Americans can be easily outraged at the sight of a naked body, particularly one presented with consent and intention. Yet I acknowledge that for most of my life I held a complicated relationship with my own form, more annoyed with its dysfunction, and afraid of it as a provocation of unwanted advances, than embracing of it as my personal soul container. Perhaps many more people than I realize experience similar disconnects that get turned outward as anger instead of inward toward resolution.

Pages 80–81: JOCK STURGES, *Vanessa*, Le Porge, France, 2002 / 2004. Gelatin silver print, made under the direction of Jock Sturges, 14 7/8 x 18 1/4 in. Gift of Jock Sturges, 2004.

I have found the work of photographers who hold the body in beauty and reverence enhances my understanding of the totality of my being. Representational photographs form the majority of the prints I see daily throughout my home, including *Vanessa* by Jock Sturges. When I first viewed Jock's work in the mid-1990s I knew little about the cumbersome 8 x 10 camera he worked with, and, like some other viewers, I ascribed most of the beauty of his photographs to the people themselves, and not to the craft and care with which he saw them. As I got to know Jock and met a few of the people he imbued with his vision of them, I began to understand the significance of all he brought to the equation. That became even clearer when we started the edit for what became *Jock Sturges: Notes* (Aperture, 2004; see p. 166).

While the majority of my professional engagement through teaching and Aperture West focused on creating experiences—classes, lectures, panel discussions, dinners, and exhibition openings—I continued to design a few books when given the chance, to hold onto the comfort I'd found in the creation of beautiful, physical objects. The direct collaboration with photographers kept me grounded in what I loved the most about photography, and reminded me of why I was fighting for the art form to be valued in our culture.

When I arrived at Jock's home and studio in Seattle in the fall of 2003 to discuss ideas for a book, he'd just received his proof prints from photographing in Montalivet, a French naturist community where he lived and worked each summer. He was understandably anxious to review his previous months' work, so, with my assurance that I would not make so much as a sound, he did a first pass of the images as I looked over his shoulder. The images he immediately pulled as rejects were technically more perfect than most people could ever aspire to create.

Jock is well versed in the history of photography and speaks easily of visual references and the education he took from viewing the work of the masters of previous generations, including Harry Callahan and Paul Strand, as well that of his peers. Like Mary Ellen Mark, he regularly contacted me to speak of people he taught or mentored that he felt were making strong photographs, or called my attention to women in the field he believed deserved greater attention. I came to the work of Mona Kuhn and Peggy Washburn because of him.

Notes remains one of my favorite books for its gentle articulation of process. It includes Jock's voice along with those of the friends he photographs, and visually demonstrates that most academic of differences—between photographs taken and photographs made—by comparing snapshots of inspiration with the final frames he created. It was an exercise for both of us to pare down to the essential elements that inform his work, and we worked through many iterations of the design, over countless conversations, to accurately convey the intersection of his work, home, life, and beliefs.

Jock does not get blanket model releases from the families he photographs. For each of his books, the edit of images is determined, and then every single person whose photograph has been selected is contacted and asked for permission to use the specific photograph(s). If he no longer has accurate contact information, the image is not used. If the person does not respond, the image is not used. If we add photographs, it starts all over again with the new images, even if those people have given permission already for use of other images in the book. It was a time-consuming process, but a non-negotiable when working with him. When *Notes* was complete, Jock offered me a print. It was a particularly meaningful gesture to me, because we had some critical aesthetic disagreements (including a photograph of him that I insisted upon, and he did not think necessary). I chose *Vanessa* as an example of Jock's seeing of figure and ground, and for its stated homage to Harry Callahan, with whom, as noted earlier, I once spoke on the phone in my early days at Aperture (geeky, I know, but true).

Fast forward eleven years. My twenty-three-year-old stepson sent me via text a photograph of him from behind, stark naked, arms askew, against the red soil of the

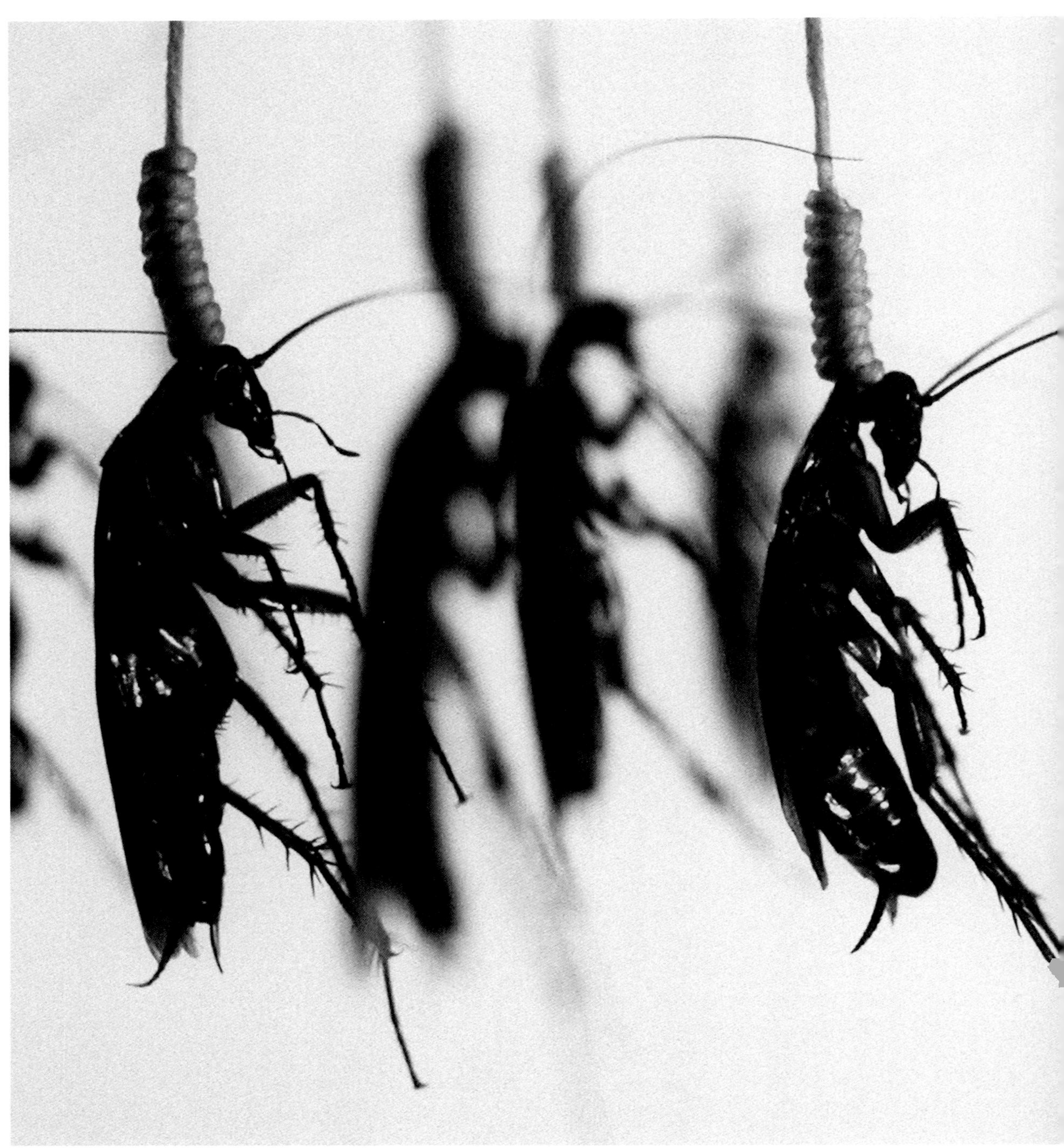

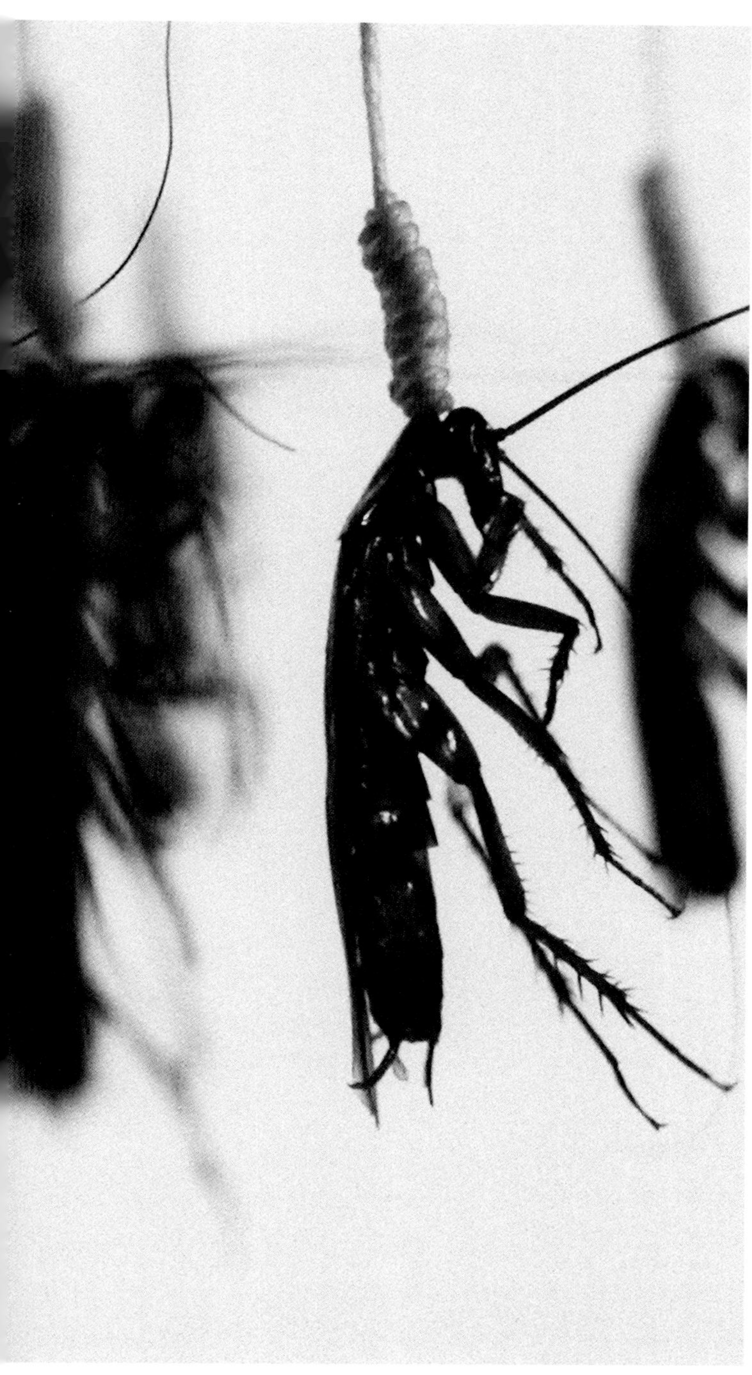

Australian landscape. My first thought was, "Thank goodness the beach culture he was raised in gave him none of the body inhibitions I grew up with." My second thought was, "Why on earth is he sending me this picture?" When, laughing, I called to ask him, he said, "You couldn't tell? I was recreating that photograph hanging above the fireplace." That he held a positive association with any of the photographs we lived with made me very happy.

Art, as a word alone and attached to an object, can be intimidating. Receiving photographs as acknowledgment, and in trade, certainly encouraged my first and subsequent purchases. But before tumbling into photography I had already bought a work of art, an oil painting by my friend Abby Bender while we were both students at Bard. She otherwise would have re-used the canvas for her next assignment, and I was still attached to the first one. The leap from an intriguing old car to a canvas was not too difficult for me to make. Functional beauty was always part of my life, from the cars to the silver and china used on special occasions. After years of using stainless steel cutlery for daily use, and silver for dinner parties, I finally decided to donate the stainless and eat with the silver every day. It's a little more work to maintain, but even the simplest meals taste a little better from a beautiful fork. Yet wine from the Waterford glasses or tea in the Belleek china I still treat as ceremonial. The self-imposed infrequency of those experiences reminds me to indulge, yet not to take all that surrounds me for granted.

Pleasing functional objects serve tangible purposes that some feel "fine art" does not. Yet once we've given ourselves permission to live with what inspires us, so much bounty unfolds. That said, I live with photographs for more than their aesthetic contributions. They are physical evidence that people I love and learned from existed, even for a short time, in my world. Books I have worked on are likewise physical evidence that I have existed, for a short time, in photography's world.

In articulating Alfred Stieglitz's concept of Equivalence, Minor White suggested that "perhaps the reader can recall some images, after the seeing of which he has never been quite the same," [*PSA Journal*, vol 29, no 7, 1963]. Catherine Chalmers's *Hanging*, 2004, amply conveys this for me (pp. 84–85). Stark, elegant, horrifying yet graphically arresting, it is an image few forget. The subject—cockroaches—turns many people away viscerally before they can take in the photograph itself. Those who do look upon it are sometimes reluctant to admit to its seductive beauty. In *Hanging*, there is no cozy corner of the frame one can retreat to, or rest in—our eyes are inexorably drawn to the ropes, the balletic antennae, the shadowy forms out of focus, and the rigor mortis of those multiple legs. This photograph has hung in one location—above my desk—for fifteen years. Catherine's work has intrigued me since I was first introduced to it in 1996; it pushes me to consider what in nature we shelter, and what we destroy.

Pages 84–85: CATHERINE CHALMERS, *Hanging*, from the series "Executions," 2004. Gelatin silver print, 24 x 36 in. Gift of Catherine Chalmers, 2004.

We all carry phobias; one of mine is rodents. When I saw the brilliant *Gene(sis)* exhibition, curated by Robin Held at the Henry Art Gallery in Seattle in 2002, and Catherine's 20 x 30 inch prints of genetically modified mice, along with baby mice, "pinkies," being consumed by snakes, I had to physically fight the urge to vomit. Yet, once I dared to look again at these creatures shown larger than in reality, their heads the same size as mine, I could begin to perceive them in a new way.

I designed the cover of Catherine's first book in 1999, and had met her a few times in addition to seeing her work exhibited. Yet I was hesitant when invited to visit her studio. A long table held terrariums of her various collaborators: snakes, spiders, praying mantises, and yes, mice. Her intelligence and calm in describing the creatures she raised and why she was drawn to them allayed some of my fears, and I could position myself without staring at the mice, which helped. When she began what became a ten-year exploration of the American cockroach and was raising those as well, she had the egg cases delivered to Aperture to minimize consternation from her neighbors, who were already wary of what was in her studio based on what had been publicly shown. I still struggle with mice, and I can understand that the fears they trigger in me are likely what cockroaches trigger in others. Yet, because of Catherine's work, and conversations with her over the last twenty years, I have greater compassion for these "lesser" lifeforms of our planet. I am more likely to observe ants busily moving a twig, or to gently right a bumblebee stuck on its back, appreciating the delicate beauty of an insect I might otherwise have been inclined to step on.

Memory, and trauma.

When I first saw An-My Lê's photograph of Tranh-Hoa, Vietnam (pp. 88–89), in 2006, it spoke to a part of my DNA that has existed beyond my years on the planet. It is in many ways a peaceful scene, and yet my appreciation for it also carried an internal response of foreboding. Tranh-Hoa, Vietnam is longitudinally separated from Mandalay, Burma, by just over two degrees south. My mother's childhood experience of fleeing Mandalay during the Japanese air raids of World War II is chronologically separated from An-My Lê's childhood experience of fleeing the Tet Offensive by just over twenty-five years.

When I first heard An-My lecture I was struck by the calm with which she spoke of being a refugee, and the intensity of her artistic engagement probing various aspects of the residue of war and conflict. Part of me wanted to ask more about how she navigated it all in her being, and another part of me felt that was not a question to be asked in words. The answers may perhaps reside in some of her photographs.

While I sensed that perhaps An-My's stories paralleled some of what my mother's family had experienced in Burma, my mother rarely spoke of her childhood, so I didn't really know for sure. My first and only glimpse of what my mother lived through in 1942

Pages 88–89: AN-MY LÊ, Untitled, Tranh-Hoa, from the series "Viet Nam," 1998 / 2006. Gelatin silver print, 12 x 17 in. Number 12/40. Produced by Aperture Foundation and purchased from them, 2019.

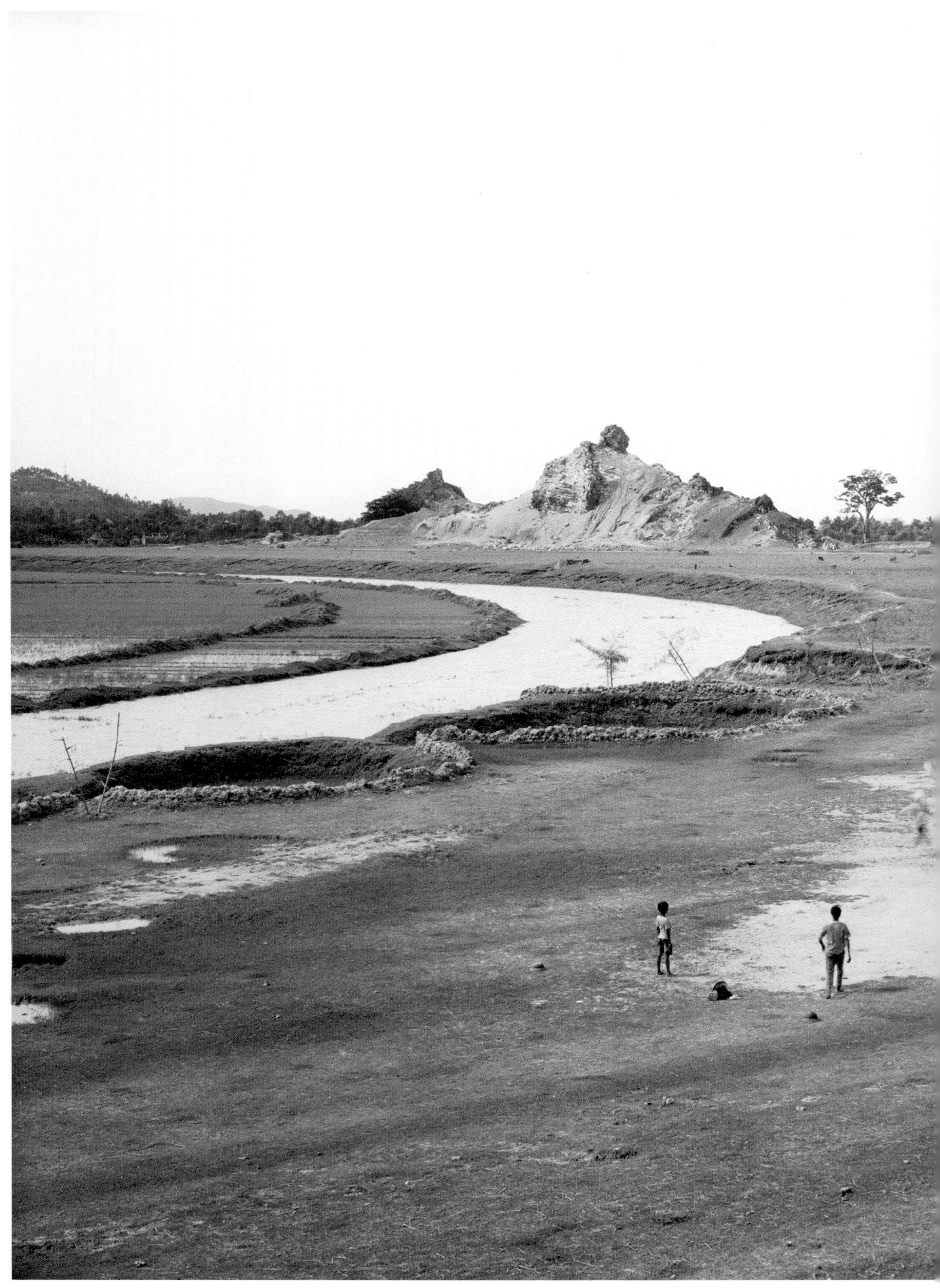

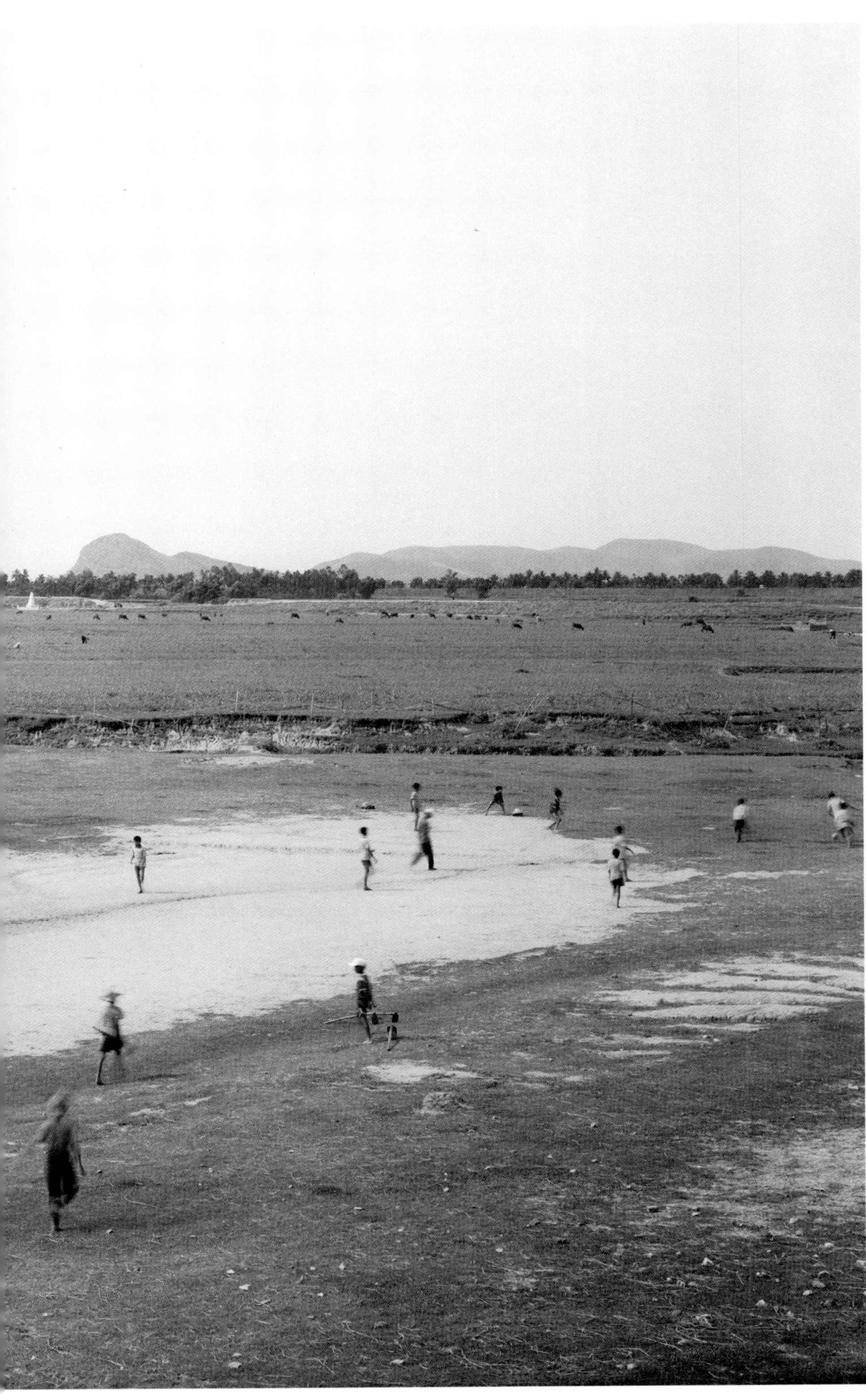

came around 2007, from showing her a book a friend had completed on the Ayeyarwady River. Looking at a map within it, she pointed out a city I'd never heard of, Myitkyina, and said that was where they'd been airlifted out of Burma to Calcutta. She was seven years old at the time. I knew her family had been living in Mandalay, which appeared to be quite a distance south (over two-hundred-and-fifty miles, it turns out). When I asked how they'd gotten to Myitkyina, she looked surprised and said, "We walked!" She then told me a story that added one more layer to our complex relationship.

As political rhetoric escalated and Burma engaged in discussions with both the Axis and Allied Forces, my grandfather kept two suitcases at the ready, one packed with gold and money, and the other with clothes and family photographs. When the heavy bombing of Mandalay began in April 1942, my grandmother was in the kitchen, cooking while holding her youngest child. From the shock, her hand froze around the handle of the pan. She held onto the baby, and the pan trapped in her clenched fist, while my grandfather managed to grab one suitcase before they ran with their other young children. Days later, it took three men to pry open my grandmother's hand. The valise my grandfather had been carrying was also opened. Instead of the money they needed for food, they found wrapped in some clothing the glass plate negatives of family portraits.

I was too stunned to speak. With a sinking feeling, I wondered how often the books of photography I'd shown her over the years, for which she rarely showed any enthusiasm beyond the placement of my name, perhaps prompted subconscious feelings of hunger and fear she does not otherwise recall? Then again, maybe it is the opposite, and my life in photography fulfills a cosmic circle from that moment. I will never know. After the briefest pause, she asked if I wanted another cup of tea, and completely changed the subject.

I have asked a few times what became of those glass-plate negatives; she waves vaguely and says maybe her older sister kept them.

Trauma, and memory.

I do not know An-My well. We were to travel together from Los Angeles for the lecture series in 2006, but moments before I was to pick her up, I tripped at a gas station and broke my leg in multiple places. She made her flights and delivered lectures in San Francisco and Seattle; I had surgery in California and a multi-day allergic reaction to morphine. Her mother brought me sushi in the hospital.

Nearly a week later I was cleared to fly back to Seattle, and over the next six months faced that the world functioned just fine without me as I lay in a cloud of pain, willing my tendons and bones to fuse faster. The accident had occurred on what would have been my father's eightieth birthday, and I knew it was a sign from him: *slow down.* But as Michael Hoffman used to say sometimes, "I heard you, I just didn't perceive what you were saying." As soon as I could walk again I was right back on the road, making up for "lost time."

Over ten years and many life lessons later, I had finally learned to breathe a little. With support from the PCNW board I then reported to, I extended a professional trip to

India in 2017 to do some personal travel there, as well as visit Burma for the first time. When I saw children playing on the semi-arid plains around Mandalay, An-My's photograph hovered in my mind. I knew it was one I needed to possess, a remnant of memories I had accessed—An-My's and my mother's—to which I had added experiences and memories of my own.

The regional designation of Aperture West—three-quarters of the continental United States, plus Alaska and Hawaii—made it, and me, a large island within Aperture, yet one that was connected to everything that happened through the foundation. Though there were earlier efforts to create an office for Aperture in San Francisco, my hire in 2002 and the subsequent fiftieth anniversary events we organized down the coast marked the beginning of frequent engagement west of the Mississippi. I continued to place traveling exhibitions at museums, organize book signings, give lectures, and staff booths at west coast art fairs, selling books, subscriptions, and limited-edition prints. Managing the lecture series included contact with the institutional partners and our sponsor, making hotel and travel arrangements, and planning ancillary dinners or meetings. I also took every opportunity to be present throughout the region, especially if the invitation came at another institution's expense.

Photographers and institutions in the west consistently expressed that they would like to see themselves better represented through the foundation's core programs: the magazine, and books. Given our outreach efforts, I initially asked Aperture's editorial team to commit to selecting at least one new photographer or book project a year from the region. They said photographers and projects were not evaluated geographically, so agreeing to this request posed an unreasonable limitation on their selection process.

Though I respected my colleagues, I found their position on this matter intellectually territorial, and not reflective of the curiosity we otherwise tried to foster. Of the countless western-based photographers I met through Aperture West and brought to the table in New York over five years, very few piqued the interest, or met the "standards," for publication. One of my greatest challenges was trying to articulate to the photographers whose work I believed in why proposed projects were not moving forward. I think perhaps my colleagues in the west saw sooner than I did that some of the factors at play were not solely about the work itself, but how it was feeding into the channels of consideration.

To try and achieve visibility for more photographers through the book program, I proposed, received the director's approval, and secured some funding to initiate a short-lived Aperture West Book Prize. A nominations committee of west coast tastemakers recommended people; I compiled a shortlist; and the New York editors were given final choice. Two books were produced through this program, *Pitch Blackness* with Hank Willis Thomas (his first, in 2007) and *Invisible* with Trevor Paglen (2010). As far as I am aware, the copyright page of Paglen's book is the last reference in print to Aperture West.

Those battles in New York regarding the relevance or value of a west coast program reveal many of the same challenges that are occurring within gatekeeper environments today. The foundation wanted to export exhibitions we had developed, books we'd published, and photographers we'd invested in (including Robert Adams and Richard Misrach, who resided in the west) to existing and new audiences, but the internal perception was that "we" (the editors in New York) already knew what was good, and "we" were paying attention to the whole world, so "we" didn't need additional suggestions of important work being made in the west that might not be getting the attention it warranted. If the work was excellent, "we" would of course notice. Most of the editors at that time had little direct experience in, or familiarity with, the region.

That same thought process has limited the inclusion of many underrepresented practitioners in photography, because the "we" at the table does not often include people who have cultural familiarity with and could pick up on nuanced and unique elements in the work. I think in some cases it comes less from a place of malice than from an assumption that the standards of excellence are fixed, rather than societal and cultural waves to be examined and refreshed. When people at the gatekeepers' tables have lived knowledge of different ethnic, class, geographic backgrounds, and are in positions of power to expand what is considered excellent, new standards are formed. That is where hiring is essential. That is where many institutions are still struggling. Because that is where the true power dynamic shifts. Extending agency to the viewpoints of the many from the few does not mean lowering standards, but interrogating them, and bringing new visions to the table with authenticity. It is limiting to imagine that we can only interpret or appreciate work made by people who are similar to us. It is equally limiting to imagine that a group of people who share the same cultural, class, and educational backgrounds are going to accurately reflect diverse views.

SYLVIA PLACHY, *Hungarian Wedding* or *Marika's Wedding*, 1964. Vintage gelatin silver print, signed, 11 ¹¹/₁₆ x 7 ¹¹/₁₆ in. Not editioned. Acquired through work trade, 2006.

A longtime trustee at Aperture, Robert Anthoine, once gave me some sage life advice: "Never pass up the opportunity to meet someone you admire. " I maintained the multi-institution "dream list" of well-known photographers for the Aperture West lecture series as names came up, and it was my often my responsibility to make contact and obtain a reply. Relationships mattered in the family of photography: who introduced me to a particular photographer could be the difference between silence and a response. I'd gotten a few months of "maybe" from Sylvia Plachy before I enlisted the support of her primary editor, Melissa Harris, to see if there was any chance of securing Sylvia's involvement. Infamous for avoiding public receptions, Melissa nevertheless suggested we meet at Sylvia's opening at the June Batemen Gallery so she could introduce me. I remember little from that loud and crowded evening, but Melissa's endorsement carried weight, and it was enough to get Sylvia to agree to the west coast tour in 2005.

Sylvia's first talk was scheduled for a Saturday morning in Seattle, and she was dubious. Who there would even know who she was, let alone get up early to hear her talk? I am not a morning person (though the population of the Northwest tends to be), so I was

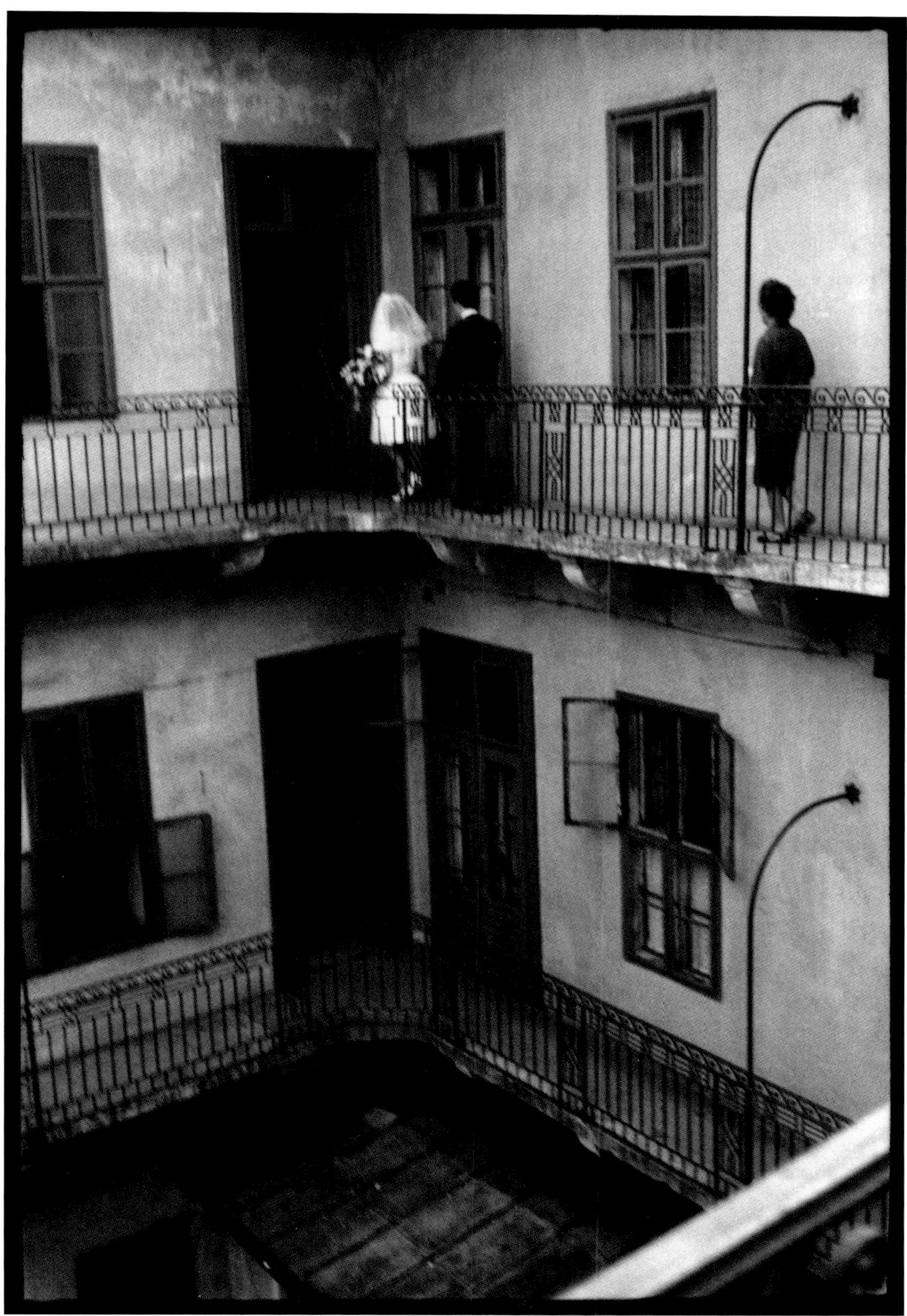

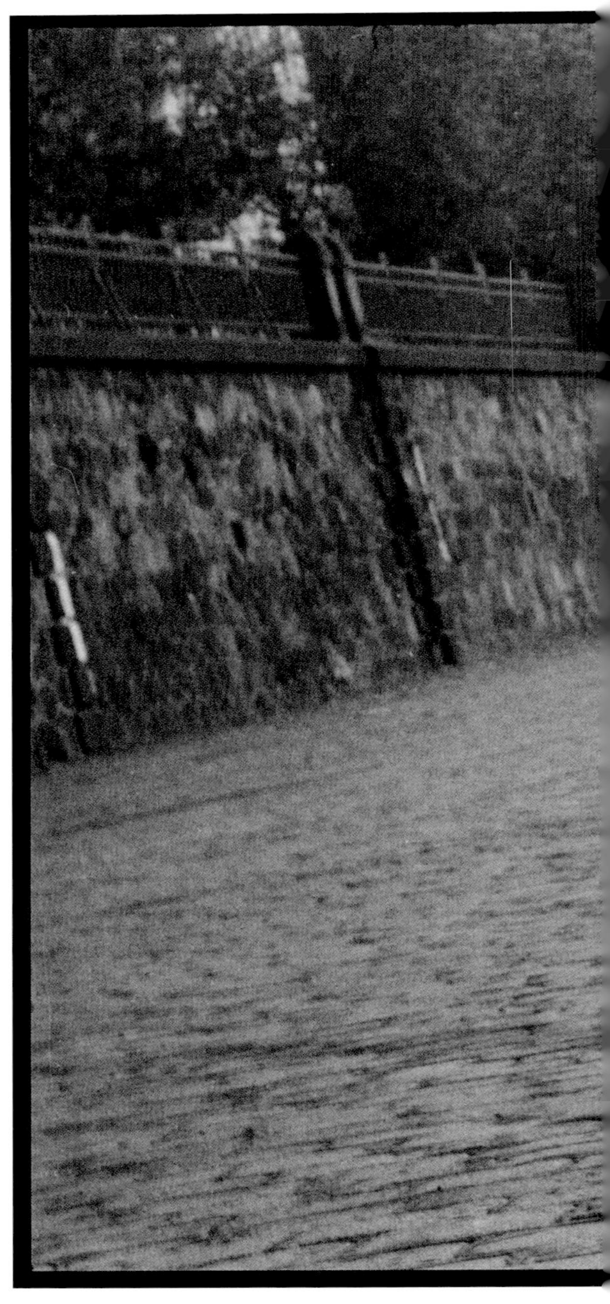

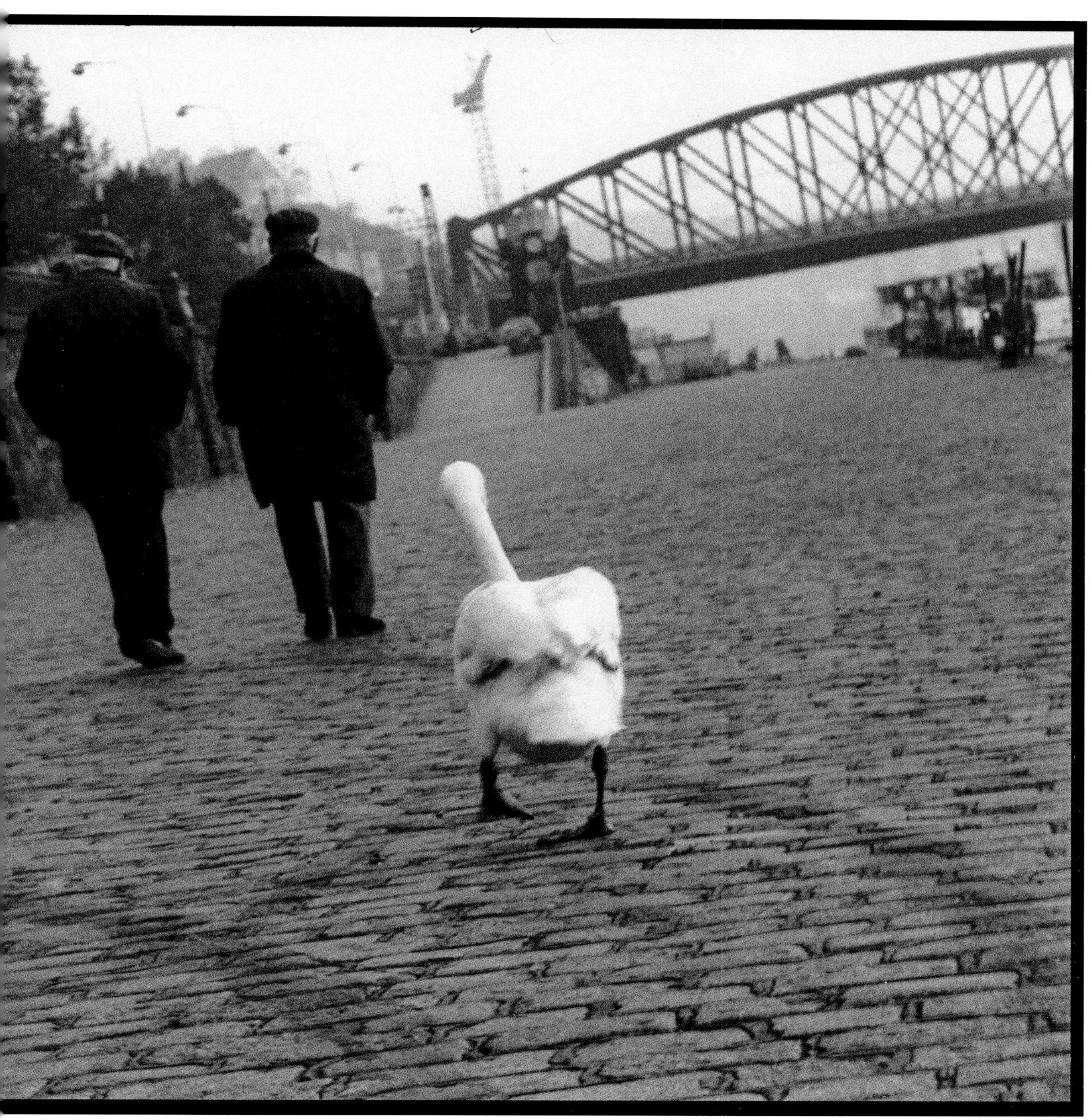

fighting my own internal response to this schedule while trying to assure her that there would be a good crowd. I said something along the lines of "Just wait—some former New Yorker who loved your column in the *Village Voice* will be there; you'll see."

The auditorium was blissfully full, and Sylvia gave a spirited talk from her forty-plus years of work. When we began the Q&A, the first man to raise his hand started with, "I have more of a statement than a question," which is usually a moderator's nightmare beginning to a public dialogue. Yet he was succinct in saying that he was originally from New York, and he just wanted to share that he always looked forward to weekly issues of the *Village Voice* just to see her photographs. Sylvia looked at me, eyes wide—and I just shrugged, smiling. That was the auspicious beginning to a dear friendship.

From before I met Sylvia I was mesmerized by *Marika's Wedding* (p. 93) , an Escher-esque concatenation of lines, anchored by figures entering a void. Are they striding into a new universe? Falling through a black hole? There is stillness here, and so much motion. I continue to learn from this print as I contemplate what rituals we participate in and reject when it comes to love, and ways to represent commitment.

It is a photograph I use often in introducing people to reading photographs, as it immediately triggers subjective responses. Nothing in the photograph immediately places it in time or geography. There are three figures, two in dark clothing. Some windows are open. It is a black and white photograph. Nearly everything else, even that we may associate a veil and flowers with a wedding, is a story we tell ourselves.

Sylvia is also a great writer, and her images are characteristic of that—short stories within a frame. We were entering the Museum of Modern Art one morning when she was drawn by a stranger who was coming out of the same revolving door we were about to step in. She spun out, camera in hand, cheerfully asking him questions and complimenting him on his extraordinary face as she snapped away. Before he'd regained his composure from this butterfly hovering around him, she thanked him and stepped inside. The rest of the afternoon, we told each other new details we imagined about his life, all stemming from that one brief encounter.

Pages 94–95: SYLVIA PLACHY, *Swann's Way*, Prague, 1991. Gelatin silver print, 8 5/16 x 12 1/2 in. Not editioned. Acquired through work trade, 2007.

Swann's Way (pp. 94–95) has become shorthand for my "slightly delayed, wondering where I am and where I need to be" existence. Sylvia and I had concluded some work together, and she asked which print I wanted in exchange. When I said the one with the goose, she looked confused, so I went on: "It's waddling, it looks kind of lonely, or at least like it's trying to catch up, chasing after these guys. That's how I feel, that I'm chasing after life right now—one of those guys is my marriage, one is my career, and no matter what I do I think I'm falling behind both of them." She then realized the image I was talking about, and said, "Michelle! That's not a goose! It's a swan out of water, and that's where you are. But you and that swan, you are both going to find your way back to the river." From the moment it came into my life, I couldn't live without this print. *Swann's Way* traveled with me from New York to San Francisco to

Seattle. When my sister first saw it, she said, "Can I have that when you die?" (She later acknowledged that perhaps she could instead purchase another print of it. But now it's slated for her in my will, so she'll just have to wait, and hope I die first.)

Years later (seven, actually) as I was about to preside over my second gala as an executive director, I received an envelope from Sylvia—who had recently been in Prague—containing a handful of white feathers. No note; no need. I knew exactly what those feathers were, where they came from, and what they meant. I had found my way back to the water. I wore some of the feathers in my hair the night of the auction and dinner, and we set a new institutional record for funds raised.

There is a strong Hungarian foothold in twentieth-century photography, a lineage Sylvia is part of by birth and culture, and one Lisa Kereszi extends as a third generation American of Hungarian descent. Though we shared a few classes at Bard College early on, Lisa (or Lavish, her college nickname that I have never been able to abandon) and I became friends working together as interns in the college's publications office. In those environs we discovered an unlikely commonality—junkyards. She'd grown up in and around the one her family ran in Pennsylvania, and I had nosed around many in Washington as my father sought various car parts for his restorations. Both intended literature majors when we met, she went on to pursue photography (due in part, I think, to Larry Fink's positive responses to photographs she'd made "down the yard" as a teen).

Pages 98–99: LISA KERESZI, *Joe Jr.'s Belly*, 1998 / 2008. Archival pigment print of Polaroid negative, 15 1/4 x 19 3/4 in. Artist proof. Acquired through work trade, 2008.

In the decade after we left Bard, Lisa worked for Nan Goldin, completed her MFA at Yale, co-authored a book, and had two monographs published of her work. She had highly regarded gallery representation, was exhibiting, and teaching. I occasionally asked her about the junkyard pictures. I pitched them to a few publishers to no avail; she'd done the same. By 2007, we decided to trade skill sets and develop a book ourselves.

The imagery she was most drawn to from her many years of photographing that familiar space had the appearance of highly constructed still lifes, even if it was her seeing, and not the environment, that had been so carefully honed. I, on the other hand, loved the gestural rawness of some of her earliest photographs of her father and grandmother. We pushed one another to justify our choices over the four to five years we spent exchanging edits and sequences. The resulting book, *Joe's Junk Yard* (Damiani, 2012), breathes with images of both her intuitive and her educated eye.

All of the portraits of her father in the book are gripping—but when it came to the prints I chose as part of our trade, this (pp. 98–99) was one I had to own. Though she was in her mid-twenties when she made it, I feel the loving gaze of her younger self in its composition, accentuating Joe Jr.'s solidity, his roundness, all arms and legs and meaty hands as weighted and stable as the pile of tires on which he rests. This, to me, is a photograph made by a child who loves, and is loved by, her father.

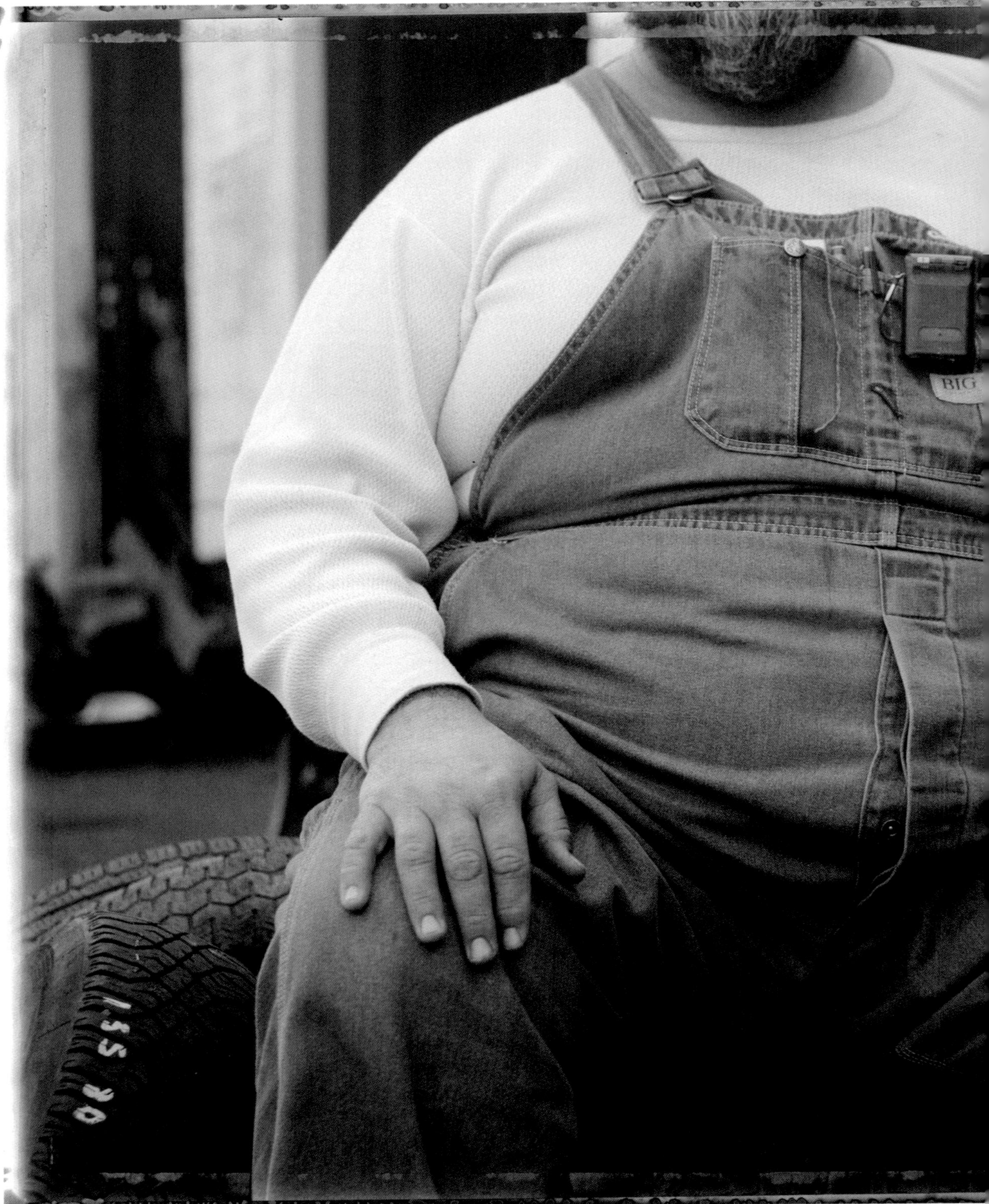

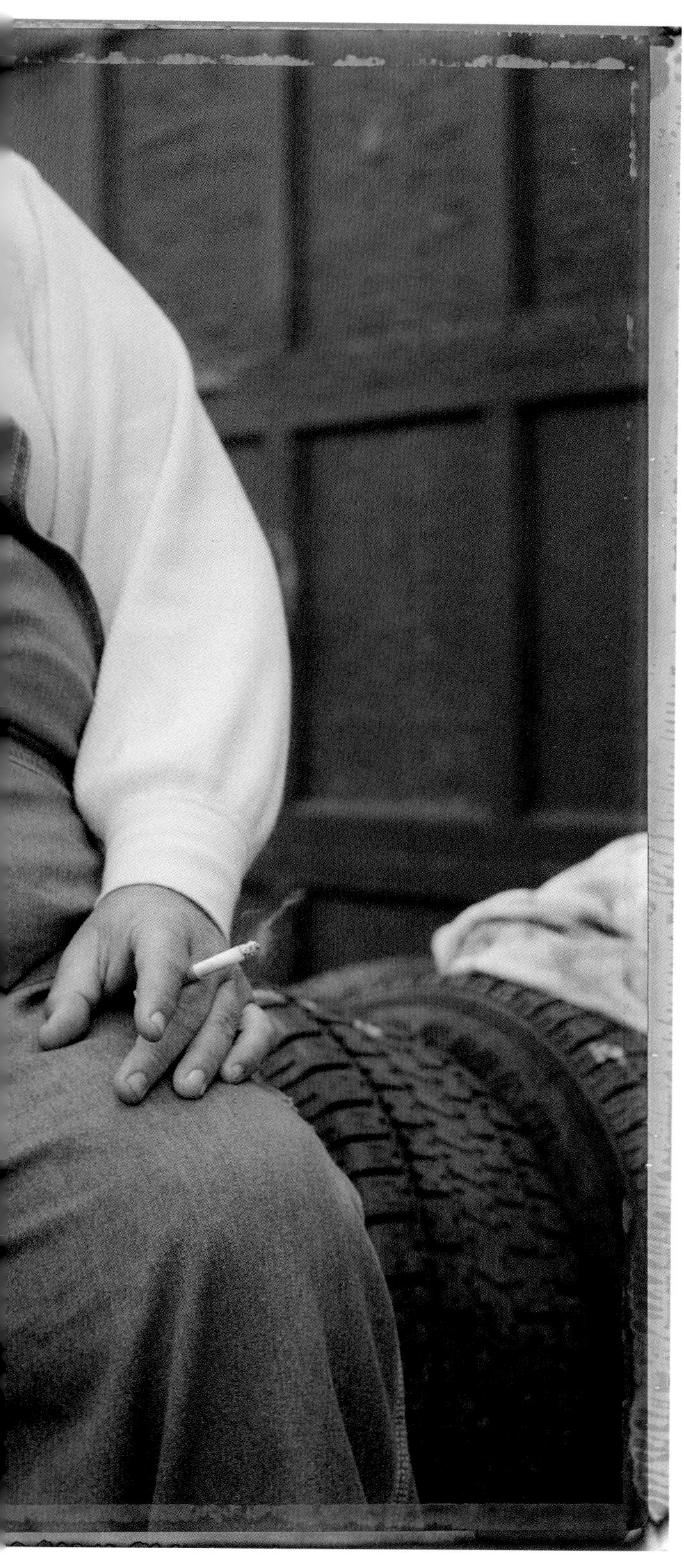

When Jeff Dunas launched the first Palm Springs Photo Festival with Hossein Farmani in 2005, one of his priorities was facilitating social time amongst peers, as well as with aspirants in the field. People making pictures often work alone. So it was somewhat surprising to me that so many of them, when they emerged from their solitary spaces, were also a lot of fun, especially when with others of their ilk. Jeff had described to me what he loved about Les Rencontres d'Arles, the international festival of photography that began in France in 1970. He wanted to create a similarly inspiring experience in the United States.

The Palm Springs Photo Festival has been an annual point of education and rejuvenation where, thanks to Jeff, I have had a platform to feature the work of over forty imagemakers and cultural contributors through panel discussions. Equally, or perhaps even more important, many years of networking in that relaxed and social environment fostered not only projects, but genuine friendships. With one group of late-night conversants, who all came from different parts of the industry, I made a pact to never discuss work. Our integration to each other and to the field was such that, five or so years into this agreement, curiosity was too strong, and we quietly began inquiring of one another, "What is it, exactly, that you do?" It was a relief, at that point, to have a truly free-flowing conversation that moved from pets, cigars, and favorite meals to an exhibition opening or new lighting technology.

Directly transactional events—trade shows, art fairs, and portfolio reviews—also had social components. Portfolio reviews, a form of speed dating where photographers paid for one to four days of twenty-minute sessions with industry professionals, were a mix of interview and therapy. On average, my colleagues and I who attend them take in a minimum of five hundred images per event. That's actually not a lot, considering most of us are experiencing five hundred or so images daily, but the daily images we mostly forget. The images from reviews, if strong, I tend to remember. Though with the many reviews that took place online during the pandemic, I became aware that my retention of images through the screen, even those I found powerful, is not as intense as what I hold onto from a physical encounter with a print.

LARRY FINK, Sylvia Plachy, Michelle Dunn Marsh, and Charlie Harbutt, 2007. Gelatin silver print, signed, 9 7/16 x 9 7/16 in. Artist proof. Purchased from Larry Fink, 2007

I first attended one of the industry's big trade shows, Photo Plus Expo, in 2006. Having been to book trade shows a few times, I thought I was prepared. But the lights, models, and fast-talking salespeople felt like sideshow barkers on the midway of the Puyallup Fair. While some advertising negotiations occurred "on the floor," far more got done over dinner or while sharing cabs between the multiple parties each night.

The elegant atmosphere of art fairs, with the quiet burbling of champagne flowing throughout the day, is no less of a deal-making environment, but here one encounters a genteel vibe and different methods to close a sale. A large part of being present is networking, but art fairs, more than any other gathering, are also delicious visual feasts. New objects debut and are swept up into private or public collections immediately thereafter; secondary market dealers unearth treasures from past decades and centuries.

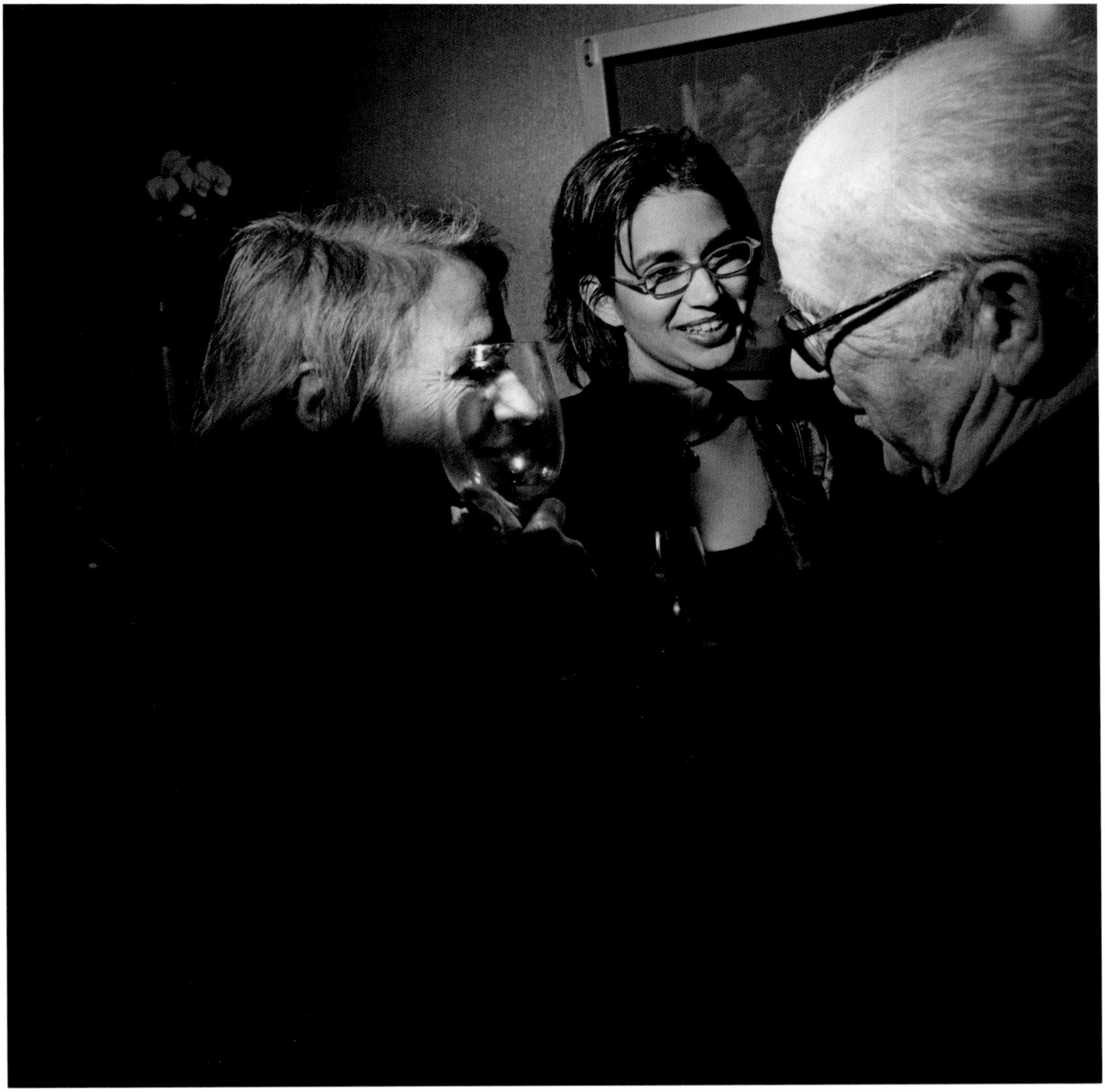

These traveling circuses within the United States, complemented by related programs internationally, have been a year-round cycle much of the last two decades of my life. The adrenalin from travelling, speaking, and socializing is addictive, a constant and justifiable high. A Saturday or Sunday afternoon goodbye after a three- or four-day extravaganza usually ends with "Are you going to. . . ? OK, see you in . . ." with a myriad of fill-in-the-blank options. Chance threads that begin over dinner one night might be picked up again in a hotel parking lot months later, as if no time had passed. Though the hours are long, the idea exchanges are always interesting. Someone I met in Santa Fe, or Houston, or Portland would turn up at an exhibition opening or a party in New York, and the conversation continued.

Larry Fink's photograph (p. 101) is evidence of such fruitful collision. Sylvia Plachy had been invited to a private book launch, and, as I happened to be in New York that week, took me along. As she introduced me to her friends Joan Liftin and Charlie Harbutt, I shyly reminded Charlie that I'd met him while working in the publications office at Bard. He, Joan, and Sylvia laughed as I recounted being brought to his studio, along with fellow intern Lisa Kereszi, to be strapped into whalebone corsets for a shoot related to an article on Victorian literature. Speaking of Bard, he said, "I think Larry Fink is around here, also."

I didn't know Larry when I was a student, since I didn't study photography, but I had met him a few times. I was glad to reconnect with him when he stopped over to say hello to my companions. He'd agreed to photograph the party as a favor to its featured guest and was ducking around the crowd with his camera and handheld flash. Larry exudes a combustion that also exists in his photographs. Watching him work was a strange mental ballet for me. He was moving through the room we were in, but I was imagining him making the pictures I knew of Studio 54 or the Met Ball from his first book, *Social Graces*.

I was distracted from watching Larry when Sylvia suddenly raised her empty wine glass next to her face and held it there as she talked. I reached for it, saying I'd go to the bar, but she just shook her head. After another few moments of this rather strange gesture I finally asked her what she was doing. Without moving the glass, she responded, "Giving Larry a photograph." Somehow, through the din and bustle of the crowded room, she'd sensed where he was, and that his gaze was on us. Then the moment passed, and she handed me her glass saying cheerfully, "Let's have more wine!"

Having exchanged contact information with Larry, I couldn't resist asking if he had indeed been pointing the camera our direction, as Sylvia sensed. His answer was a jpeg; that led to an email correspondence between us as to what we each valued in the image.

Friends of mixed ethnicities agree with me that it is challenging to understand how the world perceives us. What we notice about ourselves is largely informed by our relationships with our parents, and not the specificities of physical features that passersby might see. From the little I know of view cameras (where a composition from the world, in color, appears upside down and backwards on the ground glass) photographers who work with them probably hold the closest way of seeing to the kaleidoscopic complexity with which I see myself, in mirrors and in photographs.

Though Larry kindly offered me this print as a gift, I preferred to buy it from him, so that it was a transaction carrying no future obligation. He did not understand my insistence, but agreed, and gave me an industry discount, which I accepted. We had not worked together at that point; that was the loose condition under which I felt comfortable accepting a print, especially from a well-known photographer. It was a personal choice on my part, but one influenced by being a woman conducting business in a largely male world.

Surprising and disappointing experiences early on in my career—my enthusiasm for a project being met with sexual advances by older male colleagues; older female colleagues alleging that my promotions must be tied to sleeping with decision makers—undermined my sense of who I could trust in the workplace. Like most women, I ended up managing unwanted and unexpected power plays on my own. It was confusing, and embarrassing, and inevitably I blamed myself for somehow doing something "wrong," though all I had done was be young, and smart, and female. I also had very positive and respectful relationships with male and female colleagues of different generations, so I tried to forget the bad and focus on the good.

I am mostly able to distinguish between banter, respectful acknowledgment of attraction, and abuse of power and authority in the workplace. I have experienced all three. As I moved into senior positions, dynamics did not necessarily diminish, but they did change. The heavy press coverage around the #MeToo movement in 2017 forced me to face memories I had long tried to avoid. I ultimately made a list of the twenty-plus men who had used their professional power to make sexual advances, or gain control of a negotiation, and waited for one of them to acknowledge their actions. I'm still waiting.

Ellen Harris started as the first female executive director of Aperture Foundation in 2003, its third director (though I don't think Minor White ever officially held that title) since the magazine began in 1952. Under her administration the brownstone at 20 East 23rd Street was sold, and the offices and gallery relocated to Chelsea, on the extreme west side of Manhattan. With both a publishing and museum background, Ellen was interested in the potential of exhibitions and educational public programs, which aligned well with my efforts through Aperture West. She was supportive of those efforts and of me, though among the many initiatives needing financial support, the benefit of its regional focus continued to be questioned by some members of the staff and board.

In 2006 I regained part-time status after four years on retainer, by taking on the title of associate publisher of *Aperture* magazine. I was responsible for business development, primarily through advertising and sponsorships, in addition to managing Aperture West. The dual position gave me a stronger foothold in the New York office from my remote location in Seattle. Before I took on the role, a consultant had been brought in to evaluate the magazine and determine how it could be more profitable. When the recommendations—make it a standard physical size, spend less on the printing, add how-to content, move to six times a year to attract more advertisers—were summarized, the basic conclusion was that we should publish a different magazine.

Melissa Harris, the magazine's editor-in-chief, felt that my knowledge of the magazine and the foundation, combined with the outreach I'd been doing, could be harnessed to greater financial potential. Using the consultant's findings, we developed subscriber profiles to target who we wanted to add to our base and revised our media kit, recasting perceived weaknesses—publishing quarterly, limited ad pages—as assets. Perhaps most significant, we stopped begging potential ad clients to be charitable toward a venerable photographic institution, and instead spoke to the distinction of over fifty years of bold editorial choices, and the significant purchasing power of our subscribers.

One full-time senior staff member, Dana Triwush, was dedicated to circulation, which included management of all the subscribers, plus newsstand sales. A part-time assistant supported her. Freelance advertising representative Spyro Poulos taught me the ropes of ad sales, and sometimes the simplest methods were the most effective. During meetings with potential clients, he would open the conversation, then kick me under the table to start talking about Aperture. When he was ready to close the deal, I got another nudge and stopped talking. Dana had already launched an online advertising component to the website, which quickly generated income. By mid-2007, we were developing custom events and sponsorship programs tailored to ad clients, with a required purchase of print advertising, ideally for multiple issues. It led to a 35 percent increase in revenue over the previous two years. Those commitments saved us when the recession hit that fall.

The staff at Aperture had shifted, for the most part, from people making photographs to people thinking, writing, and talking about photographs. The latter were reluctant to "reduce" conversations of the medium to the tools of the craft. Aperture had rarely concerned itself with *how* photographs were made, as much as on their emotional and cultural impact, and on the distinct viewpoints of the people expanding the expressive capabilities of the medium. At the same time, photographers themselves were not averse to discussing papers, film, and cameras that remained costly and were practical realities of their chosen art form, particularly if we could assist in getting them access to those materials for free or at a lesser cost.

EUGENE RICHARDS, *Blind Elder*, Guinea, West Africa, 1988 / 2008. Gelatin silver print, signed, 13 x 8 ½ in. Edition of 100, produced through *Mother Jones* magazine. Gift of Eugene Richards and Janine Altongy, 2008.

Through the magazine's custom media proposals, we developed programs with at least ten international brands ranging from luxury watchmaker Raymond Weil, to Levi's, to "endemic" partners like Epson and Sony, tailored to the client's goals, and featuring over twenty photographers. Editorial ethics were a constant consideration in the "pay to play" content we developed, particularly because Aperture was a nonprofit entity contributing to the public good. Would we let one advertiser buy out all twelve pages of advertising in a single issue? What message does that send to the subscribers? Do we accept cigarette advertising? What about alcohol? These iterative conversations formed the boundaries of our creative proposals, so we did not present, and a client did not become attached to, an idea our editor-in-chief would find compromising to the magazine.

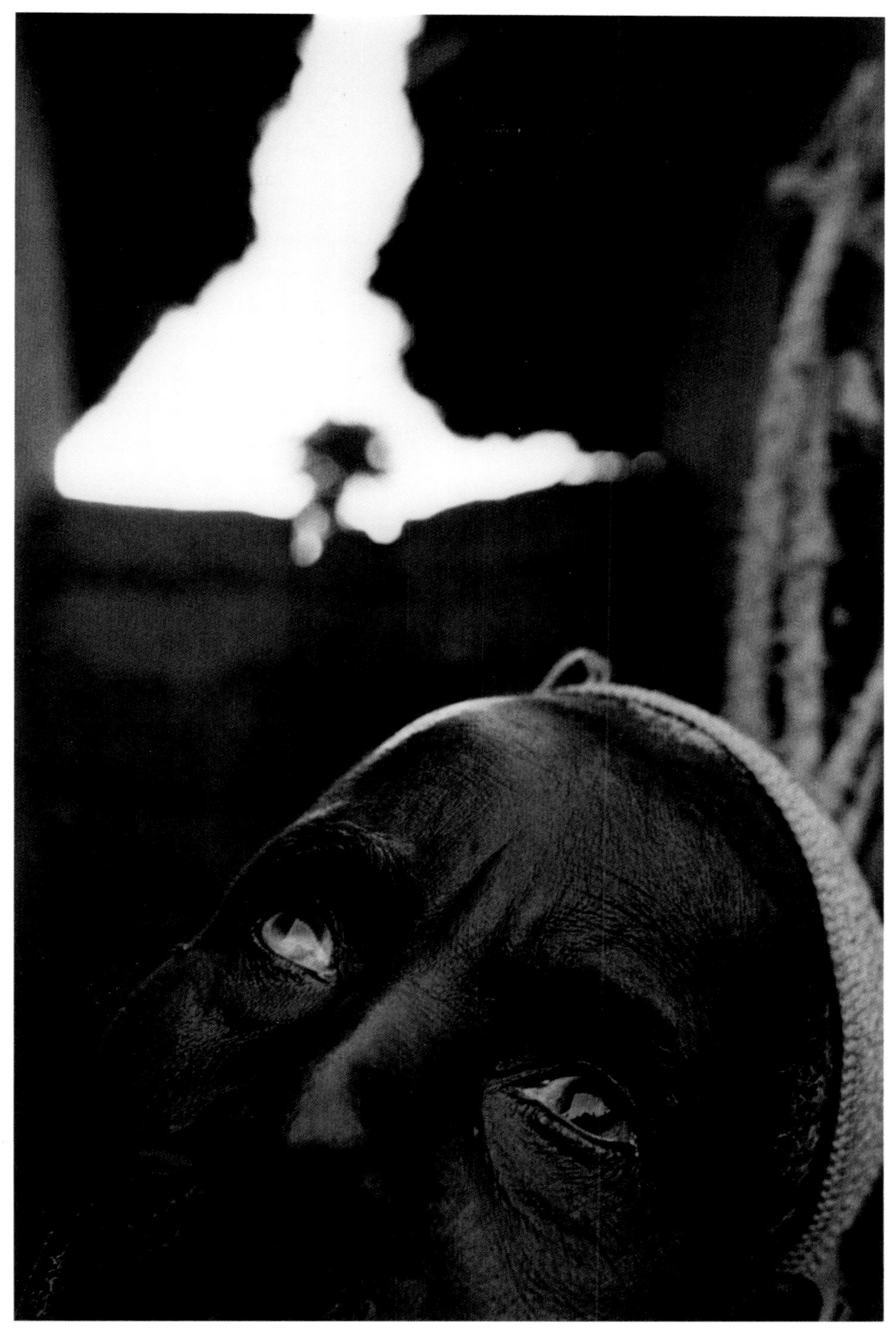

My previous interactions with the photographers came in handy. I made an effort to stay informed and in touch about what personal projects they were working on, so if they needed film, for instance, we could keep that in mind when pitching ideas to Fujifilm, Ilford, Polaroid, or Kodak, and tie a product donation to the photographer to an advertisement purchase in the magazine. Mary Ellen Mark, Sylvia Plachy, Bruce Davidson, and Eugene Richards's names came up often with ad clients as "desired headliners" for custom programs.

In 2007 we developed a custom magazine program for Kodak, a west-coast film launch featuring Eugene Richards, along with a younger Bay-area photographer, Ray Potes. SF Camerawork hosted. I had traveled with Gene for the lecture series in 2004, so to be back in San Francisco with him and his wife, Janine Altongy, a few years later felt like positive testimony to the work of Aperture West. Two nonprofit institutions on different coasts, a major corporate brand, photographers of two generations, and a local community all received benefit from the free public program. It was exactly the kind of synergy and collaboration I had begun with the lecture series, and aimed to continue.

Those collaborations required a chemistry that became harder to achieve over the next decade as print magazine circulations declined, more interactions moved online, and corporations, as part of their marketing strategies, began developing their own educational programs where they had complete control of the content presented. This led to a change in the number and types of external programs they sponsored through nonprofits.

In 2014 I thought of bringing together Gene's series "Stepping through the Ashes" (see *Firefighter*, pp. 54–55) with his subsequent series "War Is Personal," to mark the fifteenth anniversary of 9/11 in 2016. He agreed. Yet after nearly two years of effort, I'd secured little funding. Gene was not surprised, having had other exhibitions delayed or canceled for the same reason, and assumed we would also cancel. But the possibility of engaging the public, including veterans in the Seattle area, with his work felt too important to let go, so with Gene's agreement to payments over time, PCNW, the host institution I was leading then, funded much of it internally. That exhibition, *Enduring Freedom*, was an example of eking abundance out of scarcity. It was also an awakening that past sources of support to produce bold photography exhibitions may be unreliable in the future.

Viewer comments to the exhibition consistently highlighted the fraught beauty and pain they connected with in his photographs. In "real life," as in his pictures, Gene gets physically close and stays there, a gentle crossing of the barrier of personal space that, the first time I had a sustained conversation with him, was overwhelming in its intimacy and openness. Gene has intentionally and repeatedly gone into spaces of great pain and suffering, and finds a whisper of human resilience, a thread of light, in what he sees there.

Executive director Ellen Harris parted ways with Aperture in the summer of 2007. The board asked me to spend a few months full-time in New York to assist with day-to-day operations during the transition, which extended into a year, during which time I negotiated the title of deputy director. The foundation's bylaws stated that in the absence of an executive director, the CFO would automatically serve as interim director. The CFO was not consulted when the board brought me in to support him, nor was the staff informed as to what my new role entailed. In my sudden oversight of multiple departments, two major fundraisers, and many of my peers, in addition to my existing responsibilities, I was navigating some understandable confusion.

In 2001 Maria Décsey, the board liaison at Aperture, had gently noted to me then that though the foundation was in jeopardy, not everyone seemed as concerned about that as I was. For some, it was a job, and if the job ended, they would find another job. She felt deeply invested in Aperture's continuance, as I and some others did, but she could also see, where I could not, that some of our colleagues resisted my requests of them, and my "anything to save the ship!" mentality. Six years later, I at least knew not to make the same assumptions. I have sometimes landed in leadership roles because I articulated pressing concerns on which others stayed silent; I have also lost leadership roles for the same reason. When humans feel threatened, the dynamics can be dangerous.

While daily dealing with tension at the office, I was also back in a love triangle with my spouse and Aperture. Though I regularly kept an eye out for opportunities in Seattle, interviews with multiple arts organizations there had not yielded a full-time job offer. That made it easy to dive further into my advocacy of Aperture, which often took me away from home. He worked for Harley Davidson, and on his own, building custom motorcycles, which was sporadically lucrative, and personally fulfilling for him. We both had occupations we enjoyed, but they did not always meet our financial responsibilities.

Our intense love for each other was as volatile as it was deep. As the months in New York extended, I was torn. My husband was clear that he did not want to live in Manhattan, though he liked visiting. I felt ready to lead Aperture, but I did not want to lose him. The bikers treated me with better manners than he was often shown in photographic spheres, and he expressed concern sometimes that my life with him was holding me back professionally. I was aware that very little held him back from his own impulses, which was an ongoing concern for me. After many discussions, we decided together that I should approach the board and ask to be considered for the executive director position, and we would work out what was best for us personally depending on the outcome. When I did so, responses from board members were vague. Shortly thereafter, the staff was informed that a new executive director had been hired.

Musician Tori Amos, whose lyrics guided my early adult years, once said about the record industry that she had learned too late it was sometimes better to be smart than to be right. I can think of many circumstances that year where being smart would have been more politic. Had I been smart, I would not have pointed out that the actions of some board members could be viewed as compromising to the institution's integrity. That was a board-to-board consideration, not a staff-to-board observation. I might not have pushed the staff to be more strategic and collaborative in how we used our programs to introduce emerging photographers in a visible yet fiscally conservative manner, even if that changed the decision-making structures. I might not have made the decision to return valuable prints of unclear ownership to the photographers who made them, instead of auctioning them on eBay. I was not smart then. Just right.

Aperture West was mostly dormant while my duties expanded in New York, and by 2008 the program was officially concluded. When the new director started, I retained the title of co-publisher of the magazine to manage a few key client relationships, but stepped back from public visibility with Aperture.

I was surprised to be offered the position of senior editor of art and design at Chronicle Books in San Francisco, but when it arrived, the timing was right, and I accepted. I had long respected Chronicle and had even applied for a design internship there as an undergraduate student. From San Francisco I could commute to Seattle every weekend, and hopefully form some new patterns in my marriage. He and I had vacationed a few times in the Bay area, and liked it. There were professional opportunities there for him as well, if an eventual relocation seemed the best next step in our life together.

I had not really considered the financial impacts of the recession when I agreed to move to one of the most expensive cities in the United States on a lower salary than I'd been earning in one of the other most expensive cities in the United States. I paid taxes in 2008 in New York City, New York State, San Francisco, and the state of California, on top of my federal taxes. I was also audited, a fear I'd carried for years, for my freelance design business, and learned that one mistake I'd made repeatedly (related to travel expenses) meant I owed over $20,000 in back taxes. It was an educational year.

The role of editor—one I had not yet officially occupied in my decade in publishing—was a fresh and welcome shift. Chronicle's books were acquired and published with the goal of reaching a much broader audience than I was familiar with, and in setting the initial goals by which my performance would be evaluated, my manager asked me to acquire a title that would gross a million dollars. I couldn't think of a single art title I knew, let alone had worked on, that might even come close to that. When I asked her for an example, she demurred at first, saying, "Think big!" A few weeks later she acknowledged that the only art book to have done so on Chronicle's list was *The Mexican Muralists*, published a decade earlier. So, my goal was to travel back in time, and originate one of the first mainstream books about a major art movement? No problem. Building a list of twenty to thirty titles annually for a commercial publisher with loose content constraints but clear financial goals required research and new ways of thinking, particularly against the backdrop of the tanking 2008 economy.

The finance team at Chronicle had clear templates for evaluating project profitability. With their pointers I arrived at the financial benchmarks I needed to propose projects, even when that came about through methods less traditional at a larger house: raising a retail price point to compensate for a luxury package, adding a limited edition print as we did with the reprint of Elinor Carucci's *Closer* and a few other titles, or negotiating an institutional buy-back of a quantity of books, which made possible the collaboration with Experience Music Project on musician and photographer Graham Nash's book and exhibition, *Taking Aim*.

For the first time in my life, I let go of my fear of numbers. It turns out I was pretty adept with them. I had always thought I was bad at math, though looking back there is little evidence to support that—my grades in chemistry and algebra were similar to my grades in English. Maybe I conflated my fear of the junior high math teacher (Mr. Hansen smacked a paddle on his hand for emphasis while lecturing; he was pretty scary) with fear of the subject? Regardless, setting down that long-carried stereotype was an important step toward respecting my own business acumen.

Producing over three hundred titles a year, Chronicle was one of the largest independent publishers in the United States, yet maintained the office culture of a smaller, close-knit entity. Once every quarter, senior leadership called a company-wide meeting and reviewed the top-level financials with the entire staff, from the publisher to the receptionist. I'd never been in an environment with that level of transparency; it tied each of us and our daily responsibilities to the well-being of the company as a whole. It was an openness I later sought to emulate as a director. From Chronicle's owner, Nion McEvoy, and president Jack Jensen, I observed that weighing risks and rewards is essential in the business of publishing, but so is decision making. If you were not comfortable with the first, you would never find your way to the second.

Involvement with a trade publisher meant coming face to face with what the general public responded to, which tended to be books less complex than what I personally found interesting. All publishers were also reckoning with what the future of physical books would be, given the exponential onslaught of free content online. I acquired or edited several books at Chronicle that I am proud of for different reasons. Yet what I hold as my most important accomplishment there came from my brief mentorship of Bridget Watson Payne, the assistant editor of art and design when I started. Subtle shifts to her presentation style, my encouragement of her savvy taste in projects, and the strategic work we did together led to her achieving the position of senior editor (she has since progressed even further), the role I briefly occupied that she had long deserved.

You never really know what seeds are being sown that may yield perennials; sometimes all it takes is one chance beam of sunlight. I first met Graham Nash at a fundraiser in New York in 2003, and after being introduced to him I lingered, along with a few other photographers, in his presence. A woman stood quietly to my left, listening but not really participating in the conversation. I turned to her and said, "Hello, I'm Michelle," and shook her hand as she said, "Oh hi, I'm Joni." I scrolled through my mental Rolodex and I couldn't think of a single photographer I knew or had heard of named Joni. After exchanging a few pleasantries, I turned my attention back to the larger group, which disbanded shortly after to be seated for dinner. When the presentations portion of the evening began, the emcee announced that Graham's award would be given to him by none other than Joni Mitchell. I almost fainted. Joni. *Of course.*

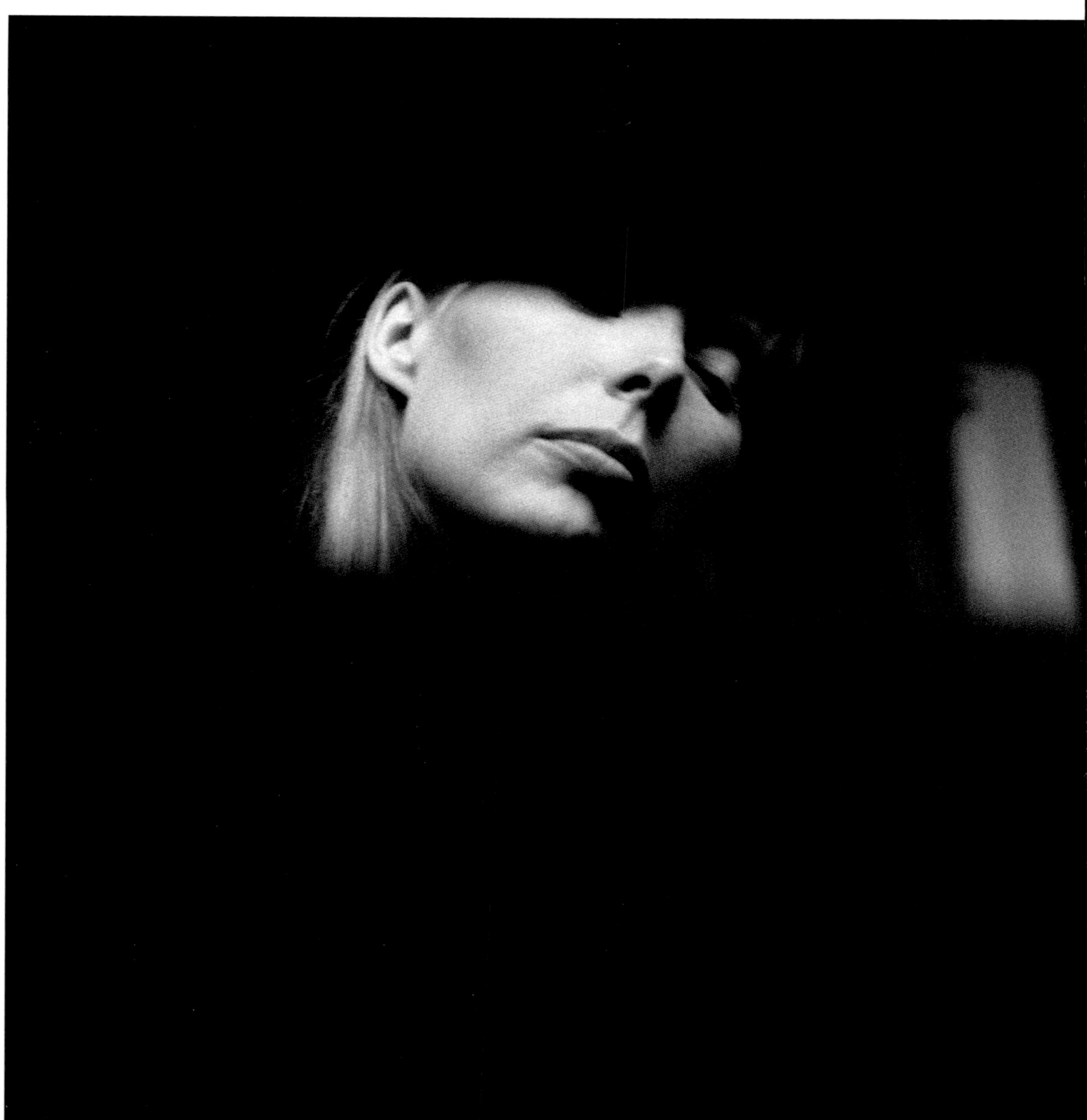

The following year, Marita Holdaway of Benham Gallery in Seattle mounted a solo exhibition of Graham's photography, and she invited me to be on a panel discussion with him. That public exchange, and conversation at dinner after, led to a continuing friendship with him, and with his business partner and fellow photographer, R. Mac Holbert.

Staying in touch with Graham reconnected me to the energy of live music. But the ultimate marriage of music and photography awaited in the irascible entity of Jim Marshall, the defining relationship of my time in San Francisco. Though I'd first met Jim at the Palm Springs Photo Festival, and again at Photo Plus Expo, he permanently established himself in my life upon my arrival at Chronicle in September 2008. Chronicle had published three books with him and had hopes for many more. I was warned that he was both an important and a difficult author, so when he called I immediately accepted a lunch invitation with him and his assistant, Amelia Davis.

Within two weeks of our lunch meeting, Jim called again, inviting me to the premiere of a documentary that included his photographs. After the screening of *Johnny Cash at Folsom Prison*, Jim shuffled up on stage with the director and one of the producers for a Q&A. At first, he couldn't hear well (he was very deaf, a consequence of years next to speakers at concerts) and mumbled answers. But within a few moments he found his stride, and a charismatic, animated personality pushed forth from this short, stocky man with a cocaine-disfigured nose and some of the most persuasive brown eyes I'd ever seen. I saw the personality who had captured iconic images of Jimi Hendrix, Janis Joplin, the Rolling Stones, Ray Charles, and, of course, Johnny Cash.

As I found my way back to my apartment that night, I realized that Jim carried much of the energy, brilliance, and complexity of some of the other geniuses I'd worked with, including Leon Botstein, Ginger Shore, and Michael Hoffman. I could foresee that I would learn from him, love him, and be transformed by him, but that knowing him could carry a steep emotional cost.

When I began in the field there was a tacit acceptance of bad behavior by talented people. That should not be considered a recommendation to engage in it, or accept it—times have changed. In some ways, my exposure to people who yelled, cut off conversations, and were physically threatening helped me find compassion for flaws in myself, and others. In other ways it heightened my sensitivities to people prone to verbal and psychological abuse. Occupying positions of power means sometimes being a target, and as a multi-ethnic woman less often seen in such positions, I am more so. The stronger I am perceived to be, the more likely it is that someone feeling insecure or threatened will seek to tear me down. I am human, and it hurts when this happens, but I am getting better at identifying the circumstances when this occurs, and not taking it too personally. Creative fields are necessarily rife with emotion, and often include intellectual conflict as a necessary part of working through ideas. Maintaining that within reasonable social and human boundaries is an ongoing exercise.

Knowing Jim was every bit as wonderful and as miserable as I anticipated. No photographer told me to fuck off more than he did, and no one said I love you, and meant it, more than he did, either. While I was commuting between Seattle and San Francisco I had dinner with Jim every Tuesday, often at the same restaurant, followed by wine or whiskey at his apartment around the corner. We talked about photography, which was refreshing for him, since most people around him wanted to hear stories about the famous musicians he photographed. He wanted to know what Bruce Davidson and Gene Richards were like as people; I asked about being around Robert Frank on the Stones tour in 1972.

Jim was unabashed about protecting the use of his work, and had intellectual property lawyers at the ready when he discovered illegal posters, t-shirts, or other reproductions made from his photographs. He made his living from licensing his images, and he understood the capitalistic reward of money. At the same time, he frequently offered to exchange his prints for kisses from attractive women (I guess a priceless kiss is equal to a thousand-dollar photograph, if you desire one and have plenty of the other). I permanently declined that offer early on, though I witnessed many women take him up on it. He always followed through on having his assistant Amelia mail prints to them.

Jim trusted that the money he earned, and the positive relationships he maintained with the musicians he photographed, demonstrated the importance of his work. He had achieved international visibility through the record industry, and while he enjoyed books, museum exhibitions, and print sales, he saw them as bonuses, putting little stock in what didn't pay. We openly discussed money, and he was fascinated that I existed on the salaries and freelance income I earned. I have never had much in the way of cash reserves, but I have also very rarely been in debt, choosing instead to live well sometimes, and austerely others, as the cash flow allowed. I knew, thanks to Steve Baron, that photography would pay in many ways but traditional currency was unlikely to consistently be one of them. Jim constantly pushed me to ask for more money as recognition of my professional skills. When I told him that I took a sense of accomplishment from the book itself, or the successful panel discussion, he rolled his eyes and said, "That's not going to keep your old car running, or the whiskey flowing, Dunn Marsh!" What Jim and I both agreed on was *respect*. Though I did not demand it with a gun or define it through what I was paid, as he did, it was no less important to me. After many conversations with Jim, I better understood how, and why, to articulate what my time and knowledge were worth, establishing that it was my choice, not someone else's successful bargaining, if I worked for less than that.

The only book I originated with Jim, *Pocket Cash*, stemmed directly out of Graham Nash's *Taking Aim*. Jim had nine photographs in the book and exhibition, more than any other photographer. Two were wildly different images of Johnny Cash. In one of the most illegally reproduced photographs in the world (aside from Michael Korda's portrait of Che Guevara), Cash's tough-guy persona was cemented as he flipped his middle finger for Jim's camera at the San Quentin concert in 1969. The second photograph was a quiet, intimate closeup of Cash with his wife, June Carter, taken at their home in Tennessee. When I asked Jim how many times he'd photographed Cash, and if he'd ever

Pages 114–115: JIM MARSHALL, **Johnny Cash at Folsom Prison, Represa, California, 1968 / 2010.** Gelatin silver print, estate stamped, 12 x 18 in. Number 8 / 25. Gift of Amelia Davis, Jim Marshall Photography LLC, 2012.

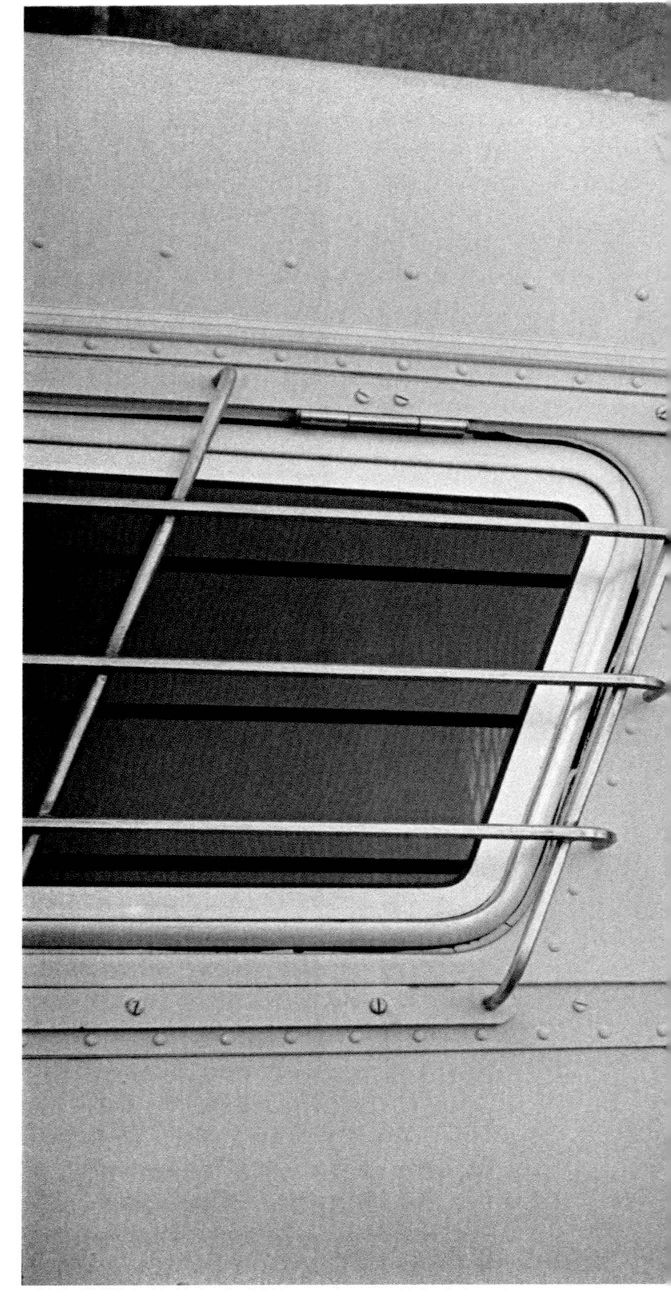

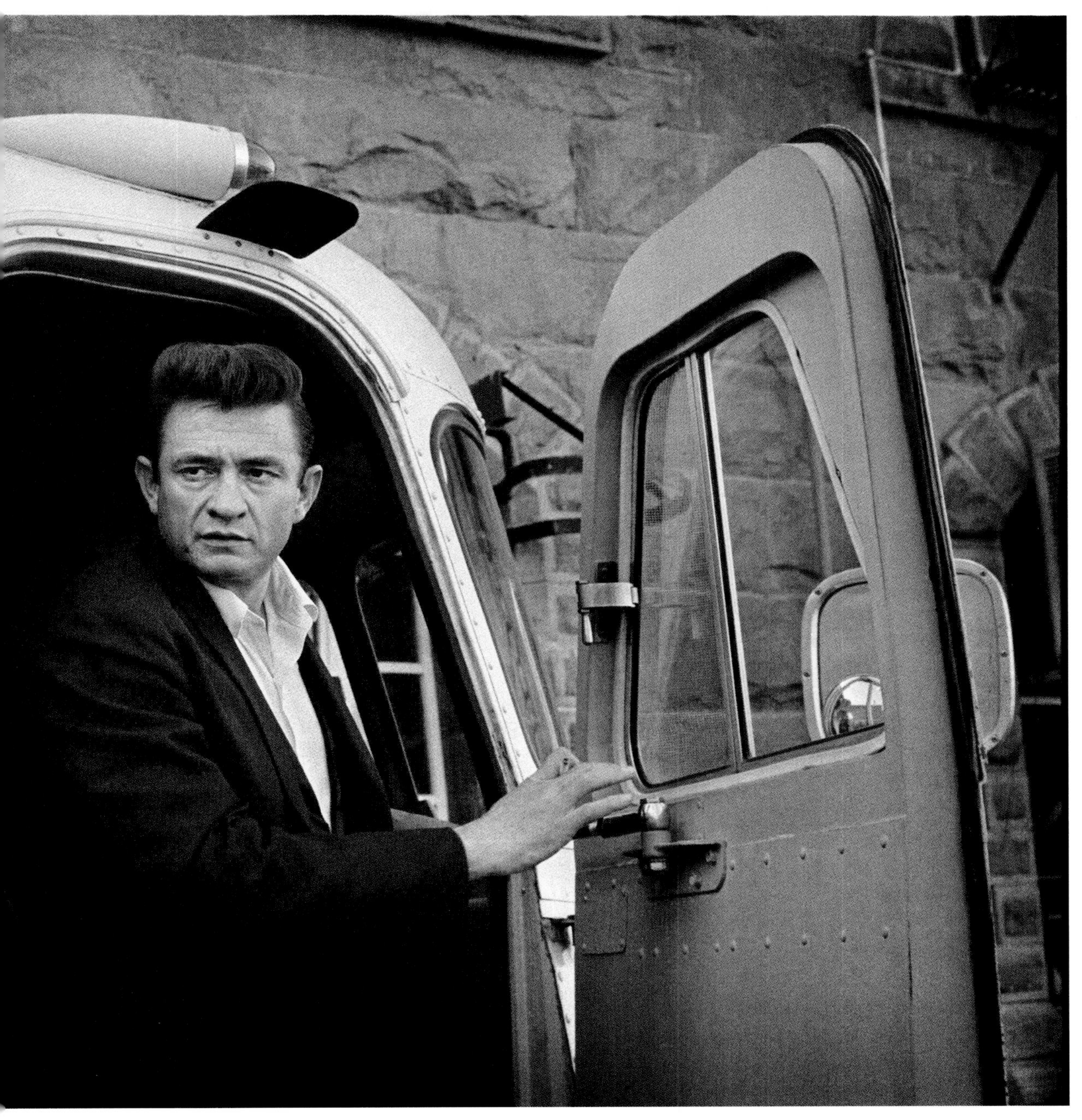

thought about doing a book or exhibition of those images, he dismissed me on more than one occasion with, "There's not enough there."

One rainy afternoon, however, he called me at Chronicle, insisted I drop what I was doing, and come to his apartment. Half of the office floor knew when he called, as I had to shout for him to hear me. His temper was well known there (he had placed a gun on the table during one of his contract negotiations with Chronicle's president Jack Jensen). Leaving work to meet him seemed kinder than continuing the conversation at the office and distressing my colleagues. As was typically the case when he got what he wanted, he was all smiles by the time I arrived at his apartment. I followed him into the kitchen, where, next to an open bottle of wine, was a giant stack of contact sheets. I knew exactly what they were. For the next few hours, we went through each one with a smudged magnifying glass and marked with grease pencil additional frames he had not previously printed over the nearly twenty-five years he'd photographed Johnny Cash.

After dinner at his usual spot around the corner, we continued the conversation back at his apartment. He said, we should get Kris Kristofferson to write something, he really liked Johnny. I said sure. Then he said, oh, I think Billy Bob Thornton should write something too, they both grew up in Arkansas. Eyes wider, I said sure. He started rattling off more names, including musicians Cash performed with. I said that's probably enough to get us started, and I'll prepare the editorial proposal right away, but don't we need some sort of permission from the Cash estate? Within minutes he was on the phone. "John? John, is that you? It's Jim Marshall. I want to do a book of my pictures of your parents. Is that OK with you? OK, great. Would you write the introduction? That would be nice. OK, here's my editor." And just like that, I was on the phone with John Carter Cash, who couldn't have been nicer considering it was probably 11 o'clock at night his time. He told me he'd fax a note over saying he was on board, and to let him know when I'd need his text.

The next morning I stopped by the desk of longtime editor Steve Mockus, who had acquired and edited many of Chronicle's successful music and pop culture books, to ask if he'd ever done a book about Johnny Cash. He said he'd tried a few times but getting approval from the House of Cash had always been a problem. I knew what had transpired the night before had all been a bit too easy, but I asked anyway, "If I have John Carter Cash's approval to do a book with Jim Marshall, would that help with the House of Cash?" He said, "Michelle, he *is* the House of Cash. How could you have possibly gotten that?"

Jim Marshall.

Jim never saw *Pocket Cash*; he died suddenly in March 2010, a week after he signed off on the final layout and image proofs for the book. Some of his ashes are above my desk, and when I hold the whiskey bottle they are in, I am transported to the most memorable time I saw him make a picture. It was during my going-away party from San Francisco in 2009, when Nion McEvoy spontaneously spoke about some of my contributions to Chronicle. Listening, and getting emotional from Nion's nice words, I felt, more than saw, a flutter out of the corner of my eye, as if a sparrow had momentarily found itself indoors. Nion finished speaking, people clapped, and I saw Jim shuffle back to his seat, Leica in hand. Though I love the print he sent me from that scene, the visceral feeling of his presence in the moment will always transcend.

I had just returned from Jim's memorial in San Francisco in May 2010 when I got the phone call that my professor and mentor Steve Baron had passed away; within hours I was back at the airport and headed to New York for another memorial service.

Just a year after he retired from Aperture in 2003, Baron was diagnosed with lung cancer. After one of his more intense treatments for it, I stopped by to see him, bringing an audio recording of Minor White that Portland photographer Stu Levy had graciously shared with me. A multitude of feelings flashed across Baron's face as he heard his own mentor's voice for the first time in thirty years. It was clearly a private moment, and I slipped out quickly. For all Baron had given me, it was a gift I was honored to deliver.

In 2006, Baron made arrangements to meet at Aperture's Chelsea space with a select group who had worked together at the 23rd Street office. Rarely emotional, his hands shook a little as he handed out carefully wrapped pieces of foil. He explained that he'd exceeded the average survival rate for his form of cancer and wanted to note the occasion. In the foil were clippings from a spider plant given to him by Minor White. That living gift directly connected us to his past, and him to our futures. It is the only houseplant that I successfully maintain; I fear a rift in the universal life force should I fail to do so.

I usually pay attention to three-year and seven-year cycles in my life. But occasionally they combine, and I don't notice until it's too late to prepare myself. 2001 was devastating. Ten years later 2011 delivered another round of life-changing tremors.

I was back in Seattle, and my spouse and I were piecing together freelance work as the recession continued to upend both of our industries. It was a lot to manage, but pleasant to be designing books for a few clients, working on projects from Jim Marshall's archive, and back at Aperture part-time, managing ad sales. Aperture's latest director had approved my teaching about Aperture, at Aperture, for the MFA in photography program at Parsons School of Design | The New School. It was a professional practices course I had developed with a professor there, and I was excited to see it through.

A week before the class began, I was laid off from Aperture as part of a staffing reorganization to reduce the company's expenses. The news came hours after I had gotten the initial green light from Sony on a major custom media program I conceived over many years with Kayla Lindquist, director of Sony's Artisans of Imagery program. My ongoing involvement was made a client condition of the final agreement. So immediately after Aperture laid me off, I was temporarily hired back to see through that project.

Over the next five months, I flew to New York every three weeks at my own expense to teach a class at a company where I was no longer on staff. I chose not to tell the students right away; it was too emotional for me, and I did not want that to distract them. The class became a form of therapy, revisiting the history of the organization and sharing its ups and downs with a group of smart, enthusiastic imagemakers and budding publishers, while considering the fullness of all I had experienced over fifteen years there.

Throughout the spring of 2011 I was also leading the execution of "Sony Photo Camp,"
itself a culmination of nearly every aspect of my various roles with Aperture. Over two separate weekends, first in Los Angeles and then in New York, faculty-nominated students from
seven to ten college programs in each region had a day of photographing in small groups
with master photographers. Professional editors did one-on-one reviews with the students
the next day. We ultimately mounted an exhibition at Aperture showcasing all the student
participants. A couple of the Parsons students from my class were selected by their professors
to attend, which brought some of our class discussions to life in real time.

As occasionally happens with a particular group of people, the students from my
Parsons class connected with me and with each other in a lasting way. Though my class with
them did not involve examination of their work, the students asked to show me what they
were developing, so I arranged brief portfolio reviews with them outside of class. I am glad
they took that initiative; I have worked with, or exhibited the work of, at least nine of those
fourteen individuals, beginning with Charlie Rubin.

I had seen versions of *I Love You, Rock* a few times; it was one of Charlie's favorite
pieces. But when I saw his thesis exhibition, his decision to fold the print along the rock's
edge jolted me. I was horrified (the
sanctity of the print!) and delighted that
through his intervention he had released
a sculpture. It reminded me of my complicated response to Catherine Chalmers's
Hanging (pp. 84–85), a revulsion and
attraction not easily processed, and therefore a duality that lingers. Charlie's print came to me
straight from his show, pinholes and all, bearing the specific kind of imperfection I love.

CHARLIE RUBIN, *I Love You, Rock*, 2012. Archival pigment print
on Fuji Crystal Archive paper, folded, 27 x 20 ⅛ in. Edition of three,
each unique. Purchased from Charlie Rubin, 2013.

At the last class at Aperture, I told my students that I had been laid off as the semester
started. Their heartfelt reception of this information made the pain slightly more tolerable as I
sat with the cold fact that the longest institutional relationship in my life was over.

Six months later my marriage ended.

A different me emerged when that man said he loved me, and with his son, formed a family
with me. That me was at first stronger, more inspired, and more beautiful than any me I'd
known before. It was an essential and defining relationship of my life. And it was never easy.
His ultimate decision to leave, an act of strength on his part, even if poorly executed, was
more than I could bear. I felt I had lost everything I lived for.

My adult stepson mirrored back to me many of the values I'd attempted to teach him
throughout his adolescence: Accept the unconditional love around you. Apply perseverance,
you can lift yourself up no matter what is happening. Try new things. He added truths of his
own: Sometimes you try too hard. Trust the people you love. Stop making excuses for other
people. And, perhaps the most important lesson: ride more rollercoasters—*confront your
fears*. His encouragement, and his sense of humor, were both critical to my taking the first
steps toward what would be a long healing process.

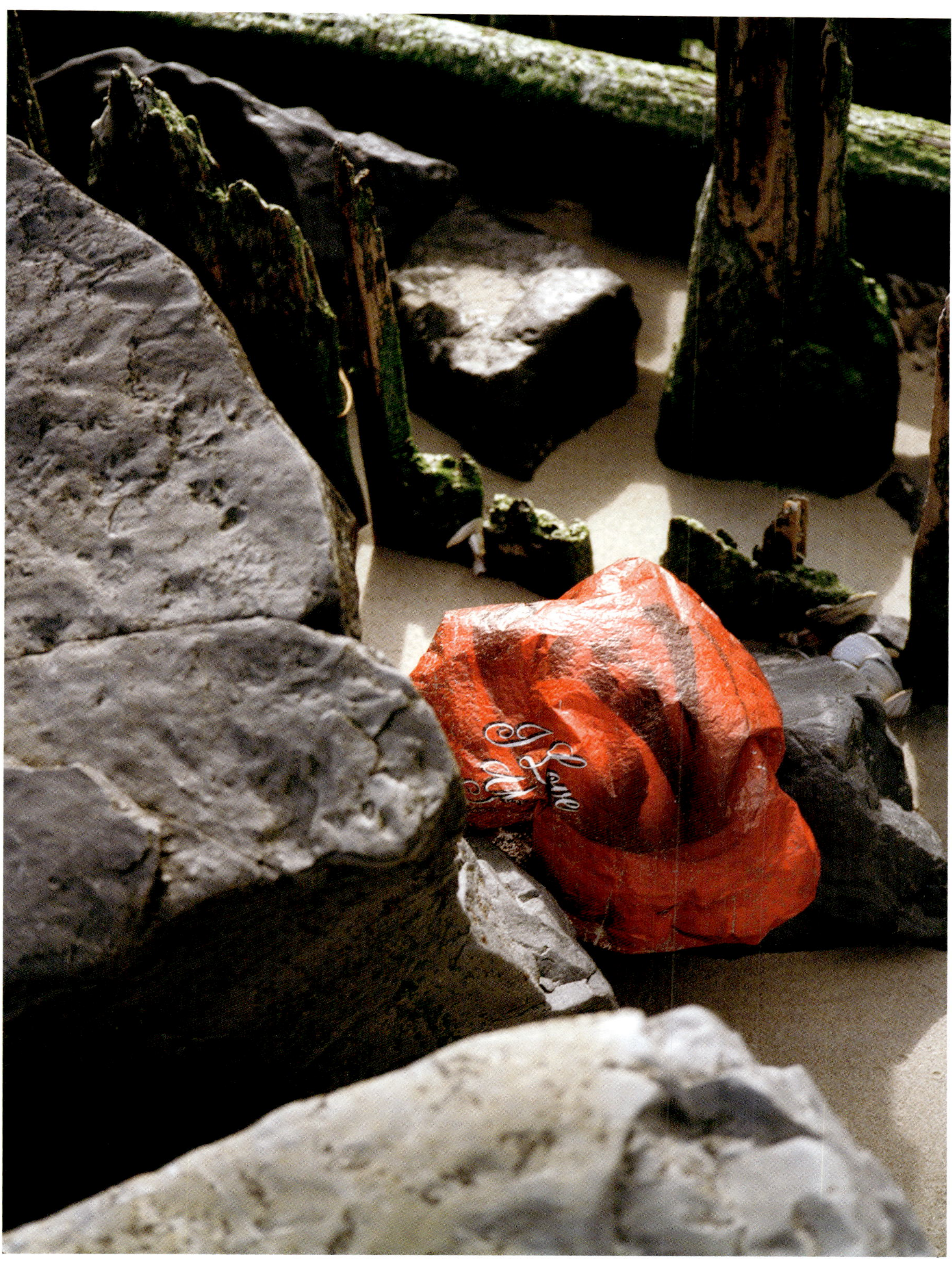
I Love

I carry a genetic condition that over the years has occasionally resulted in debilitating physical ailments. As I processed the end of two major relationships in my life, I struggled to consume enough calories to keep my body functional and stave off a serious health decline (I had no health insurance, so it was an inopportune moment to need doctors). At nearly forty, I had dropped to my adolescent weight. I was often told how great I looked, a compliment of salt in gaping wounds. If, wracked with every level of pain, I was considered attractive, it was a reminder of why I had never aspired to be.

What is beauty, anyway? And how does it relate to a woman's sense of self? If attraction is subjective, is beauty even definable? Elinor Carucci's bold color photographs in her first book, *Closer* (Chronicle, 2002), revealed, among other things, arduous layers of construction to achieve an ideal of femininity. Plucking, curling, waxing, bleaching—who came up with all this? *It's so much work.* My lack of interest in most of those rituals as a teen fed what became a lack of knowledge as I aged. When my hair began graying in my thirties, I was alarmed, and asked my sister why she didn't have any gray hair yet. She laughed and said, "Because I dye!" I really had no idea how many women, who had always looked "natural" to me, invested consistent time and resources to present that way. Elinor's work probes being a woman in all of its richness, and she has continued that visual exploration with honesty and courage throughout her own life and aging process.

Two Eyes (next spread), an image of Elinor and her mother, subtly speaks to me of intergenerational notions of beauty, while holding the parallel tension I feel with my own mother, and the ferocity of love I feel for my stepson. This photograph obliterates everything around it. It lives on a wall where I must choose to encounter it, along with the dynamic rush of emotions it stirs. Very occasionally, I can step back from all those feelings, and see the Cubist-like forms that first led me to choose it.

When I think that perhaps we've reached the visual end of what can be accomplished through "straight" photography, I think of Elinor's photograph, and of Adrain Chesser's portrait series "I have something to tell you," and know there are still untapped resources for practitioners to mine. The bravery Adrain brought to his 2003 series felt like that of a conflict photographer. They are some of the hardest, gentlest portraits I've ever experienced, made while he told each friend sitting before his camera of his AIDS diagnosis. I saw them for the first time shortly after they were made, and they have possessed me ever since.

Adrain was one of a few people with whom I had open conversations about processing my simultaneous losses: Aperture, my husband, my marriage as an entity tied to but separate from my husband and, at the base of it all, the absence of any sense of self. In the spring of 2012, he suggested I join him for a weekend of ritual and photography, at the same time asking if he could have the large, ornately framed mirror hanging over my fireplace to use in one of his rituals. I was taken aback—his asking for an heirloom object he knew I never really liked, yet also had no intention of parting with, felt invasive when I already felt so vulnerable. I had known him long enough, though, to trust his spirit, which very much includes an element of the trickster. Perhaps granting his unusual request would foster some transformations.

Nervous, I steeled myself to attend a portion of the weekend he had planned, and agreed to his taking the mirror provided it return to me in some form as a work of art. The raw photograph of me on the following page fulfilled that condition. I dreamt this moment, and wanted to live it, to lie down cold and naked on the wet sand, inside the mirror's frame, and be reborn. In the moment I felt so strong.

What I thought of as my truth in that moment did not translate to the film through the eye of my sensitive friend. He saw I was a heart detached from its soul, more corpse than newborn. The photograph held so much more of me than I could. As soon as I saw this image, I asked for the largest print he could make; I needed this physical evidence of my pain. I woke up next to it for a long time, yet after just three days, it ceased being me. I opened the blinds one morning and thought, "she looks better with a little more light." In that moment the person in the photograph became "her," a character from the past, one I was trying to love, learn from, and move beyond.

Many around me kept telling me I was going to be fine. But I was seeking a role model for failure, someone to keep me company so I wouldn't feel so alone in my abject state. When I looked within my own family, all I saw were overachievers, triumphing against the odds—those are the histories we tend to retain, burying the narratives that don't come with happy endings. One likely candidate emerged, though: my grandfather, Thomas Gabriel (T. G.) Dunn. All I had been told about him was that he drank, and that he'd left his family. I eventually learned this was a partial truth. He did drink, but he did not exactly leave. He couldn't pull himself together to save their farm during the Depression, despite my grandmother's support and extraordinary efforts. Eventually she moved west without him, taking my father with her. I'd found my man.

When T. G. died in 1953, he'd been estranged from his wife and son for over a decade. Yet they arranged his burial in a Catholic cemetery outside of Los Angeles, and on my next trip there I paid him a visit. The headstone was simple: his name, the year he was born, and the year he died. No one claimed him. Finding him gave me comfort. It was also a little kick in the pants. My siblings and I are all that remain from this guy, a guy who seemingly did only two things right by marrying my grandmother, and fathering, even if not parenting, my dad. If I was going to add some meaning to his existence, let alone my own, I had to find a way back to the surface.

I was invited to lecture at Parsons, and I wanted to demonstrate the importance of risk to the graduate students in the audience. With that in mind, I was contemplating sharing Adrain's portrait of me, and sent it to Sylvia Plachy to get her thoughts. She expressed concern about so publicly sharing my body, and my pain. Her hesitation furthered my own. I was scared, and that was part of the point. But I also trusted Sylvia's sense that perhaps I could say, "be brave," without so personally demonstrating what I meant.

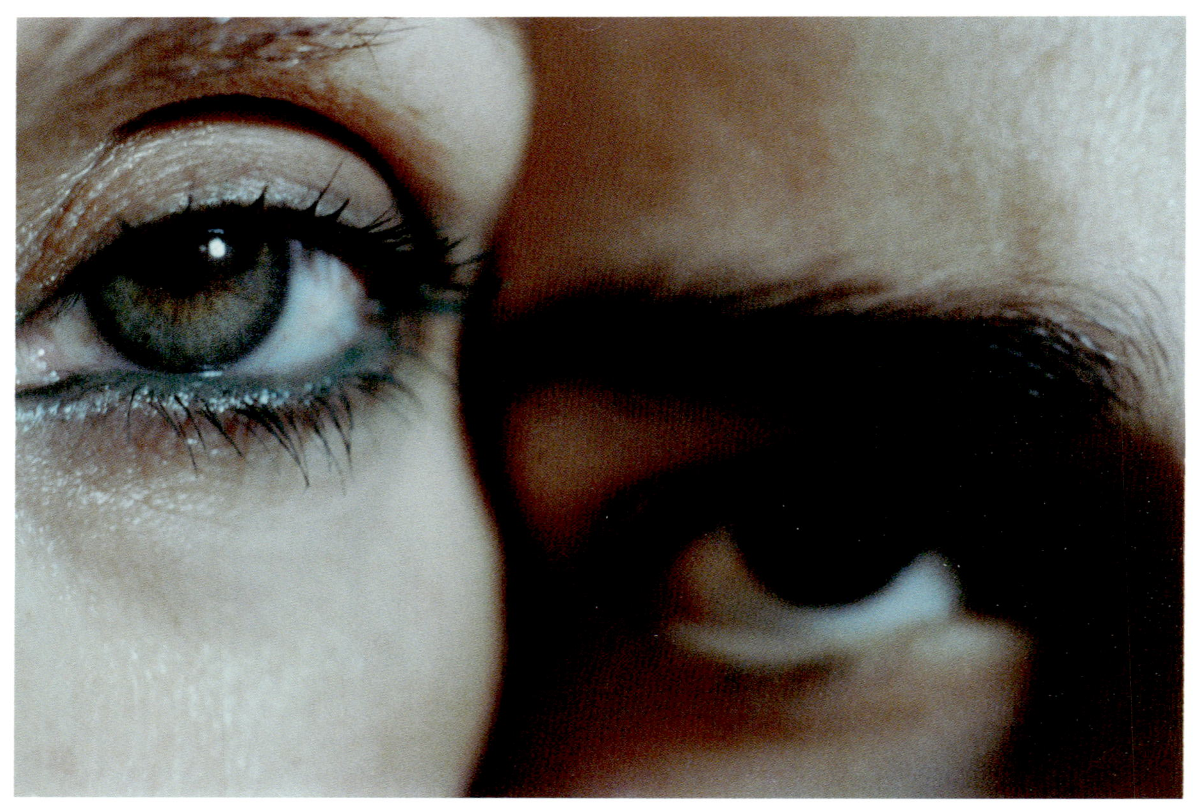

SYLVIA PLACHY, Michelle Dunn Marsh, Woodhaven, New York, 2012. Archival pigment print, 4 $^3/_4$ x 7 $^1/_8$ in. Artist proof, signed. Gift of Sylvia Plachy, 2013.

In the end, I did show it briefly, though I was clearly emotional as I did so. Some of my students (from the year before, and what would be the year ahead) thanked me for trusting them, and believing they had the capacity to receive and express deeply.

Sylvia came to the lecture to support me and to see if I'd choose to show the photograph. Afterwards she said she was glad I did, but that she saw me differently, and that perhaps she should show me who she saw.

On a breezy December afternoon, in the familiar space of her backyard, we made pictures together. Though there are many wonderful frames from that session holding the dynamic energy of our friendship, this one contains the elegance and fortitude that she wanted me to see—that of a swan who has found its way back to the water.

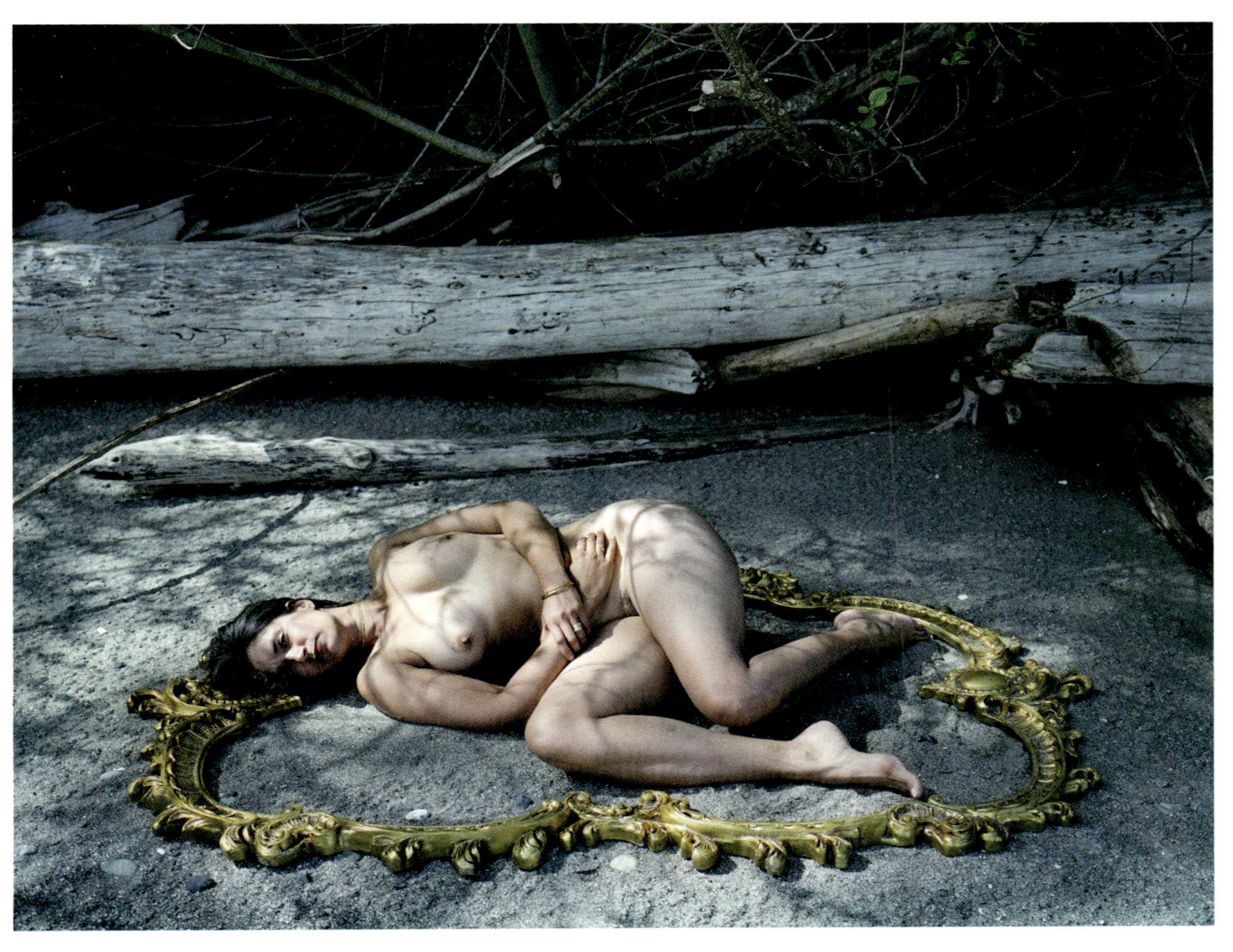

ELINOR CARUCCI, *Two Eyes*, 1993. Traditional C-print,
12 x 18 ¹/₄ in. Number 2/8. Gift of Elinor Carucci, 2009.

Overleaf: ADRAIN CHESSER, Untitled, 2012. Archival pigment
print, 31 x 40 in. Unique. Gift of Adrain Chesser, 2012.

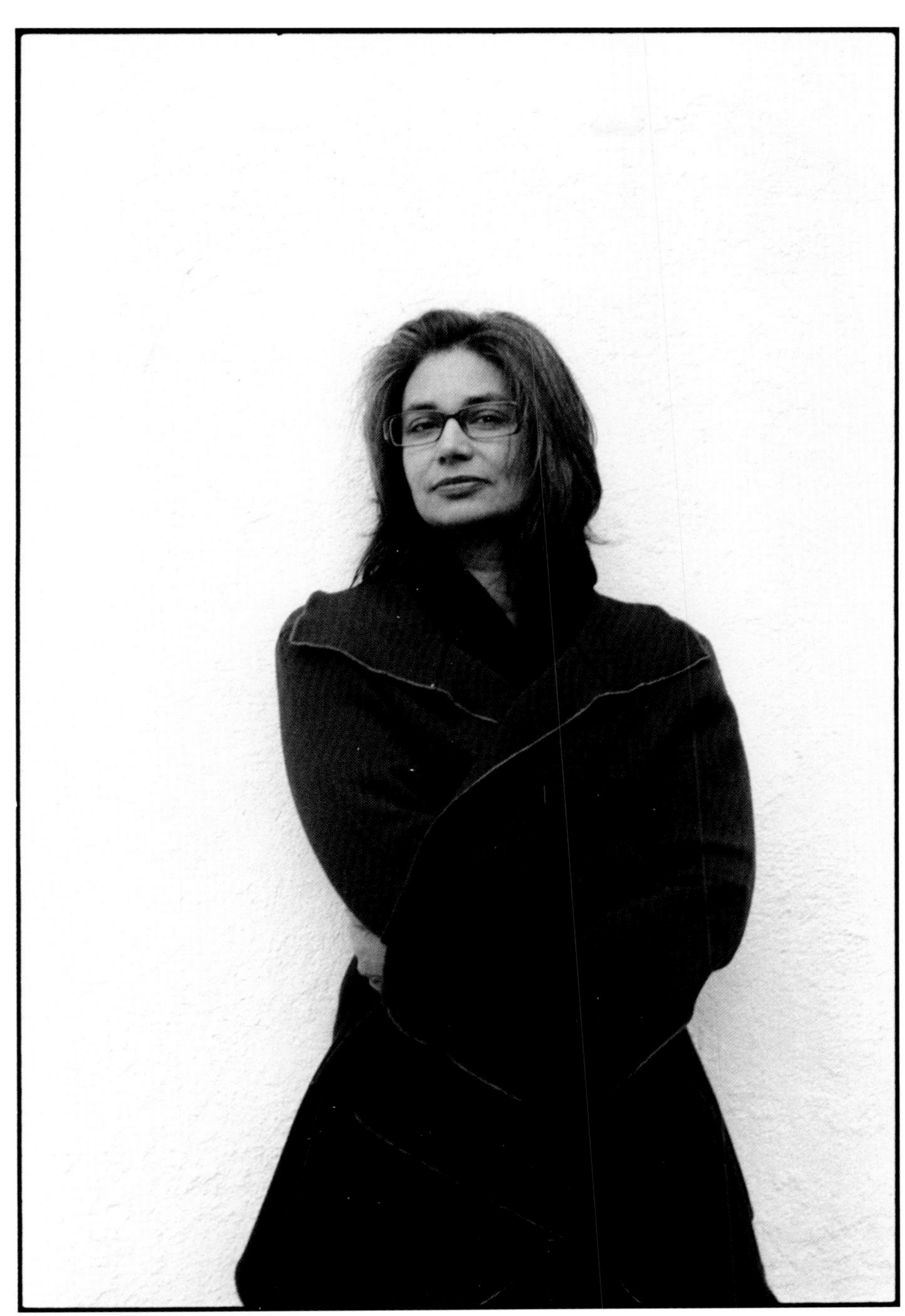

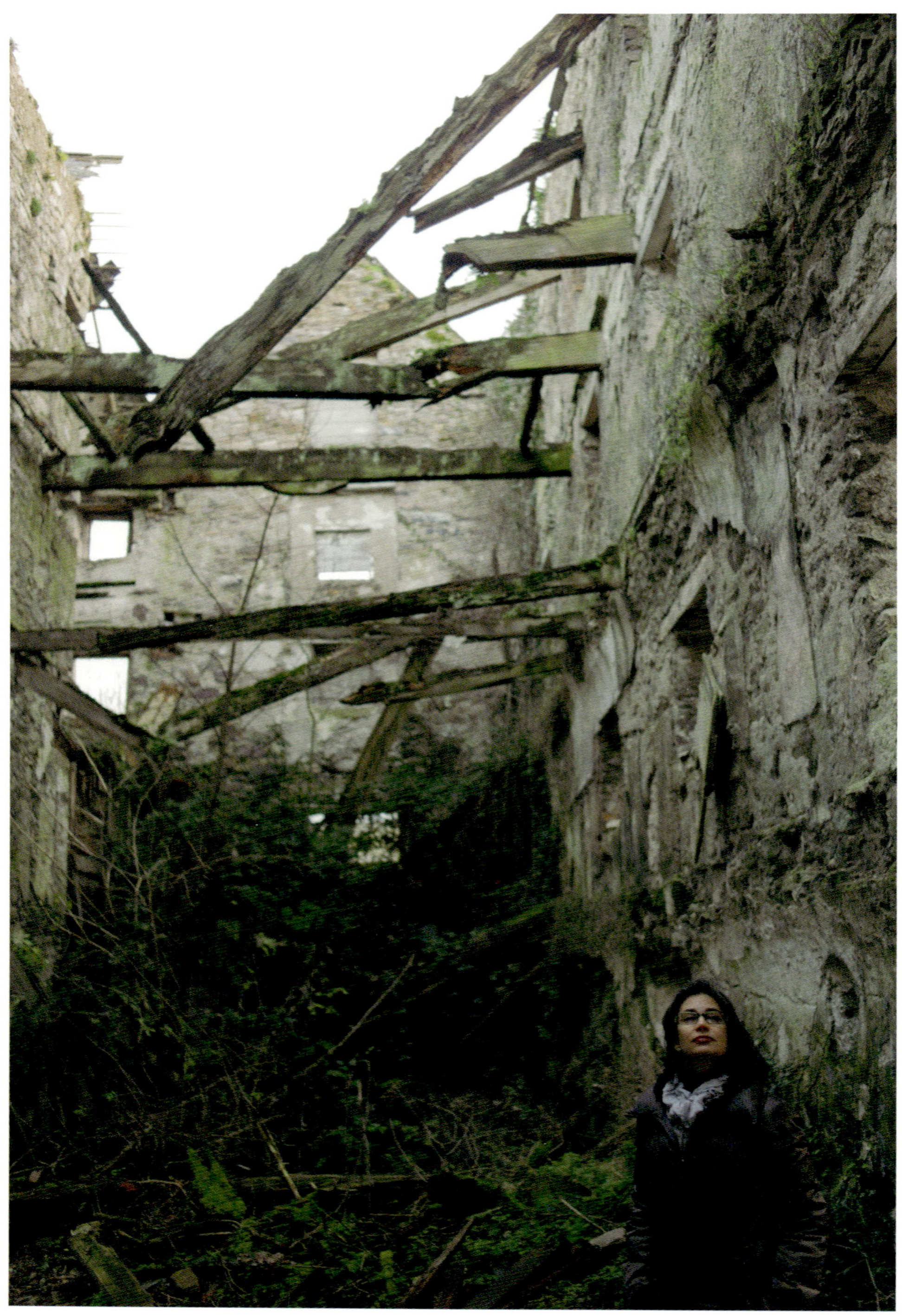

I wanted to mark my fortieth birthday far away from everything that had transpired over the previous two years. A lot of frequent flier miles got me to my sacred place in the southeast of Ireland. When I arrived at the Salmon Pool, the family pub above which my grandmother was born, I was greeted by my father's cousin, Dick, with two powerful words: "Welcome home." My spontaneous invitation to Sylvia Plachy resulted in her arrival a week later, just in time to participate in a joint New Year's Eve and birthday celebration organized by my cousin Irene. Bright-eyed, Sylvia darted around the pub with her Leica, as various cousins quietly pulled me aside to say "Should we tell your friend it's too dark to get a good picture in here?" Their comment came both from genuine concern (most not knowing who she was), and a subtle rebuke at being photographed. I assured them that she knew what she was doing, and very little could get in her way when she decided to take pictures.

I made merry into the wee hours, but followed through on a promise to Sylvia, and to myself, to get up for sunrise on New Year's Day. Though we started walking around Jerpoint Abbey, a thirteenth-century Cistercian monastery and one of the most visited destinations in Kilkenny, Sylvia was more interested in photographing the remnants of a building near the bed and breakfast where we had stayed the night. As she roamed around, I thought about what was on the other side of this holiday. Solitude. One freelance project. No full or part-time job. A business plan with no attendant funding. Bills I probably couldn't pay. A house I probably couldn't keep. No clear next step. Stay in Seattle? Move to New York? Return to teaching? Drive a UPS truck (the benefits were astounding)? Hide in a pub in Ireland? The last idea sounded the most appealing. I tried to stay engaged, while I could, in a place I loved with people I loved. I had a long plane ride back to Seattle, with a break in New York, to figure it out. The angel on my shoulder kept whispering that perhaps it was time to be brave on another level.

What became Minor Matters—the collaborative publishing platform I conceived, and then co-founded—evolved over nearly two years, informed by everything preceding it. From fits and starts and a different name in 2011, through a business plan and possible investors in 2012, we officially established our partnership with $100 in a bank account, deposited by Seattle Central Community College alumni Steve McIntyre, and me, in early 2013. Our business model was based on pre-selling books online directly to the public, establishing that a base audience for each title existed before bringing a project to print. Audiences used their purchasing power to determine what books we produced. We acknowledged their role by listing them as our co-publishers in the books that achieved the necessary pre-sales, and made it into printed form.

Amazon's rapid growth and the concurrent demise of many brick and mortar bookstores led me to consider the role of the buying audience and its influence on publishing. I'd interviewed with the founder of Amazon, Jeff Bezos, in 1996, and though I opted not to work for him, I was curious about (and dismayed by) the ways Amazon was disrupting many aspects of what had been a fairly placid, polite industry. Their extreme price discounting, sometimes selling books to the public at a loss to build audience loyalties, affected many parts of publishing. As their customer base grew exponentially, they began leaning on publishers to give them bigger wholesale discounts.

For visual books, consistently expensive to produce, there was not a lot of wiggle room on the profit margins. Publishers were seeking ways to reduce costs through adjusting physical sizes, paper choices, and printing techniques, while testing higher price points to compensate for the discounts they had to offer their primary retailer. Though there was no shortage of photographers pitching interesting projects, they had high expectations for how a book of their work should look and feel and were less interested in the financial challenges the publishers were facing. More independent publishers began producing photography books, though it was unclear if the buying audience was increasing at the same pace. From publishers paying authors a cash advance to publish their work, the model flipped, and photographer authors were routinely asked by an increasing number of publishers to contribute upwards of $30,000 toward production as a condition of the contract. Many authors did not realize they were unlikely to ever earn that money back.

By 2010, print-on-demand technology had also opened "self-publishing" to the masses. It was truly evolutionary to be able to produce a single-copy hardcover book for less than $100, and if the end result did not demonstrate great color fidelity, or was not on luxury paper, it was nonetheless a book. Everyone could produce books through iBooks, as well as platforms like Blurb and Lulu. As my professor, Werner Linz of Continuum Publishing, once said, though, a book isn't truly published until it's *sold*. While the technology was accessible to *make* books, there was still the matter of getting them out into the world, preferably through a paid transaction.

Jeff Dunas had long encouraged me to start something on my own. I had never seriously considered it, knowing how challenging it was to generate revenue even when I was doing so on Aperture's behalf. He kept bringing it up. I loved sequencing photographs, and considering what texts could add insight to a viewer's relationship with the work.

While I had been a freelance designer and production manager for a decade, and an editor at a major house for three years, I had never attempted to edit and design a book. Those roles are separate in traditional book publishing, and "crossing over" from being a designer at Aperture to an editor at Chronicle had been controversial to the teams I worked with there. Could I apply my skill sets simultaneously? Did I want to?

Two books published by others in 2012 became test cases: Jim Marshall's *The Rolling Stones 1972* (Chronicle Books), and *Joe's Junk Yard* by Lisa Kereszi (Damiani). I handled editorial development and design for both. I knew some independent book packagers and publishers served in those dual capacities, but I felt the pull of tradition, and was so unsure about "breaking the rules" that I listed myself in Jim's book as the editor, and in Lisa's book as the designer. I found I could navigate by compartmentalizing, doing one role at a time. I did so easily when working on freelance projects, designing books for one client and editing for another. So it was possible that I could become a service provider to myself, if I were to actually start publishing.

I shared elements of my pre-sales concept with Chronicle and Aperture, hoping one of them would take it on and I could manage it, instead of starting something on my own. Neither were interested in turning over control of what books were produced to the buying public. I started to grasp that if I wanted hold the books I was imagining, I might have to try and publish through this new model myself.

I dissected what I knew about the financials of publishing. Could costs associated with warehousing and distribution be reduced, if we knew in advance of printing how popular a book might be? Could that savings be invested into better paper? Online sales had gained public acceptance; people were used to buying what they had not seen. Bookstores had ordered books that did not yet exist from catalogs for years. How could that common practice be used? Kickstarter was gaining traction, but the Securities & Exchange Commission was apparently observing the unregulated arena of crowdfunding, and lawyers advised me against using that term at all with our model (apparently the SEC has bigger fish to fry. Crowdfunding remains an unregulated market).

From freelance production experience, I knew the costs to produce 500–1,000 copies of a hardcover book was about $25,000. My design and editorial expertise contributed an additional $15,000 to $20,000 per book in-kind. The average retail price of an art monograph over the last four decades was $50.

From there it was just math. I'd need to sell 500 copies, at retail, to cover hard expenses. $50 x 500 felt achievable, sort of. Five hundred copies sold would certainly represent a meaningful audience of interest. And that repetition of fives and zeroes worked nicely visually. If we sold 500, and produced 1,000, we could give the artists 100–200 copies so they had plenty to use for their own purposes. But to generate any income, we'd need to sell the rest. Could we avoid Amazon and still do that? *How?*

The business model I formulated brought together elements of everything I had learned thus far, but what made the venture possible was recognizing what I *didn't* know. That was the online world, an arena I'd mostly ignored since leaving it professionally in 1996. Steve McIntyre, who had assisted me on a few book projects while he was a student at Seattle Central, and had even worked with me in New York for a few weeks during one summer break, was the first person I contacted. I had followed his success as a web and app developer, and asked him to review the proposals I'd solicited to build out a commerce-driven website. He confirmed that it was not a simple site, and the $10,000 estimate was reasonable for what I was asking for. I shelved the concept shortly thereafter.

Nearly a year later, I finally saw that what I had conceived was as much about e-commerce as it was about publishing. The books first had to be *sold*, and for that, I needed someone who understood the use of screen-based environments as well as I understood the printed page. I went back to Steve, asking if he'd consider adding his knowledge and sweat equity to mine to get this off the ground. I knew nothing about start-ups, but he did, and he was willing to take a risk. From his initial yes, he kept saying yes. Yes, I'll build it out with you. Yes, we can launch without the investment that you'd hoped for, money gets committed but falls through all the time. Yes, you can change one more word, one more time, this isn't print! Yes, that great press came earlier than we had planned, and yes, people will come back to the site when we have a book to sell. Yes, we should do this. Yes.

There's are scraps of paper filed somewhere that have the all the words I noted to arrive at the name "Minor Matters." I'd been listening to music, looking at photographs on the walls, and thinking about who inspired me. I wondered why the word "minority" was so often associated with inferiority. It represented quantity, not value. In music, major and minor chords and keys are equal, just different. Could minority represent something rare, or special? "Minor" and "Matters" were in different phrases

MINOR WHITE, *Nude Foot*, San Francisco, 1947 / before 1963. Gelatin silver contact print, 4 x 5 in. Edition unknown. Purchase from Stevan Baron, 2003.

and separate columns, but at one point I circled each of them, and it just felt right (the alliteration helped). I had some concern that photographers might find the name diminishing, but after discussing it with several people, they all said they first associated the name, and me as part of it, with Minor White, and no one had an issue with "Minor" mattering. That worked for me on both the levels I intended: if Minor the man mattered, then my minority viewpoint could also matter.

The next two considerations came out of my past professional experiences. Should Minor Matters be a nonprofit organization? And should it be exclusive to photography?

There was a purity I associated with the nonprofit sector that was primarily a construct in my mind, but one that I wanted to be a reality. From my occasional ventures into the commercial world, I valued the simple baseline of profit, noting it did not have to be the sole priority of a business. Could I run a for-profit guided by integrity? I considered the challenges of convincing people to support photography as a cause, versus the capitalist motivation of buying what you want or need. I wanted people to *want* our books. Was that asking too much? We would probably attract a small following, if any (art books are niche, photography books a niche within that). Would it be enough? Could we develop an audience that saw itself as a different type of shareholder,

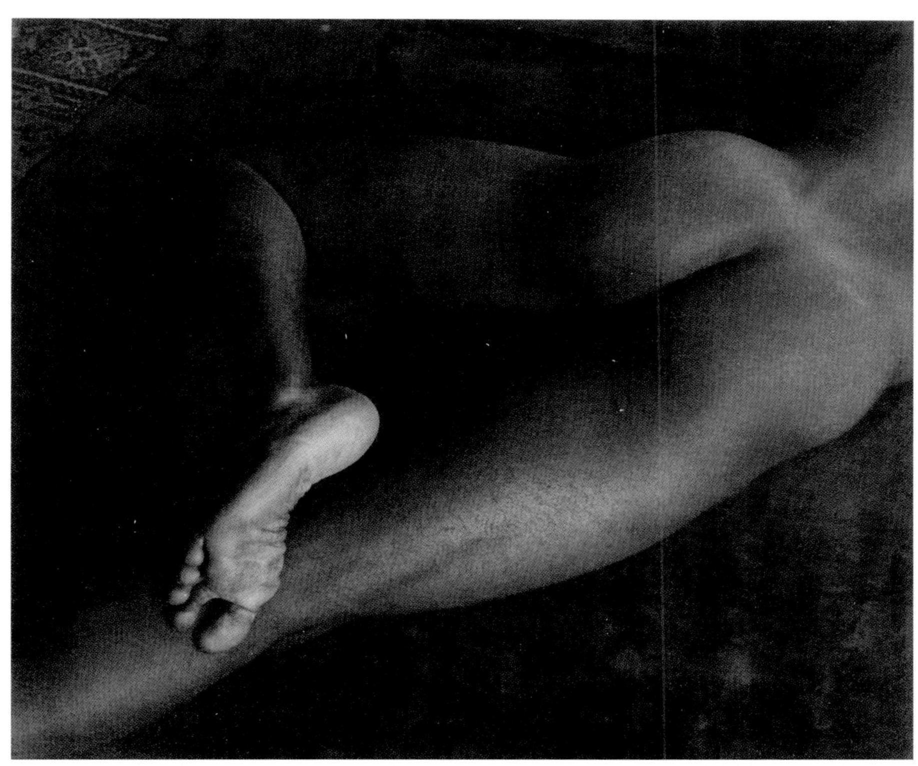

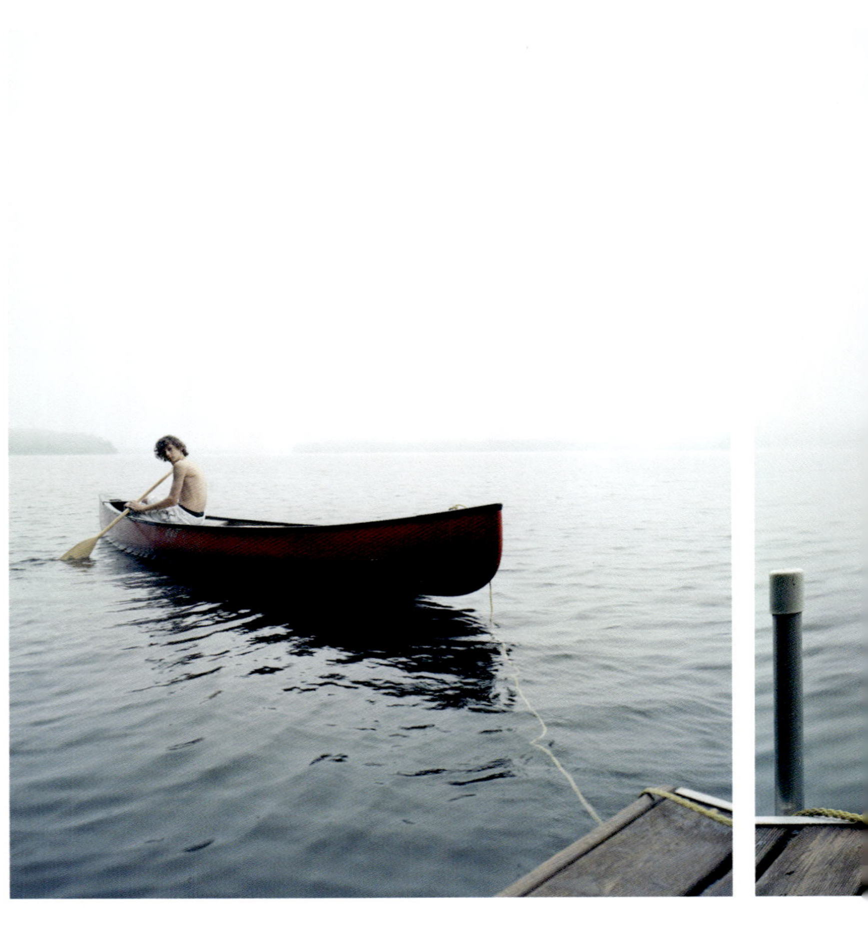

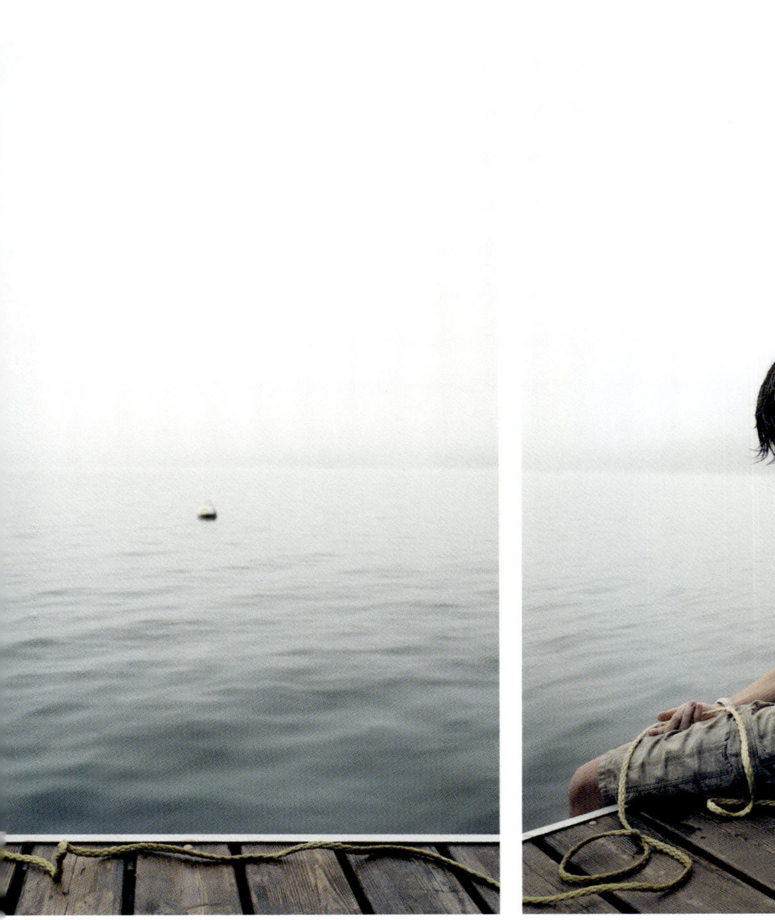
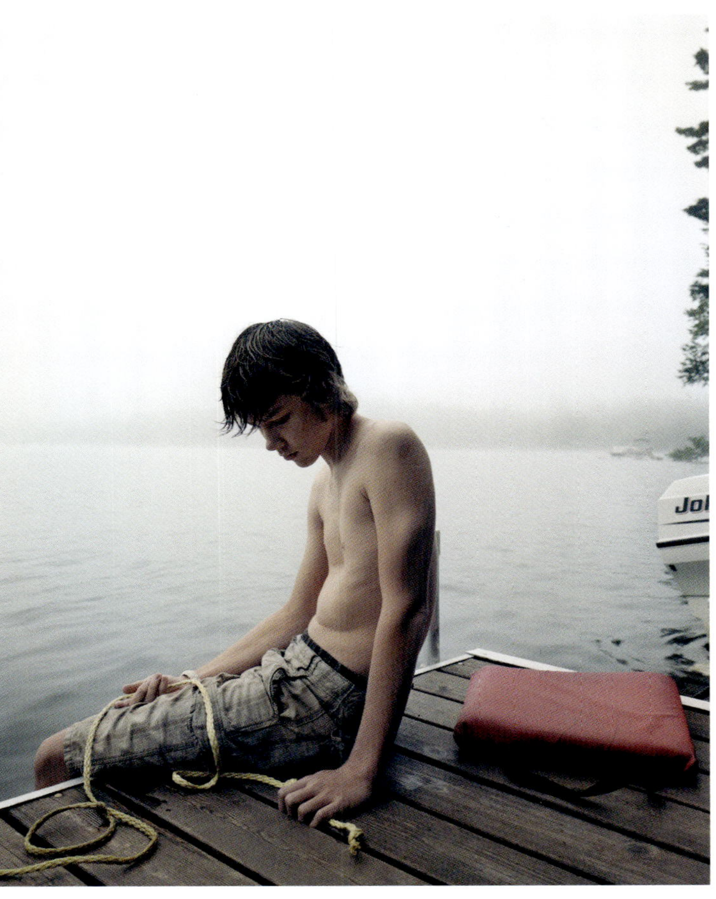

rewarded not through cash dividends but personal affirmation in seeing their names in print? Would it matter to them to know they were essential to the creation of the book?

Likewise, what would it mean to make space for art forms beyond photography? I had privileged photography in my life. Would I be abandoning the flame I'd tended for so long if I did not isolate and dedicate this new venture to it? I found the paintings of Joe Park, a colleague from Seattle Central (and also Steve's professor), extraordinary. I had successfully brought Joe's work to Chronicle through a small postcard book, but he was worthy of a larger monograph. If we were exclusive to photography, it would eliminate him from our potential roster. That concern answered itself: for him, Minor Matters could make space for more than photography, while still championing it.

As was sometimes the case when I was wrestling with matters of philosophical importance, I called Robert Adams to talk through the decisions I needed to make, and my inclinations. Some part of me was seeking permission from the universe to take this next step, and in his thoughtful responses I found that. In formulating a mission, I settled on an open-ended intention to publish projects that reflect the surface of life, drawing from Bob's eloquent words (in a letter to me, but also in one of his essays) that "photography will always be interesting, because the surface of life keeps changing."

We sought and secured agreements to launch books for pre-sales with five authors—oil painter Joe Park, and Eli Hansen, who works primarily in glass. Photographers Anna Mia Davidson and Larry Fink

Pages 128–129: DAVID HILLIARD, *Boys Tethered*, 2008 / 2015. Archival pigment prints face-mounted to plexi, 24 x 60 in. (each of three panels, 20 x 24 in.) Artist proof. Gift of David Hilliard, 2015.

represented the emerging and master ends of the spectrum; David Hilliard was a mid-career photographer with gallery representation in the United States and abroad, and a first monograph already published. The trust and acceptance of risk from these artists completed the net I needed to take the leap and announce Minor Matters. Steve and I decided that if we launched ten books and none of them went into print, we'd call it quits.

When David Hilliard first got in touch with me, through our mutual friend Lisa Kereszi, about doing a book, I didn't do a very good job of promoting my new venture. I offered to put him in touch with Chronicle, and at the end of the conversation mentioned Minor Matters. He liked that he would be directly engaged in the editorial process with us, and was excited he could assist in the formation of a new model in publishing.

We met in New York to develop an edit and sequence of his work. It was an intense and emotional two days, discussing why he made pictures, what types of men he was drawn to, and what his photographs of his father and his mother meant to him. As we selected and discarded images, a rhythm appeared. Only the title took us a few more weeks of correspondence and conversation. When we arrived at *What Could Be* (Minor Matters, 2014), *Boys Tethered* (pp. 128–29) emerged as the essential cover image.

David's multi-paneled works push the cinematic in his photographs. Barely perceptible shifts of light or weather from one image to another mark passages of time not immediately apparent; I saw this more clearly as we printed his book. While on press together in

Iceland (my first visit; he'd been there before), he made a point of getting me out of the plant, first into the soaking pools for which the country is known, and then on a day-long drive to see some of the landscape. David revels in joy and beauty in his life and in his photographs, one of many reasons that an enthusiastic audience responds to his work.

Working "from the fringes" was a declared intention of Minor Matters from its inception. As the mainstream changes, we leave malleable our definition, giving ourselves room to look at well known themes or subjects from previously unconsidered angles, while also seeking out underrepresented artists worthy of greater attention.

I rarely state publicly how my identity as a multi-ethnic, bicoastal woman, in addition to my professional expertise, influences the books we develop. On one hand, it is obvious to me, so I do not need to state it. On the other, I recognize that in my desire to be seen for my mind in professional spheres, I have sometimes succeeded in rendering invisible this tea-stained female body. But it is here, and I am in it, a double minority. I am also a middle-class, well-educated Caucasian American, of which there are many in publishing. I both fit in and stand out, depending on who is paying attention, and to what.

Loose demographics of the United States show that half of the population identifies as female, and an aggregate 25 percent are not of European descent. We bear these in mind when considering what projects to take on. We have published gay and straight white men, Black women, queer identifying people under forty, right or left-coasters of Indigenous and multi-ethnic backgrounds, spanning five generations. We choose our authors because they have demonstrated excellence in their craft, they have something timely to say and have done so in a compelling manner, and they are multi-faceted human beings. We engage with them in their totality.

With all the opportunities to self-produce books, publishers still hold relevant knowledge of the bookmaking process. To some people, publishers retain a position of privilege, granting a kind of cultural affirmation to the authors they endorse. It can seem an impenetrable world when it comes to how decisions are made. That is partially because, as in many creative endeavors, there are steps of logic, and then leaps of love.

Alice Wheeler was high on my list of possible authors to approach for Minor Matters. Her photographs have an unmistakable and rare flair informed not only by the people she is drawn to but how she sees them. I'd been following her work since I returned to the Seattle area in 1999. Ten years later, I reached out to her while I was at Chronicle about possibly doing a book, though we did not end up moving forward then. She had clear stipulations for what she did and did not want—a book needed to reflect her vision, not exploit her friendships and encounters with Nirvana, Bikini Kill, and other high-profile bands from the Seattle music scene.

Alice holds a personal sense of integrity to her work and her subjects that is reminiscent of the generation before her. When she agreed to work with Minor Matters, and delivered the one hundred photographs I had requested to begin an edit for her book, she left out the majority of her best known images. It was necessary to see what works *she* felt were most important to realize a sequence that was authentic to her.

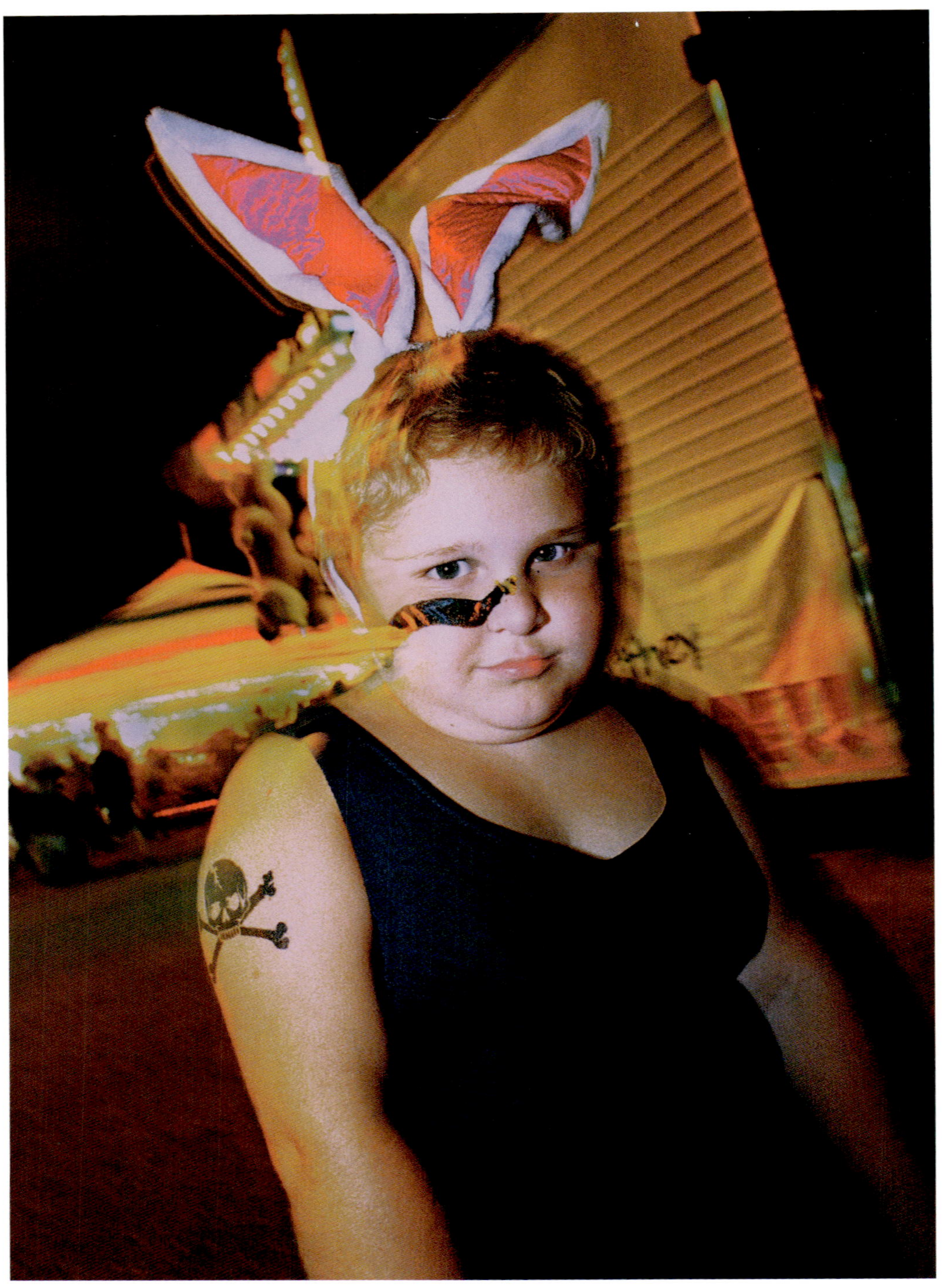

When I showed Alice the first duotone press proofs of her black and white images, she said, "these look great; they just don't look like my photographs." On a conference call with separator Thomas Palmer, she explained her high-contrast images, noting she sometimes "pushed the film" on certain photographs. Thomas knew exactly what she was talking about (I didn't), and the next set of proofs was spot on. Of the many books I have worked on with Thomas, he has only ever asked for additional copies of Alice's *Outcasts & Innocents* (Minor Matters, 2015).

In the early part of 2013, just after Steve McIntyre and I opened the bank account for Minor Matters, Photographic Center Northwest (PCNW) in Seattle posted a job description for its next executive director. I ignored it for as long as I could. A publicly accessible, accredited art school and exhibition space, PCNW had existed in some form in Seattle since the late 1980s, and I had partnered with the institution a number of times through Aperture West, as well as attended other programs and fundraisers there. Friends and colleagues locally encouraged me to apply again. I was not eager, having been a finalist for the position twice before.

Practical factors weighed on me. I needed to secure a mortgage by myself to keep the house I'd previously shared with my spouse. No bank, not even the one holding the existing joint mortgage and seeing my consistent payments, was willing to refinance a single, self-employed woman (I tried). If I ever wanted to see our years of investment in it pay off, I'd have to hold onto it. That meant I'd have to apply for full-time work. The PCNW opportunity was in my field, and in my

ALICE WHEELER, **Boy with Rabbit Ears, Evergreen State Fair, Monroe, Washington, August, 2006 / 2009.** Traditional chromogenic print, 18 ¼ x 23 ¼ in. Purchase, 2015.

backyard. It was a chance to use the leadership skills I had developed through various administrative and management roles. Judging from my research and conversations with previous board members, the institution appeared to be financially stable. I was offered the position, and with the board's understanding that I would still be launching Minor Matters, I accepted. I negotiated a lower salary and fewer vacation days to dedicate time during the week to my other professional obligations. That tactic ended up being far more necessary than I knew.

I began my role at PCNW remotely, while I was in New York teaching for the summer. That gave me two months to think conceptually as I got to know the staff and programs in increments. I developed a white paper noting PCNW's distinction as an accredited educational institution and a publicly accessible space, and positioned it amid peer organizations regionally and nationally. Having time to research and prepare this was a rare circumstance, one that made a difference in successfully navigating my first year.

Yet with its million dollar operating budget, a staff of twelve to fourteen people, a rotation of adjunct faculty, and no endowment, PCNW as a business was, in accounting terms, not a "going concern" when I began. We did not have the cash to make payroll a month after I arrived on site. Having been on the receiving end of a surprise re-org at Aperture, I did not want to lead one, but immediate measures were required. The dedication of PCNW's staff during that period will long stay with me. Though furloughed for two weeks, nearly everyone contributed time and skills, without pay, to begin the fall quarter on schedule, and execute a forthcoming fundraiser—once again, a single evening on which so much depended.

Had the gala merely *met* the minimum financial projections, a quarter of the staff would have been permanently laid off a week later. Thankfully we avoided the worst-case scenarios by raising far more, achieving a stretch goal that bought us three months to implement a new staffing and budgeting structure. I reduced our public hours. I reduced our full-time work week from 40 to 35 hours, reducing the payroll accordingly—a permanent pay cut to a team that had just demonstrated tremendous effort and commitment. I moved a few positions to part-time, including my own, to maximize what expertise was needed daily, and what contributions could be made remotely or through fewer hours. I still had to cut two positions. Later hiring back one of those loyal employees, Erin Spencer (she went on to facilitate our most ambitious exhibitions), was a milestone in my efforts to right the ship. Creativity needed to be applied to operations of the business itself, not just to how we fulfilled our mission.

Within my first year of leading both the nonprofit and our book venture, PCNW had somewhat stabilized under the austerity measures, and three of five titles launched through Minor Matters achieved the necessary pre-sales to go to press, which meant I was continuing in my dual occupations. Doing so was met with skepticism from some of my peers, but I had solid role models. Musician and photographer Graham Nash, Leon Botstein, conductor for the American Symphony Orchestra while also president of Bard College, and Michael Hoffman, thirty years a curator at the

MEGHANN RIEPENHOFF, *Chronograph #07 (9.22.16–10.7.16)*. Double-sided dynamic cyanotype, each side 7 3/8 x 9 5/16 in. Unique. Purchased from PCNW auction, 2016.

Philadelphia Museum of Art while also executive director at Aperture Foundation, had all demonstrated that no one has to be singular. Admiration and awe were directed at those men. In contrast, I was often told, "You just can't keep doing all of this." For me, the two roles, plus the ongoing multi-year book project I was art directing for a private client, brought balance, income, and kept me from overextending in any one direction. Sequencing photographs in the evening was relaxing after a day of meetings and spreadsheets. The creative freedom I was experiencing through Minor Matters bubbled through to leading blue-sky conversations with the staff at PCNW.

PCNW's exhibition area is also its entrance to darkrooms, classrooms, and studios, so we used the shows to extend awareness of the language and the craft of the medium to students and the public. Noting an increase of practitioners turning from digital capture to hybrid uses of alternative processes, gallery director Ann Pallesen curated *Process* in 2014, including the work of newly local artist Meghann Riepenhoff. Meghann's hand-coated, abstract cyanotypes, textural from the sediment and seaweed that attached during her ocean exposures, were landscapes I engaged with. They did not document

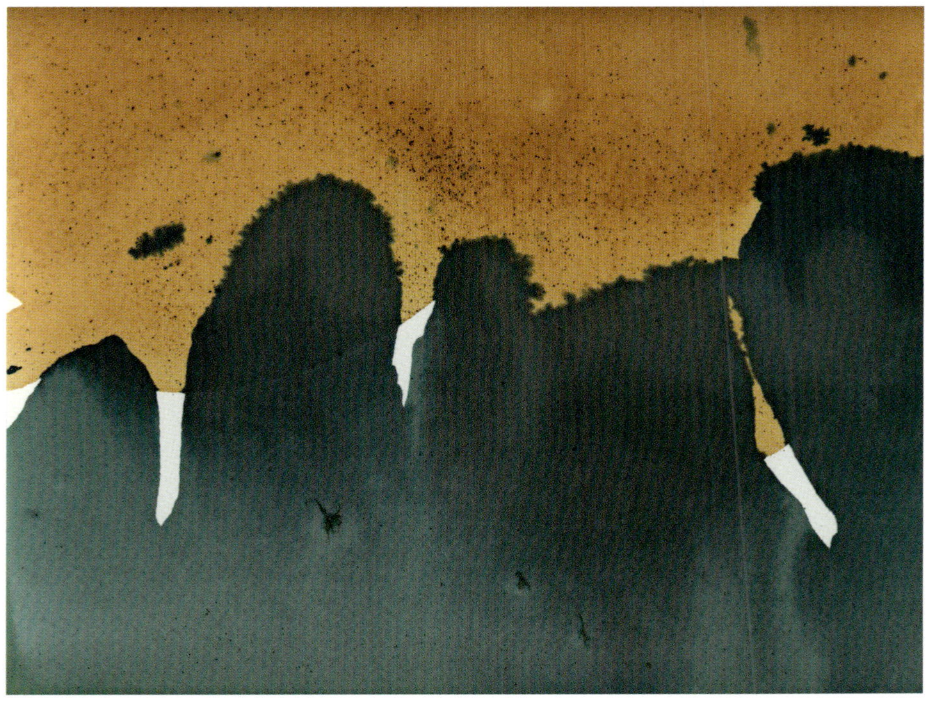

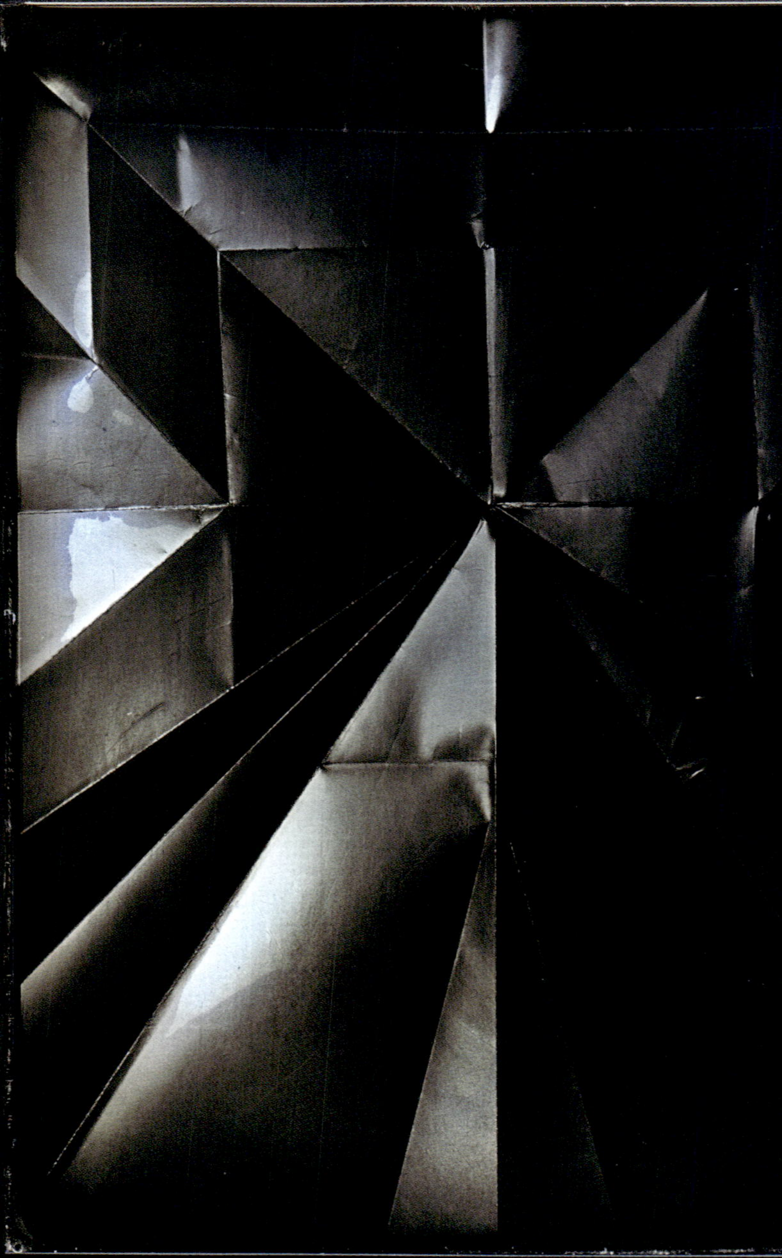

elements interacting with scenery, but instead physically embodied light, water, and wind in an unfixed chemical reaction that continues over time. *Chronograph #07* is double-sided; I turn it on the summer and winter solstice. It is a personal six-month calendar to remind me that the piece, the planet, and I are rotating together.

Process was a hyper-insider show, exciting to darkroom aficionados. It was followed by the timely *Me and My Selfie*, led by curator Chieko Phillips in 2015. An effort to apply art historical research to a current cultural phenomenon and a version of photography not often thought of as art, the images were displayed entirely on phones and tablets as the native platforms for this new form of portraiture. That exhibition drew the attention of the *Seattle Times*, as well as King5 News, Seattle's local NBC affiliate.

Other exhibitions, such as *Terminal: On Mortality and Beauty*, a group show I developed examining loss and death, explored photography's expressive capabilities as a visual language. These endeavors and their attendant public programs drew in new, and sometimes larger audiences, but often required project-specific fundraising. We pitched a few shows at a time to donors, hoping at least one idea would seduce them. The process was not so different from selling advertising, but then I was closing deals of $10,000 to $50,000. In Seattle pitching exhibitions yielded $500 to $2,500, if anything at all. I secured one $15,000 corporate sponsorship for *Me and My Selfie*, but it took nearly a year to do so. *Terminal* was courageously funded by the Satterberg Foundation, after its opening, thanks to efforts by our then-development liaison, Nichole DeMent. The financial return on investment of time was never enough. We looked to what we could achieve with partnerships, creative use of the funds we *did* have from the city and county, and sheer will, moving forward shows that best served our mission to facilitate creation, conversations, and experiences of significant photography.

DANIEL CARRILLO and EIRIK JOHNSON, Untitled, from the series "Unfolded," 2016. Daguerreotype, 6 ¹/₂ x 8 ¹/₂ in. Unique. Purchase from PCNW fundraising auction, 2016.

The Riffs residency was initiated in 2016 to extend awareness of the hybrid model of our space, and photography as an art form, locally. Artists engaged with music, ceramics, glass, painting—mediums better known and valued in the city—were selected to be in conversation with a group of photographic practitioners. The residency carried two stipulations: the artists had to meet as a group three times, and had to deliver something tangible—notes, recordings, sketches, or proofs—for the culminating works-in-progress exhibition. The daguerreotype collaboration between two photographers who did not then know each other well, PCNW Programs Chair Eirik Johnson and faculty Daniel Carrillo, was one kind of unpredictable combustion I'd hoped Riffs would ignite. Their initial trials during the residency resulted in art fair and gallery exhibitions of their "Unfolded" series.

We initiated new, low-cost programs responding to artist-defined needs within the community, including professional practices mentorship, and visibility outside of the region. Three issues of *Latitude 47*, a thirty-two-page publication, were produced and distributed to tastemakers nationally showcasing local photographers. A gala fundraiser honoring the longevity of ten photo-specific commercial galleries across the United States was the backdrop to the announcement of the PCNW Presents program, designed to provide short-term representation for artists not affiliated with galleries in the region, and to connect collectors to more artists. We developed receptions and talks to encourage acquiring photography regionally, including through local commercial galleries.

During a collecting workshop at PCNW, a visiting art consultant noted that good photography was still on the market at a reasonable price—which he defined as prints selling for $10,000 to $25,000. Upon hearing those numbers, the room in Seattle got very quiet. His comment answered a question I had never thought to ask. How do people ascribe value to art? Connecting worth to currency was one way. I tried to think of where photographic art appraised at $10,000 was publicly on view in the area. Sometimes at the museums, but never with an attendant price tag. Sometimes at local galleries. Often, nowhere at all. There was a small, loyal community who had consistently supported PCNW over thirty years, but engaging a collecting audience was proving challenging.

Having briefly explored borrowing works from local museums and realizing the limitations of their procedures and our space, I turned to artists, private collectors, and gallerists I knew. They were happy to loan works for the relatively short durations of our exhibitions, allowing us to showcase internationally celebrated photographers—Robert Adams, Tina Barney, Susan Derges, Eikoh Hosoe, Richard Misrach, Hank Willis Thomas, Joel Peter Witkin, and many others—alongside up and coming regional practitioners. We shifted our exhibition schedules to align with the academic quarters, tying not only workshops and lectures but new elective classes to works on view. We added significant photographic exhibitions regionally and nationally to our bi-annual brochures, encouraging our patrons to see with us the medium's, and the institution's, potential.

PCNW was the first environment I'd worked in where I was constantly around people shooting, developing, and printing photographs. That exposure deepened when a photographer became a part of my personal life. From my earliest days at Aperture I had avoided romantic involvement with photographers. It was intricate enough making books with them, and I did not want further complications. Yet after the ruptures I'd experienced personally and professionally, sharing time with someone passionate about the medium, and for whom it was a primary mode of expression, was new and wonderful. It also presented some challenges. Running two businesses left me with no spare hours, and nurturing a relationship required time I could not easily create. I was also concerned about a potential conflict of interest. He occasionally taught at PCNW, and though I did not have direct oversight of the adjunct faculty, I signed their paychecks, and was the final arbiter of any conflict resolution. It was delicate.

I felt ethically bound to disclose our relationship to the board to whom I reported, and absolutely resistant to doing so. From the shame and discomfort I felt from instances of being sexualized in professional contexts, I could not now—as a woman and a leader— lay my intimate involvement on the table to be discussed, approved or rejected by a room mostly full of men. It triggered deeply buried emotions I had tried to forget for over twenty years. I loved him and didn't want to end the relationship; he loved me and chose to teach less. That I didn't follow my own ethical standards weighed on me in ways hard for him to relate to. We cycled through so many rules of engagement for public and private interactions, for professional and social interactions, for break-ups and make-ups that fissures formed, then grew. This was also transpiring amidst polarized politics in the United States, increased visibility of police brutality against Black American citizens, and another wave of publicity highlighting rampant misogyny in the workplaces of many professions, including academia, the arts, and publishing.

It all added unprecedented tension to the already-challenging role I held running an underfunded nonprofit organization in Seattle. Though the city considers itself liberal, it is less so than it believes. It has long masked its history with racist policies through overatten-tion to politically correct language, rather than substantive, direct action to diversify power.

This was made painfully evident in the closing days of the *All Power: Visual Legacies of the Black Panther Party* exhibition in 2018. With board approval, a book generated through Minor Matters two years earlier became a PCNW exhibition. It timed with the fiftieth anniversary celebrations of the Seattle chapter of the Black Panther Party, which launched in 1968 twenty-plus blocks away from PCNW's current location.

The exhibition had opened to positive press at the Association of International Photographic Art Dealers (AIPAD) Photography Show, an annual art fair in New York City. The Seattle installation following AIPAD included a photographic mural by ocal artist Jasmine Iona Brown. The near-life-size adhesive photograph of her son wearing a hoodie and reading a book was installed on the front of PCNW's building. Days before the exhibition closed, the mural was vandalized—the head ripped off from the figure.

Some staff and board members did not immediately perceive it as the racist act I did. Still, the institution led a neighborhood response to re-install the same work multiple times on the block where PCNW was located. When the city's Office of Arts & Culture declined our emergency request for $1,000 to produce ten more murals, we absorbed the cost internally. Staff members voluntarily went door to door, securing permission from business owners and landlords to feature the piece on building exteriors. Of the re-installed pieces, seven of ten were torn down or destroyed within weeks. *Teen Vogue* brought national attention, picking up the story from the courageous reporting of *Seattle Times* columnist Tyrone Beason. He received hundreds of dismissive, insulting responses to the two columns he dedicated to the circumstances. I wish I was surprised.

When I accepted the position of executive director at PCNW in 2013, I had the foresight to negotiate time as a commodity. My decision to do so led some stakeholders to doubt my commitment to the role. I wonder if they fully understood what it takes to manage an institution and its staff, donors, and programs, while reporting to a rotating group of volunteers who are allies, income sources, occasionally critics, and bosses, on a salary of $60,000 gross a year? Doing it well extends into breakfasts and dinners, weekends and evening events. Gaining back some office hours I could *choose* to spend on PCNW, or on income-generating work for myself, was about sanity and necessity. The responsibilities of the job are not commensurate to that salary, as most executive directors would confirm, though that salary is all too common. Throughout my six years as executive director I shifted my hours and income a number of times at PCNW, directing funds slated for my salary toward other underpaid positions, while using my time strategically for the organization, and on external projects, to keep the institution, and myself, solvent.

The last permutation was my board-accepted proposal of a dual-leadership structure. It granted day-to-day oversight to a staff member internally promoted to executive director, and created a more flexible role for me to focus on potential site development, and expansion of visual literacy within our programs and curriculum. The position, chief strategist, refreshed my energies through presenting new challenges, and facilitating use of my institutional history in meaningful ways. Yet the board's invitation to renew my agreement a year later was contingent upon my reporting to the executive director instead of the board as initially agreed, and stepping away from the real estate component. After some discussion, I declined. It was a quick and quiet conclusion to my seven years there.

The cultural sector is heavily dependent on the generosity of individuals who give time and money to facilitate the continuance of nonprofit organizations. Board roles in particular are weighty commitments. I have great respect for many of the individuals who served on the boards of Aperture Foundation and PCNW during my years working for those organizations. I believe that a number of them also had respect for me. And yet in both environments, groups of people behind closed doors made governing decisions that did not necessarily reflect our mutual respect for one another, or for the organizations we served. On a crass level of evaluation, I financially and programmatically

JONATHAN DAVID SMYTH, FAO Schwartz, New York, August 3, 2015, from the series "Just One More." Archival pigment print from cameraphone image, 8 x 10 in. Artist proof. Gift of Jonathan David Smyth, 2017.

garnered both of those institutions more than I cost them. On a more timely one, the years I spent in leadership at those institutions added the diversity and representation both organizations now claim is important. Neither appreciated the challenges, or the benefits, that came with my polyvalent views. In some ways, neither did I, feeling limited for reasons I couldn't easily identify. I couldn't imagine that perhaps subconscious biases around gender and ethnicity, or cultural differences in communication, could be possible causes for why I could not obtain, or keep, a seat at the table. The white male in me just didn't see that.

Normalizing and integrating difference rarely happens smoothly, particularly when it challenges existing power structures and asks for new paradigms. I have sought analogies as I consider these experiences so I can look forward with hope, rather than the despair I sometimes feel that despite the talk and trainings corporations and cultural institutions are now devoting to diversity, equity, and inclusion, little of substance is changing.

Lately the formation of pearls comes to mind. Pearls begin with an irritant landing in the shell of its host. The mollusk's response is defensive, secreting a liquid perhaps to flush out the irritant, or at least to lessen the impact of its presence. Over time, though, something new and precious generates from the irritant and the host—if they find a way to co-exist. My mother's mother said that pearls are not meant for everyone; at the moment I have a better relationship with diamonds. They are formed under pressure, a condition to which I better

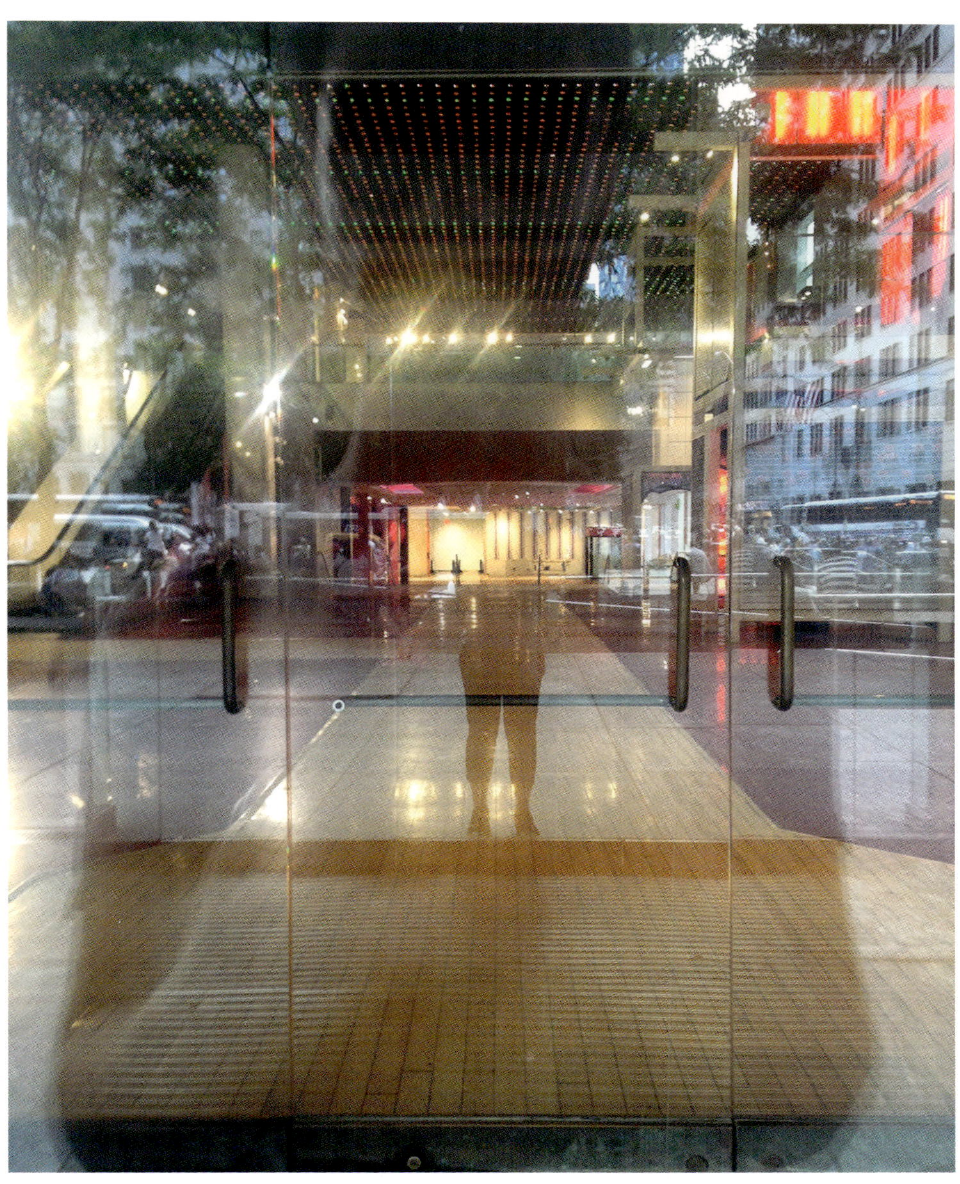

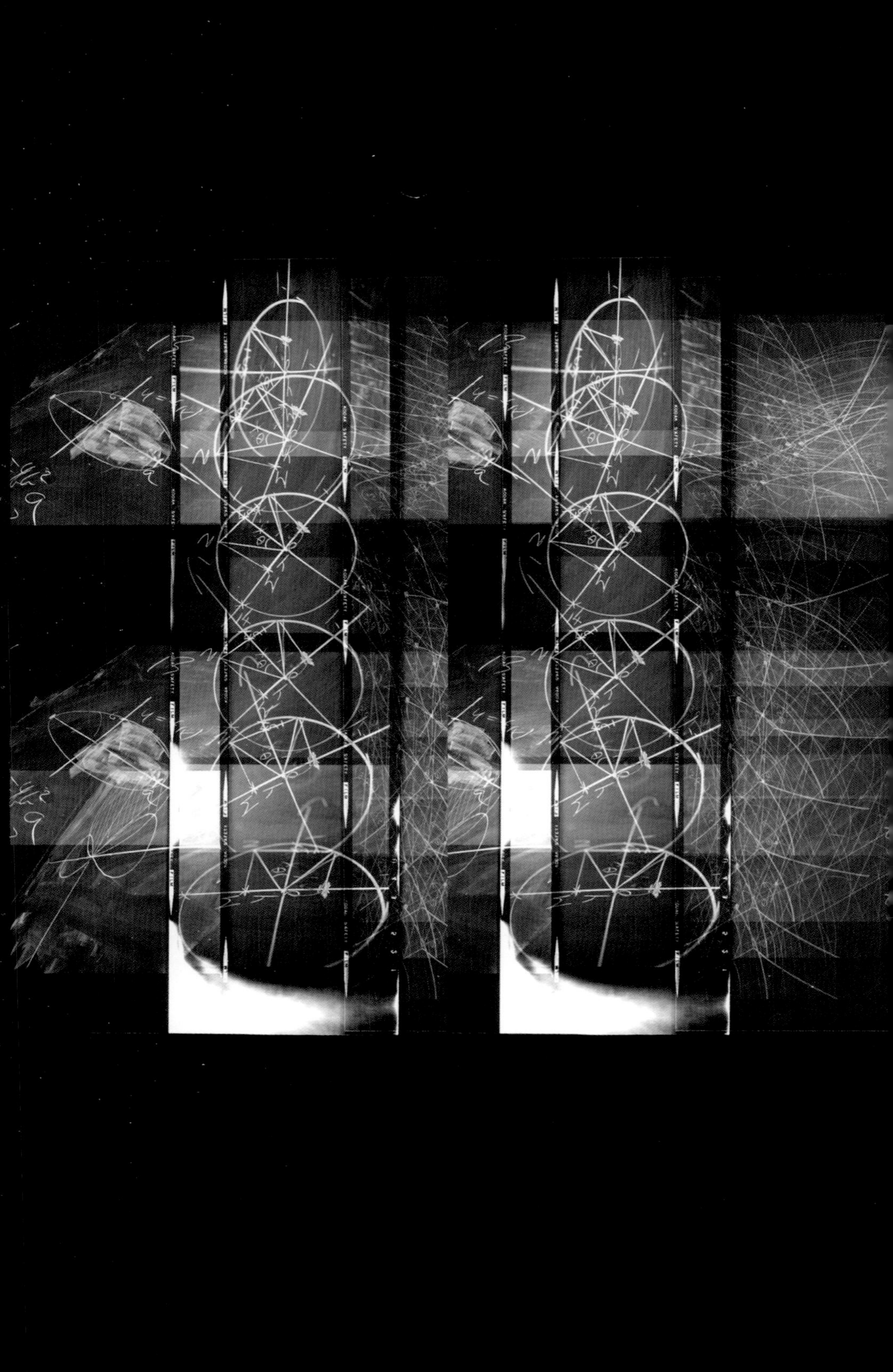

relate. I feel the presence of those who came before me, their exhortations to hold the "best" of this medium. "Best" is a subjective evaluation that those of us seeing professionally will continue to debate, given the medium's histories, and the energies of the moment.

All this pressure bearing down on the stuff of photography in the crucible of my brain adds sparkle to the projects I conceive, discuss, edit, and design. Some come with their own external pressure; with others I apply it to myself. The first hardcover monograph for Paul Berger, a practitioner of photography for over fifty years, fell into the latter category, though Paul's intelligence and sense of humor lifted much of the weight.

Berger taught at the University of Washington (UW) for thirty-five years, and is a mentor of many in the photographic field. He seemed elusive the few times I'd been invited into UW's PhotoMedia program, but not aloof, more in the manner of a mystic, or perhaps a hermit. I gave some critiques at UW in 2012, and extended an invitation to those students, and their faculty, for an annual gathering at my home. That invitation somehow got shared with the entire photo department. When Paul appeared at my door, I think we were both a little surprised. Had he walked in and turned left toward the bar, instead of right into the living room, we might never have worked together. But he came face to face with Minor White's *Sandblaster* (p. 33), and, pausing, said he'd been moved by hearing Minor speak at the Visual Studies Workshop in Rochester. Learning this, I had to look at Paul's work, which I'd previously found more heady than I could access, all over again.

His book *Multiplex* (Minor Matters, 2018) is rare for me in that when we went to press I still didn't fully understand the book we'd made, though I was part of creating it. But my goal was to present his work in a manner that was somewhat accessible, without being reductive, and I believe we achieved that. Decades from now, as the rest of the world catches up to Paul's brilliance, others will have a chance to wrestle with his ideas and his work because his book exists. Over burgers and beer to celebrate its completion, Paul casually mentioned that his grandmother was from Mexico. His mother was a quilter. His father had been a tile setter. He mused about the square scraps he and his siblings had played with as children, and how each of them had absorbed those shapes in different ways. I was quiet; these were new pieces of information to digest. After that lunch, I finally found my way into his work.

PAUL BERGER, *Mathematics #57*, 1977. Vintage gelatin silver print, mounted on board, signed. 10 ½ x 9 ¾ in. Gift of Paul Berger, 2018.

Isaac Layman (like Eirik Johnson, p. 136) was a student of Paul's. Working with Isaac on two publications cemented my awareness of his meticulous eye. Scale is an important component of many of his pieces, and when we chose a small trim size of 8 x 10 inches for his second book, *Homeschooled* (Minor Matters, 2016), I was concerned that we might lose the dizzying surface tension that is present at their original, monumental scale. Isaac made match prints of every artwork in the book, making subtle adjustments to retain the feel of each piece as it would appear within the book's dimensions. After he pointed out what he thought was a flaw in the press proof (it turned out to be the grain of the paper), I told him that he could not possibly be on press with me. Though he would love working with the machinery and the craftsmen, it is an environment that inherently requires some degree of compromise, and compromise is outside of his scope. He understood my decision as the compliment it was to his seeing; I understood his trust as the compliment it was to my experience.

I first saw *Glass Plate Negative* in 2010, at Isaac's small solo exhibition *Taking Pictures* at Lawrimore Project in Seattle. I loved its absolute simplicity, holding a horizon line of glass and plexi that light may, in time, inscribe in some way onto the black gator board. This was nothing, and everything, that I loved about photography. A few days later when I inquired with the gallerist about the piece, I was relieved and disappointed to learn that it was on hold for someone else (it turns out my dear friend Yoko Ott placed the hold and ultimately bought the piece). Those moments were always complicated. I didn't have to spend money I didn't really have, yet I wasn't going to live with an object I found profound, and would learn from.

Glass Plate Negative ended up with me after the death of its owner. The light traces from the eight years she lived with it are evidence of her, to which I have added some evidence of myself, an infusion that will continue for however long it is in my care. Isaac's creation initiated an unexpected collaboration with our mutual friend Yoko that now extends from both of them to me. I asked Isaac if he wanted to photograph it, eleven years after he made it, for its inclusion in this book. In the process of adding himself to its index, he also created a new work.

ISAAC LAYMAN, *Glass Plate Negative*, 2010. Handmade frame, gator board, half-pane of glass, half-pane of UV-protective glass, light, and time. 17 x 17 inches. Unique. Gift of Scott Lawrimore and the estate of Yoko Ott, 2020.

Though I engage with people constantly, I do not easily make friends. Some of that comes from still inherently being shy; some of it comes from the ambassadorial nature of my professional roles, which demand vivaciousness, but not always depth. I like depth. Those peers who cross over from being my colleagues to being my friends usually do, too. Dina Mitrani is one of them. I met her at a communal breakfast table while we were both reviewers during Photolucida in Oregon in 2013. That biennial event brings together dozens of photographic professionals and hundreds of photographers in timed conversations over four days. From our first conversation I just wanted to know more: about her, the artists she believed in, and her gallery in Miami. My occasional business trips to Miami led to dinner discussions on family, forthcoming projects, and how we as women and business owners balanced the many and competing priorities of our lives.

I had arranged to meet Dina at the AIPAD Photography Show in New York in 2017, and first met Marina Font there. Grasping quickly why Dina had spoken of Marina highly and often, I spontaneously proposed we three develop a book from a multi-year series Marina was continuing to explore. I was intrigued by the humor, poignancy, and visual distinctions of her hand-altered pieces, all stemming from one source photograph she made of a woman, nude, standing in a pose reminiscent of anatomical studies and religious iconography. The resulting objects, ranging from delicate 4 x 6 inch works on

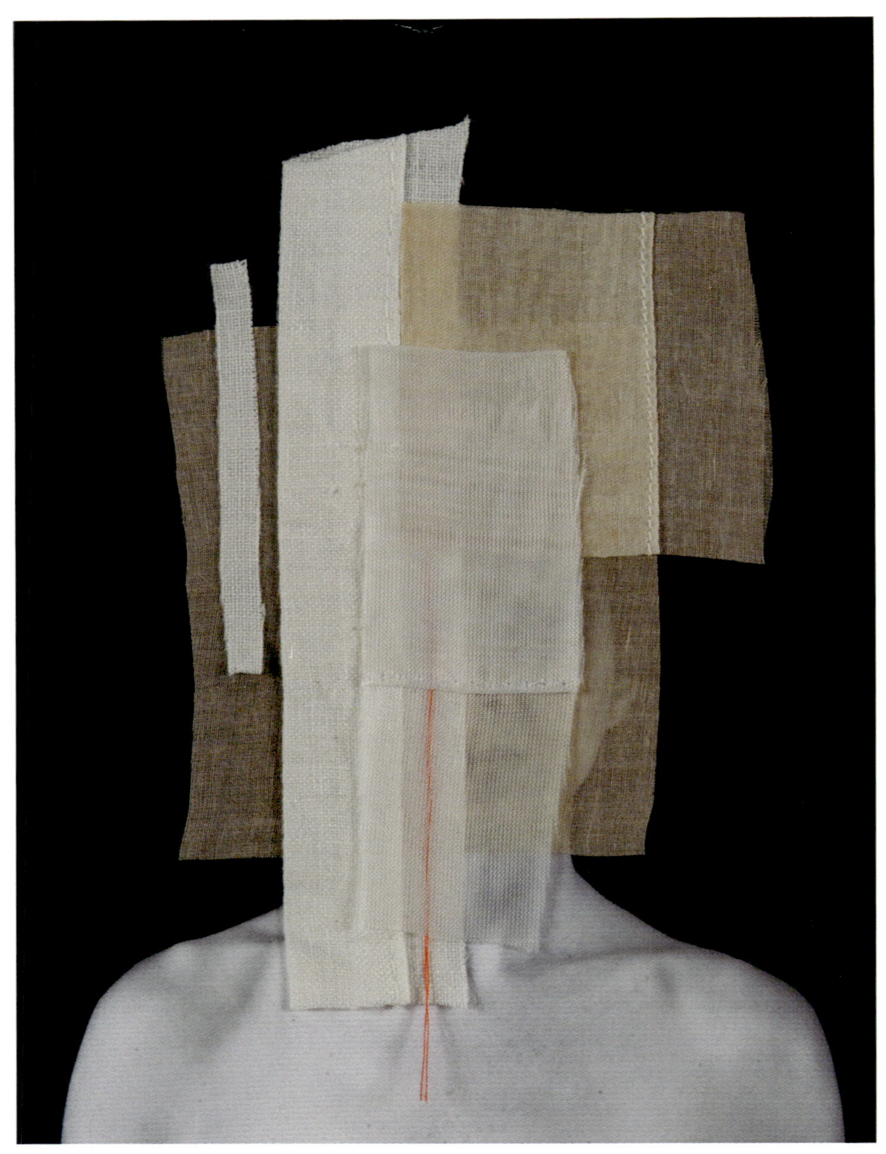

paper to eight-foot canvases, all began with some element of that photograph, and I loved the abundance she had harvested from one origin image. To its foundation she added paint, fabric, found vintage objects, or hand-embroidered patterns of thread and yarn, responding to Freudian elements of psychoanalysis, the reductive association with needlework as "women's work," and her own bodily shifts and changes in middle age.

Her resulting book, *Anatomy Is Destiny/la anatomía es destino* (Minor Matters, 2018) was in pre-sales during the first Women's March on Washington, DC. We encouraged co-publishers to name younger women within the book at a time when celebrating feminine identity, women's professional contributions, and attention to women's safety in healthcare and in society felt paramount.

MARINA FONT, Untitled, from the series "Architecture of the Mind," 2017. Archival pigment print on canvas mounted on wood panel; gesso, found fabric, and thread; 8 x 6 x 1 ¹/₂ in. Unique. Gift of Marina Font, 2019.

Marina chose for me a work that, like the three contact prints (pp. 48, 127, 154) included in this book, demonstrates the power of intentional scale. Each is petite, yet nothing about them is diminutive.

In Burmese and Irish cultures being born with "a veil" is believed to closely connect the individual to the spirit world. I am told my maternal grandfather had this distinction, and if such gifts are hereditary, I think I have been passed a little bit of that sensitivity. A cross-breeze in the room where this piece lives gently lifts the fabric sometimes, activating the spiritual and sculptural components of the piece. Like Charlie Rubin's print, it has been created as well as altered by its maker. Not broken, yet restored, throughout its gestation.

The phrase "in real life" has entered our lexicon to distinguish live interactions from communication exchanges and transactions online. For me, though, those words are immediately associated with the lyrics of "Bohemian Rhapsody," a 1975 release by the British rock group Queen (headed by one of my *desi* inspirations, Freddie Mercury): "is this the real life? Is this just fantasy?" Caught in a landslide, no escape from reality." My inability to accept my "dream reality" in 1999, in New York and in publishing, prompted an escape to a no longer present past. Many people have similarly retreated, or never given themselves permission to pursue their dreams "in real life." Working with creative people has bolstered my belief that much of reality is what we choose to construct. When the rainbows show up, ride them for as long as they last! After my divorce, I forgot that I used to bathe in all those colors, that I could live within beautiful abundance if I chose to do so. The universe tends to deliver gifts in the form of artists to remind me.

Endia Beal is one of those gifts, a woman who also believes in turning dreams and ambitions into reality. I first saw her work in early 2016, and made contact with her shortly thereafter. Following a public panel we did together, I expressed interest in publishing a monograph of her work. Her responses were polite and vague, and I assumed that she was fielding many requests and evaluating different opportunities. The press coverage around her work grew exponentially; from photo-specific spaces of *Photo District News* or Lensblog through the *New York Times*, she was crossing over to *VICE* and *Huffington Post*. I kept looking for announcements from other, bigger publishers, wondering who'd closed

a deal with her. Every once in a while, I'd send her an email to say hello, and indicate I
was still interested. When in a phone conversation a few years later she mentioned that
she'd received some funding and was working toward "a little catalog," I was, admittedly,
disappointed, but I kept that to myself and congratulated her.

We exchanged a few notes before she asked to schedule a phone call, where, to my
surprise, she shared that the idea of making a book was a little intimidating, which is why
she had not responded with greater enthusiasm to my earlier notes. Having started the
process on her catalog, she realized how much went into a publication, and wanted to
know if I might still be open and interested in working with her to publish a book through
Minor Matters instead. Since that conversation, a few other artists have shared their fear
around the finality a book represents, a response I could not have imagined until Endia
trusted me enough to discuss it.

Throughout 2020 conversations with Endia kept me moving forward. As Americans
fought bitterly with each other online, and in person, debating causes and cures for the
COVID-19 virus ravaging the globe. As defining facts seemed impossible. As protests
and counter-protests sprang up across the United States. I had been at much smaller
protests in 2016 in response to the deaths of Black citizens at the hands of the police.
*All Power: Visual Legacies of the Black
Panther Party* (Minor Matters, 2016),
edited with my colleague Negarra A.
Kudumu, came directly out of that para-
lyzing, painful summer, and includes
early portraits by Endia of her mother.

ENDIA BEAL, *Sabrina and Katrina*, from the series
"Am I What You're Looking For?," 2016. Archival pigment
print, 20 x 29 in. Artist proof. Gift of Endia Beal, 2018

The book—an intergenerational exploration of history and culture through work submitted
by sixteen Black artists—is a record of a short-lived, youth-led political party founded in
1966, and its ongoing influence fifty years later. I did not feel I was sufficiently drawing
attention to the abuse some of my fellow Americans were experiencing in 2016. Making a
book did not feel like *enough*, and in that moment I questioned the importance of the work
I had been doing for twenty years. I hesitated. I started. I stopped. Carrie Mae Weems
said "keep going." Another artist in the book, Kambui Olujimi, said "keep going." I finally
asked Negarra to help me, and she said yes. We launched that book. We sold it in three
weeks, and we delivered it in three months. It was, in that moment, what I could do.

2020 was different, and the same. I had moments of feeling paralyzed. Certainly
selling photography books felt impossible. Yet Endia never complained, never gave up,
and achieved five hundred pre-sales in advance of the established deadline. Endia and I
spoke about how we were doing, how we were feeling, about COVID-19, about politics,
about families. We reminded each other throughout the many swells of the year that our
work to complete her smart and needed book was an act of civic duty to our times.

Holding *Performance Review* (Minor Matters, 2020) five years after I was first bowled
over by Endia's series "Am I What You're Looking For?" was a personal and professional
moment of arrival. I was always excited when advances of books arrived, but this was different, made more significant from the challenging year we had survived. *Minor Matters*

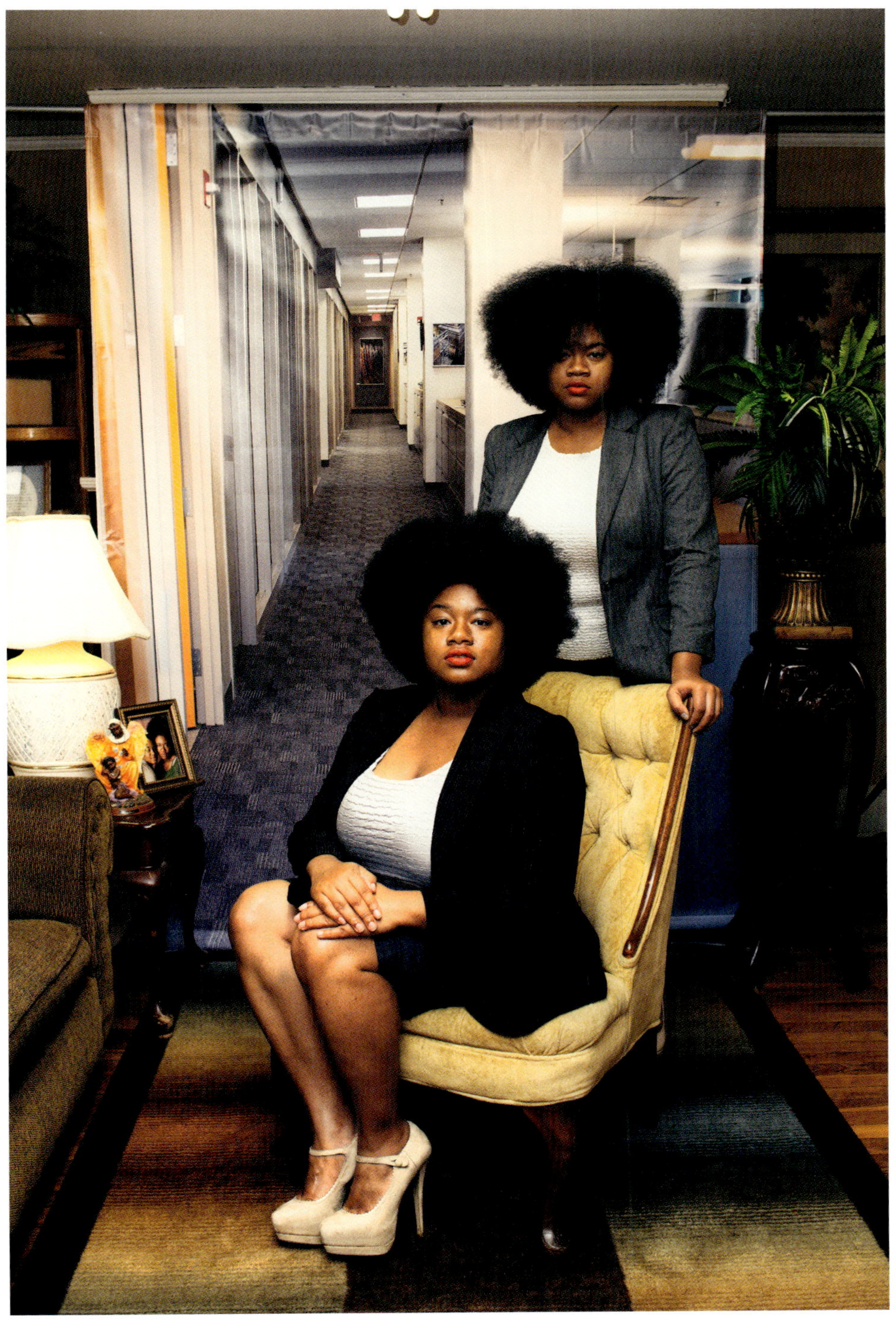

published this. I am a publisher. The important books we've produced in collaboration with
a community of breadth and depth have reached over ten thousand people around the
globe. We hit a milestone in 2020 of achieving sales in every one of the fifty states in the
USA. Given the divisions within our country the last decade, that feels pretty remarkable.

It may sound odd that it took seven years and twenty books for me to truly absorb
what Steve and I initiated. When we started, we had no idea if our model would work.
At best I hoped to learn something, possibly make and own some books I'd long envisioned, and bring attention to artists we believed in, without anyone going into debt.
When I was preparing a business plan, colleagues with venture capital experience
pushed me to imagine what kind of numbers we *could* achieve, not just what I thought
was possible given my experience in the book industry. It took me a while to figure out
that they were asking me for a plausible story, not what I was actually predicting would
happen. We did not end up taking on investors, and I kept our estimates conservative.

Five years in, I asked Chris Pichler of Nazraeli Press for some professional feedback.
Minor Matters was staying afloat solely from our substantial investment of time, but I was
not sure how to evaluate this fledgling venture, given I had previously used that time to
generate income. Chris held up an important mirror. He said I'd proven vision through
the books I had been able to publish (that compliment, from someone I deeply respected,
sent me skyward), but that I needed to demonstrate the same commitment in making the
business work. He knew me and my years in the nonprofit environment well enough to
emphasize that I couldn't, and shouldn't, avoid paying myself. I didn't set out to be a
hobbyist, I set out to be a publisher, and if I wasn't accounting for my time, it wasn't a real
and sustainable entity otherwise. His clarity hit home, and I will never forget that tough-
love conversation. Though I didn't take his guidance until I was really forced to do so,
because of his words I knew what I needed to do when circumstances demanded.

It was tough to ask someone I admire to listen to my struggles and provide advice,
to hope that I picked a person who would not use my personal and professional weaknesses against me. Then again, peers find each other. When people who are good
at what they do and confident in their skill sets, regardless of profession, connect, the
combination of curiosity and respect can be catalytic. Sometimes you have to risk a
little, and trust a little, to get there.

We have arrived here, at the end of my current past, and perpetually on the edge of photography's future. If not adequately conveyed already, I will state it plainly: I have had a rich life. It will always be somewhat wondrous to me that focused tasks of replication leading to the dissemination of knowledge, which I first discovered at Edgemont Junior High, are still a part of my professional activities thirty-plus years later.

I came into photography when it was wholly tangible, and the range of object forms it can take continues to delight me. Some of the prints reproduced here have been in my life for over two decades; others arrived recently. All have been my primary companions of the last two years, as my existence, like everyone else's around the globe, was radically altered from the pandemic. And yes, as the months wore on I eventually progressed from talking to the cat to conversations with the photographs. Pictures really are worth a thousand words, and I had plenty of time to listen to them.

These objects are inextricably tied to the people who chose to suspend particular moments of reality by trapping the light in some alchemical or digital manner. While I appreciate all of the photographs in this book for their formal qualities and their significance within the ongoing and multi-faceted trajectories of the medium, I have stayed loyal to what the original installation of *Seeing Being Seen* mandated: to place the photographs, and my relationships with their photographers, within the context of my life.

Doing so has forced me to consider my past reticence in speaking about highlights of my career. The religious environs I was raised in prioritized serving the greater good. "Tooting your own horn" was not just impolite, it was disrespectful to the Higher Power. The ancient cultures from which I descend—Indo-Burmese and Irish—also subconsciously reiterate that too much sparkle can draw the attention of the mischievous and malevolent, be it the fairies or the evil eye, and is best avoided. Many of our Western cultural associations with women and femininity emphasize caregiving and nurturing. I believe these essential traits add to women's leadership abilities, yet can also result in our sense of success, even in the twenty-first century, being tied to others we've guided, rather than to our own advancement or that of our ideas and creations.

With all of that, it is easier for me to study mistakes or failures, or to envision next goals, than to pause and celebrate accomplishment. With her gentle insistence, Nancy Salguero McKay at Highline Heritage Museum guided me to see myself through my successes. It was uncomfortable. It was embarrassing. And it was extraordinary. Since then I have thought a lot about how to better facilitate similar experiences for others, particularly women. The transparency of what I have shared in this book, from salaries to insecurities, serendipity to hard won achievements, is an effort to see myself through my fragilities *and* my strengths, as the photographers holding my energies have amply done.

The near-constant narrative today of suppression of women and underrepresented populations in the United States is important, and it is exhausting. It is time to speak of successes. Acknowledging systemic inequities can be done through uplifting long-demonstrated resilience. It can be done by focusing on the (in)actions of the oppressive systems still in place, and holding negative societal structures accountable. Those of us in the arts, and in media, bear an ongoing responsibility to research, formulate, and articulate twenty-first storytelling that mainstreams progress. The books published through Minor Matters (Nicholas Galanin's *Never Forget* is the most recent example) reflect that there is an audience committed to these necessary narratives, if we are willing to work with them.

As the photographs in this book demonstrate, there is abundance, not compromise, in fostering representation when examining the medium's significant practitioners in the United States. There is room for everyone. And diversifying worlds—not only that of photographic practitioners who are lauded but of those behind the scenes working with them—is essential to the evolution of visual culture in the United States.

Without greater ethnic, class, and geographic diversity in editorial, production, and design, corrosive effects that currently exist—though often subtle and perhaps unintentional—will be perpetuated. Giving consideration to how particular skin tones might appear ashy or uneven printed on a matte paper surface, or questioning a line edit that, while technically accurate, wildly affects a writer's meaning in describing nuances of microaggression—such habits will become norms when there are colleagues at the table who can speak with authenticity to the circumstances in question.

Without greater inclusion in all parts of our ecosystem, we risk homogenizations of vision, instead of growth. We risk being relegated to prescribed "lanes" where we can only read, see, edit, and appreciate that which derives from people who are just like us. That is not progress. That is another kind of sublimation. Publishing is a profession that thrives on the interpretation, refinement, and presentation of words and images. With a workforce that represents a full spectrum of the American population, the industry has an opportunity to lead our culture forward with integrity, one photograph, one word, one capitalized letter at a time.

In 2020 and 2021 other books engaging with the contemporary history of photography, like this one, have been published. There are few visual overlaps. Of the nearly 120 photographers selected by writer and educator David Campany in his book *On Photographs* (Thames & Hudson, 2020), only Stephen Shore is included in that title and this one. Andy Grundberg's *How Photography Became a Contemporary Art* (Yale University Press, 2021) includes nearly one hundred photographic artists, five of whom are also represented in this book.

We are three authors of distinct professional backgrounds, from different geographic regions, and generations. The incongruity of our selections certainly expands the practitioners held in our field's history; it also reflects our times. Whether we questioned them or championed them, there were a few metaphorical battlefields in photography on which we came together to fight about who, and what, was important to know, to preserve, to study. When I began to absorb a language of photography in the 1990s, I appreciated that there was a pantheon of people to know that more than one institution or individual agreed upon. I acknowledge that those lists were subjective and exclusionary; all lists are. It was a maze formed by specific entities, certainly, but there was a point of entry and a point of departure. That is no longer.

Canons have always been constructed through power, politics, and access, under the veneer of knowledge. Are we abolishing all canons? Or forming new ones? Perhaps what I perceive as a "change" to the notion of distinction in the medium isn't, really. Power, politics, and access are all still relevant. Not, perhaps, to what is *seen*—everyone can feed the gaping maw of the screen, and simultaneously consume from it. But what is exhibited, collected, and promoted, where work is held, and by whom, that hasn't changed so much. Future canons will be determined by each individual who teaches, writes, curates, purchases, funds, and publishes, and those individuals will influence whoever thinks their viewpoint relevant. Some will point out that this is how it has always been.

Books remain a technology I value. Will books be the right vessels to hold the "essential" outpourings of screen-shared imagery that increasingly flood our present? I don't know. Those who see photography as a river of ephemeral images (thank you, Charlotte Cotton, for this wise analogy), will likely guide that. I don't swim easily in those rivers. I find them cold, fast, and simultaneously shallow and fathomless. That is okay. I can observe from the banks, and occasionally someone will take me by the hand and help me wade in a little bit as they tell me of the joy they find there. Joy in the experience of images delineated (sometimes) from reality (whatever that is) will be our common ground. I recognize, as the rivers flow, that at some point in my future I may have to decide if I am truly an arbiter of the *now*, or if I am in fact adding, from the present, to the canons of the past.

These last thoughts I have struggled with the most, probably because I feel this a time of questions more than answers, of inquiries over conclusions. Thank you, reader, for making it this far with me, for the time you have invested in these words and images, for the questions we will keep pondering together.

I will close with an invitation to read again, forgoing the words this time. The simple methodology I developed for reading photographs is based on the 1950s prescience of photographers and educators Minor White, Walter Chappell, and Nathan Lyons. Reading photographs roots us first and foremost in ourselves, then in the separation of seeing from feeling, and then in the reintegration of both from the cognitive place of personal responsibility for what it is we see in, and feel from, an image. It will become clear to anyone who engages in even the most cursory use of this method why Minor White said that, in the end, it is the viewer who completes the photograph. What a responsibility. What a gift.

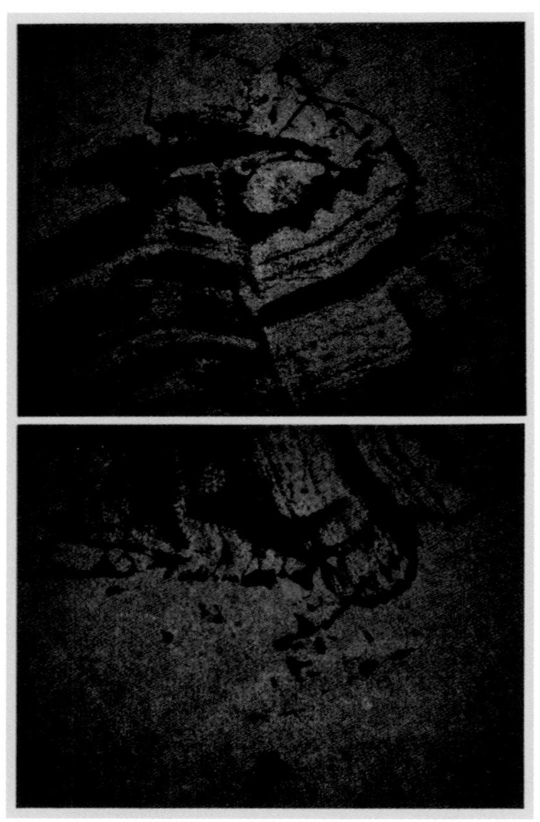

Nancy Salguero McKay

The Highline Heritage Museum opened its doors in June 2019. Since 1994—first as the Burien Heritage Society and later as the Highline Historical Society—the organization, under the leadership of Cyndi Upthegrove, has been preserving stories, collecting artifacts, installing exhibits, and providing programs for over twenty-five years.

We capture the stories of Highline, a region south of Seattle, from its earliest inhabitants (a replica skeleton of a giant sloth found under what is now Sea-Tac Airport is at the entrance of the museum), to the newest immigrant stories. History and heritage are personal matters to everyone. We believe that exploring everyone's heritage allows us to experience personal journeys that enrich us as a community.

The museum's physical opening was an exhilarating time for me to transition into the position of executive director, while remaining the museum's only employee. It truly takes a village to raise a museum. From inspiring and fiercely dedicated volunteers, to donors, board members, funding support from various sources, and amazing partnerships co-curating exhibits, this museum is *from* the community *to* the community.

Opening a new museum allowed all of us involved to experience the extremes, from joy, excitement, and happiness to heart breaking, physical/emotional pain, and challenges. How do we open a museum when there are not enough funds? When your volunteers face aches and limitations? When there are forces working to bring down the entire project? At the same time, nothing can substitute for opening a space that gives back to the community, or replace witnessing the beauty of people giving the best they can, day in and day out, evenings and weekends, to make this space a reality.

JOE FREEMAN JR., *Tar and Asphalt*, 2010. Selenium and tea-stained gelatin silver contact prints, 4 $^{3}/_{8}$ x 2 $^{23}/_{32}$ in. (total dimension). Unique. Gift of Joe Freeman Jr., 2012.

We learned about Michelle Dunn Marsh's professional engagements through a 2014 article in the *Seattle Times*. It identified that she lived in our region, which captured our attention. After our initial meeting with her, the richness of her personal story became evident, and we recognized the need to represent her voice, her story, and her work through an inaugural exhibit in our museum.

We are not an art museum, so while Michelle offered to lend us photographs for exhibition, we wanted that, but also more. Why did the photographs matter to her, both in the context of the books she has designed, edited, and published, and in her personal life? That is what we wanted to convey.

Her exhibition, *Seeing Being Seen*, allowed everyone to witness her magic, presenting her work with photography through original photographs she has collected over the years, books she has worked on, and mementos of her life. This exhibition provided a tiny window

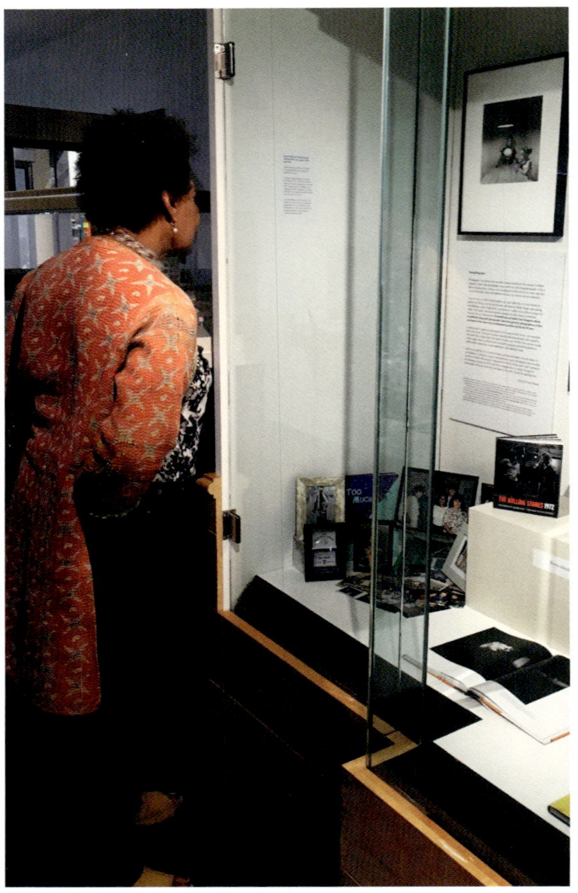
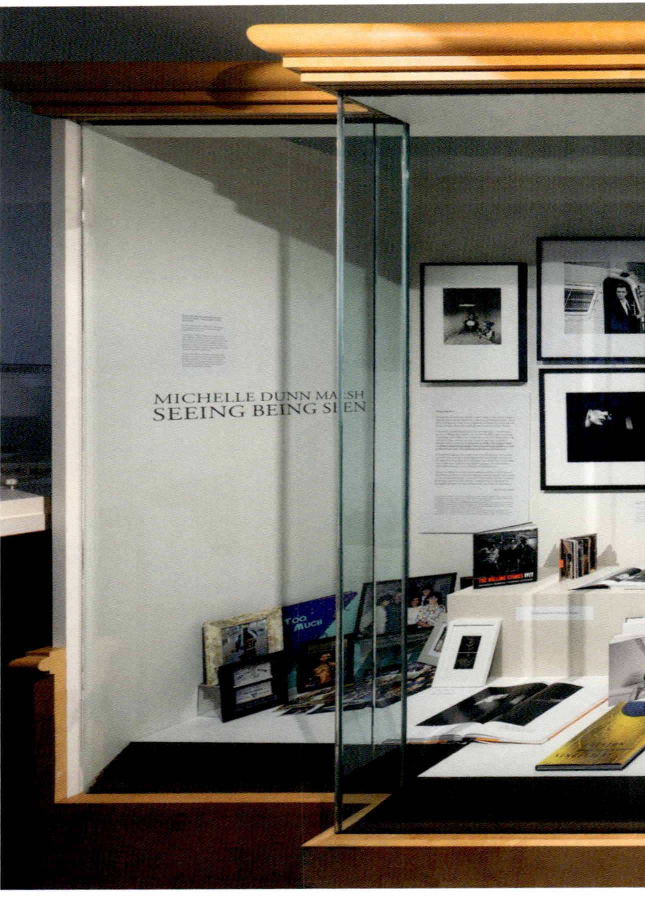

into who Michelle is. So while in this space she represented the neighborhood she lives in, she also represented artistic and creative communities, and more.

Museums are special spaces. I taught in the Museum Studies program at the University of Washington, and often work with interns from the program and with the Museology Department to foster hands-on experiences with exhibition development. I use a co-curation model to bring authenticity and representation from many voices to the objects and information presented. Museums can ignite your curiosity, and create opportunities of learning through discovery. You can explore your own heritage and history, or embrace someone else's stories. When we started to develop and design the museum, we wanted to display many unique stories—Michelle's story was one of them.

Michelle had curated photographic exhibitions, so she was comfortable presenting photographs and books, but resistant to presenting them with her life story as the guiding principle. Throughout the process, as I was guiding her while overseeing so many details of the museum coming together, I had to keep reminding her, "This has to be about you."

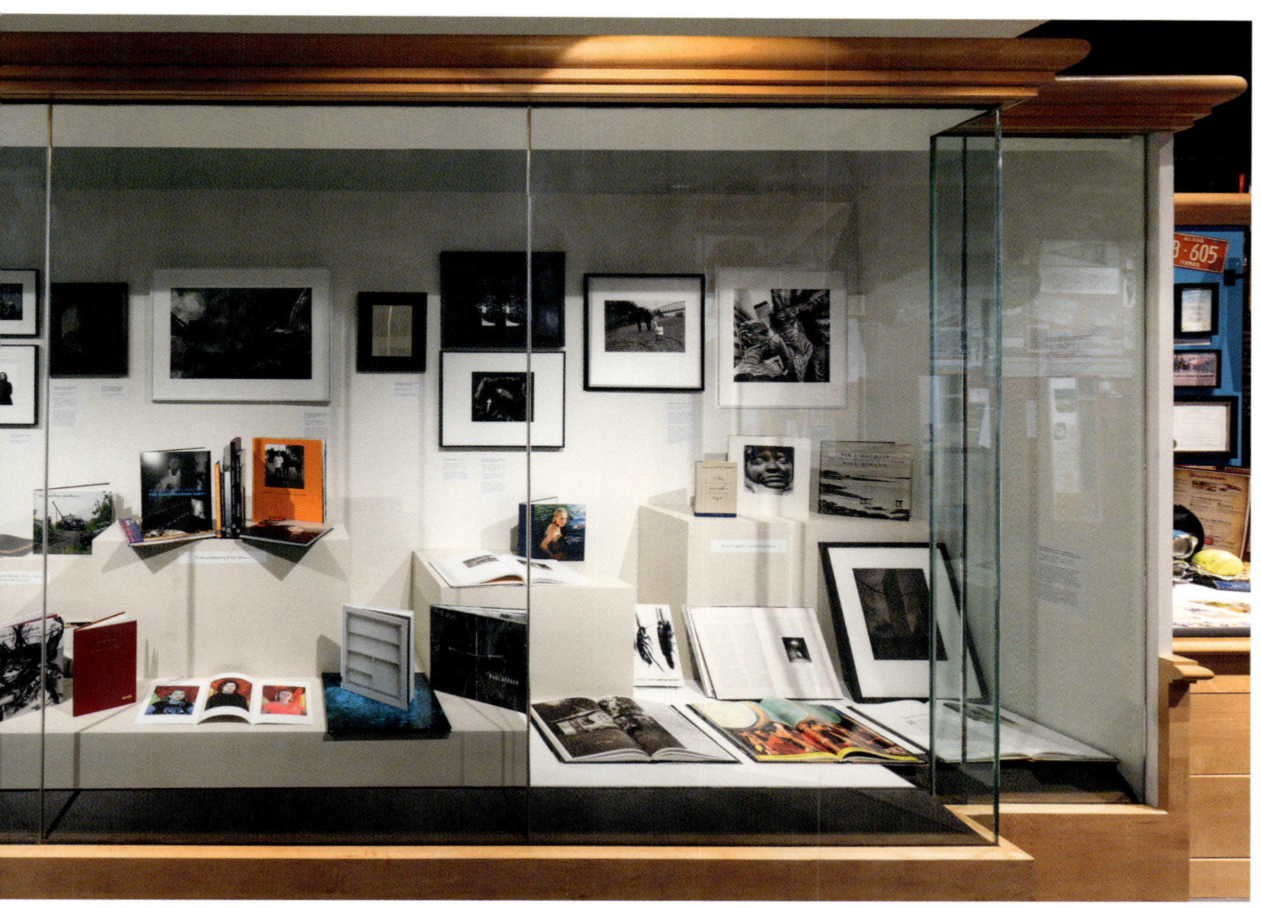

I was frantically vacuuming the space hours before the official museum opening when I had the very special surprise of meeting the amazing Carrie Mae Weems, whose photograph was included in the *Seeing Being Seen* installation. Her visit to Michelle's exhibit and the rest of the Museum just moments before we opened for the first time felt surreal.

Some of the museum's installations were designed to be permanent, while other spaces, including where *Seeing Being Seen* was presented from June 14 through December 5, 2019, were designed to rotate, so other community members's stories can be shared and celebrated. My intention is for our visitors to have access to a broad spectrum of information sources and cultural perspectives. We envision ourselves always at a round table, where stories are heard respectfully, regardless of gender, age, sexual orientation, disabilities or ethnicity. We want those stories to spark discussions and to share differences and similarities. Our approach to documenting cultural histories led Michelle to finally agree to this special installation, and we were happy to open the museum with her professional life story as one of the installations reflecting our values.

Opposite: Carrie Mae Weems visiting the *Seeing Being Seen* installation at the Highline Heritage Museum, June 2019. Above: Installation of *Seeing Being Seen*, Highline Heritage Museum.

EXHIBITION CHECKLIST: *SEEING BEING SEEN*

Seeing Being Seen was one of the opening installations of the Highline Heritage Museum, 819 SW 152nd St. Burien, Washington. The ribbon cutting was June 14, and the exhibit was on view through December 5, 2019.

Prints are listed below left to right as shown in the installation, pp. 156–157. Full object descriptions included with plate captions. Book dimensions listed width x height; all books hardcover unless noted.

PRINTS

Carrie Mae Weems, Untitled, from the "Kitchen Table" series, 1990/print 2010. p. 47

Jim Marshall, Johnny Cash at Folsom Prison, Represa, California, 1968/2010. p. 114–115

Graham Nash, Joni Mitchell, 1969/2012. p. 110-111

Joe Freeman Jr., *Tar and Asphalt*, 2010. p. 154

Stephen Shore, Graduation, Bard College, Annandale-on-Hudson, 1995. p. 30

Sylvia Plachy, Michelle Dunn Marsh, Queens, 2012. p. 121

Will Wilson, Michelle Dunn Marsh, from the Creative Indigenous Photographic Exchange (CIPX), Miami, Florida, 2019. cover

Eugene Richards, *A firefighter sits alone in the rubble*, World Trade Center site, New York, 2001. pp. 54–55

Daniel Carillo and Eirik Johnson, Untitled, from the series "Unfolded," 2016. p. 136

Paul Berger, *Mathematics #57*, 1976–77. p. 142

Minor White, *Sandblaster*, San Francisco, 1949. p. 33

Sylvia Plachy, *Swann's Way*, Prague, 1991. pp. 94–95

Mary Ellen Mark, Alex Londono and Chayanne Yate, Pride March, New York, 2008. p. 62

Edward Steichen, *The Flatiron*, New York, 1905/1973. p. 34

BOOKS DESIGNED FOR APERTURE

Paul Strand, *Tir a'Mhurain: The Outer Hebrides of Scotland,* 9 $^7/_8$ x 11 $^{11}/_{16}$ in, 128 pages, cloth case with jacket (2002)

Various, *Shooting Blind: Photographs by the Visually Impaired,* 9 $^1/_2$ x 12 in, 96 pages, cloth case with jacket (2002)

Carrie Mae Weems, The Hampton Project, 9 $^1/_2$ x 12 in, 96 pages plus gatefold, printed case with vellum jacket (2001)

Jeff Dunas, *State of the Blues,* 9 $^3/_8$ x 12 in, 176 pages, cloth case with jacket (1998)

Catherine Chalmers, *American Cockroach,* 7 $^1/_2$ x 11 in, 96 pages (2004)

Jock Sturges: Notes, 9 $^7/_8$ x 9 in, 96 pages (2004)

Candida Höfer: Architecture of Absence, 9 $^3/_8$ x 11 $^3/_8$ in, 112 pages, printed case with jacket (2004)

Jackets or interiors for Aperture

Henri Cartier-Bresson, *The Mind's Eye,* 5 $^1/_4$ x 8 $^1/_4$ in, 112 pages (1999), jacket design

Virginia Dodier, *Lady Hawarden: Studies from Life 1857–1864,* 9 1/2 x 11 $^1/_4$ in, 128 pages (1999), interior design

Melissa Harris, editor, *Tibet: Silence, Prison, or Exile,* 9 x 12 in, 184 pages plus gatefolds (2000), interior design

BOOKS EDITED FOR CHRONICLE

Joe Park: I'm Yours, 3 $^{15}/_{16}$ x 5 $^{15}/_{16}$ in, 30 postcards, paperback (2010)

Graham Nash, *Taking Aim: Unforgettable Rock and Roll Photographs,* with Experience Music Project, 9 x 12 in, 160 pages, printed case with jacket (2009)

Jim Marshall, *Pocket Cash,* 6 x 8 in, 160 pages, flexcover (2010)

BOOKS DESIGNED FOR UW PRESS AND MUSEUM OF GLASS

Preston Singletary: Echoes, Fire, and Shadows, 9 x 12 in, 152 pages, cloth case with jacket (2009)

Ingalena Klennell and Beth Lipman: Glimmering Gone, 10 $^1/_2$ x 8 $^1/_2$ in, 96-page accordion book with case (2011)

Vicki Halper, *Contrasts,* 8 $^3/_8$ x 8 $^1/_2$ in, 64 pages, paperback (2006)

BOOKS DESIGNED AND EDITED FOR OTHER PUBLISHERS

Lisa Kereszi, *Joe's Junk Yard,* 9 $^1/_2$ x 11 $^3/_8$ in, 144 pages (Damiani, 2012)

Jim Marshall, The Rolling Stones 1972, 7 x 8 in, 168 pages (Chronicle, 2012)

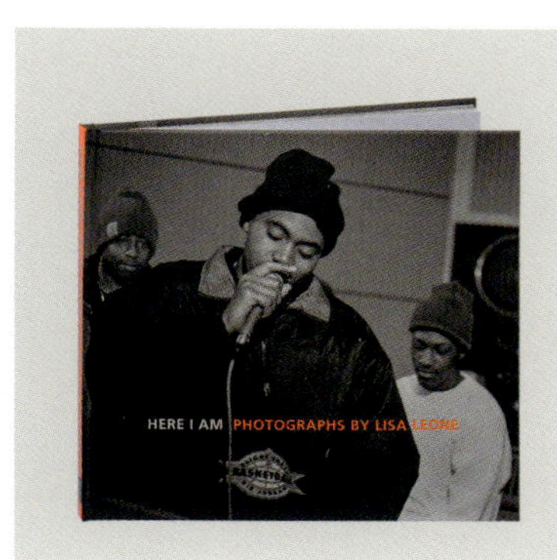

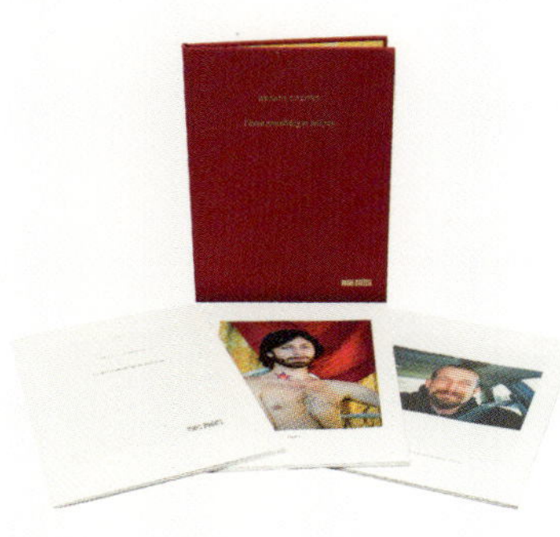

Alice Wheeler, *Outcasts & Innocents, Photographs of the Northwest*, introduction by Kathleen Hanna, 9 x 10 in, 144 pages

2016

Isaac Layman, *Homeschooled*, essay by Bob Nickas, 8 x 10 in, 108 pages plus gatefold

introduction by Merritt Johnson, artist interview with Negarra A. Kudumu, 8 x 10 in, 144 pages

Adrain Chesser, *I have something to tell you*, artist interview with Tim Wride, texts by Gloria Babcock and Vicki Carlson, 6 x 9 in, three uncut sheets

Paul Berger, *Multiplex*, essay by Rod Slemmons, artist interview with Jon Feinstein, 10 x 11 in, 128 pages, printed case with jacket

BOOKS DESIGNED, EDITED, AND PUBLISHED THROUGH MINOR MATTERS:

2014

Joseph Park, *Prizmism*, essay by Toby Kamps, 10 x 13 ¹/₂ in, 84 pages

David Hilliard, *What Could Be*, essay by Ariel Levy, artist interview with Pam L. Houston, 8 x 12 in, 128 pages, cloth case with jacket

Lisa Leone, *Here I Am*, texts by Rosie Perez, Fab 5 Freddy, Fabel, Nas, and Mare139, 10 x 9 in, 104 pages

2015

Anna Mia Davidson, *Human Nature: Sustainable Farming in the Pacific Northwest*, introduction by Sebastiaõ Salgado, essays by restaurateur Matt Dillon and Dr. Marcia Ostrom, 10 x 12 in, 80 pages

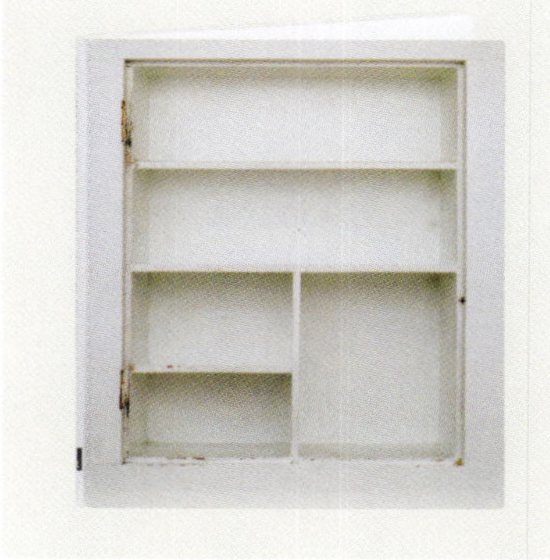

Charles Lindsay, *Carbon*, essays by Lyle Rexer and Dr. Jill Tarter, 9 ¹/₂ x 10 ¹/₄ in, 80 pages

All Power: Visual Legacies of the Black Panther Party, essays by Negarra A. Kudumu and Rene DeGuzman, interview with Hank Thomas and Dr. Deborah Willis, 9 x 10 in, 96 pages

2018

Nicholas Galanin: Let Them Enter Dancing and Showing Their Faces,

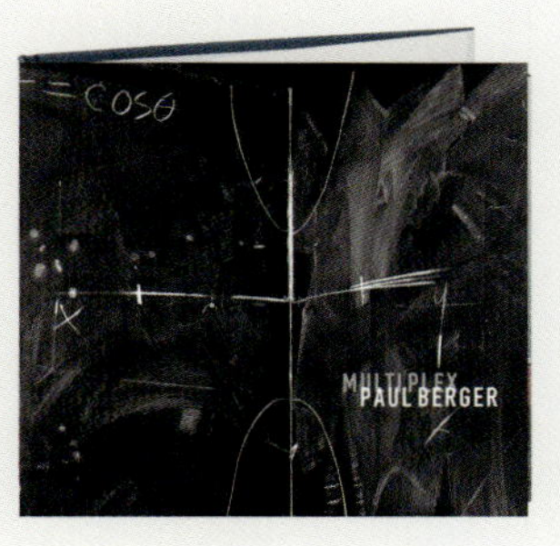

Marina Font, *Anatomy Is Destiny / la anatomía es destino,* essay by Lisa M. Volpe in English and Spanish, 10 x 12 in, 80 pages, cloth case with jacket

Eirik Johnson, *Pine*, 12 ³/₈ x 12 ³/₈ in, 80 pages plus two gatefolds, inserted 12-in vinyl record

Melodie McDaniel with Amelia Fleetwood, *Riding Through Compton*, introduction by Mayisha Akbar, poem excerpt by Robin Coste Lewis, afterword by Walter Bodle, 10 x 12 in, 96 pages

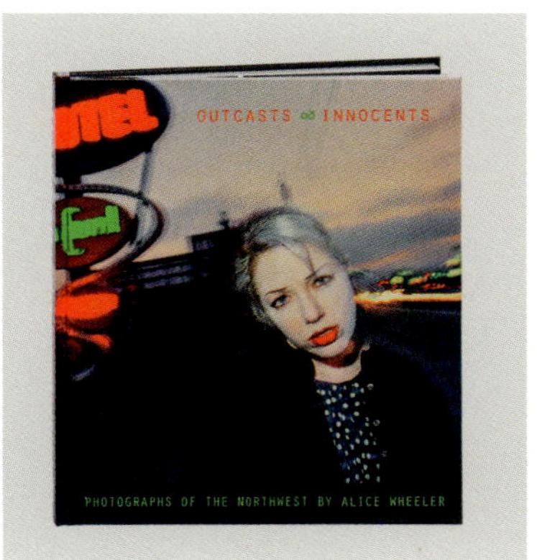

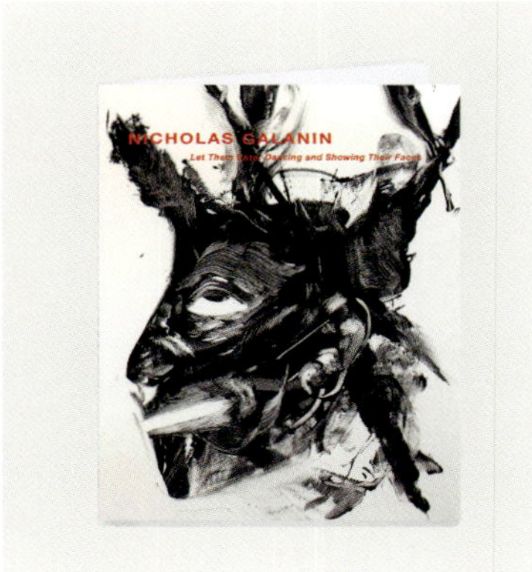

Notes in italic following each biography highlight my professional engagement with the photographer, including books (illustrated throughout), exhibitions (pp. 161, 165), and public programs I have overseen or developed.

Robert Adams (b. 1937, Orange, New Jersey; lives in Astoria, Oregon) has photographed the landscape of the American West for more than forty years. Since the 1970s, more than thirty books of Adams's photographs and essays have been published. He is represented by Fraenkel Gallery, San Francisco and Matthew Marks Gallery, New York. **See page 75.** *Coordinated and moderated a panel on Adams's book,* The New West *at* The New School, *2007; included his photographs in the exhibition,* Terminal: On Mortality and Beauty, *at PCNW January 8–April 4, 2015; his books,* Turning Back *and* Sea Stories, *designed by Catherine Mills;* Summer Nights, Walking, *designed by Katy Homans; and* From the Missouri West *and* Why People Photograph, *designed by Wendy Byrne, were exhibited in* By the Book: Nine Designers, *at PCNW September 10–December 13, 2018.*

Endia Beal (b. 1985, Winston-Salem, North Carolina; lives in Winston-Salem) examines the personal stories of women of color within the corporate space

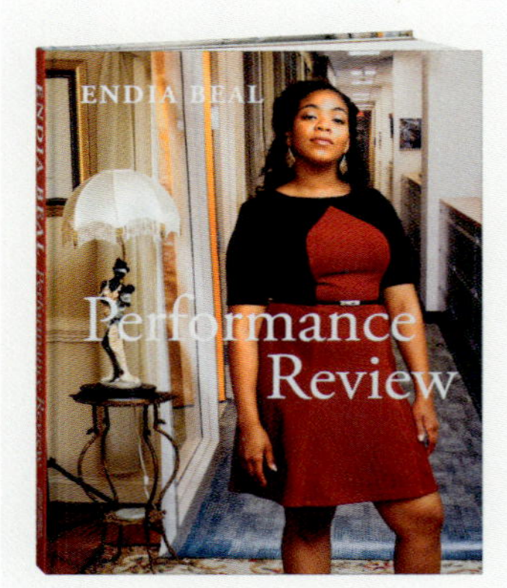

through her photographs and video narratives. Her work has been extensively published and exhibited internationally. Beal holds a dual BFA-AH in art history and studio art from the University of North Carolina at Chapel Hill, and an MFA from Yale University. **See page 149.** *Invited Beal to a panel for the Palm Springs Photo Festival, 2016; included her work in* All Power: Visual Legacies of the Black Panther Party *(Minor Matters, 2016) and the exhibition of the same name (AIPAD, New York; PCNW, Seattle; and Central Washington University, Ellensburg) in 2018. Published her first monograph,* Performance Review *(Minor Matters, 2020).*

Paul Berger (b. 1948, The Dalles, Oregon; lives on Whidbey Island, Washington) has been working in the photographic medium since 1965. He taught at the University of Washington's School of Art for thirty-five years, co-founding the photography program in 1978 and initiating digital imaging classes in 1985. He is represented by G. Gibson Projects, Seattle. **See page 142, 159.** *Published his first monograph,* Multiplex *(Minor Matters, 2018).*

Daniel Arturo Carrillo-Lozano (b. 1973, Mexico; lives in Seattle) is a photographer specializing in the daguerreotype and wet-plate collodion processes, as well as astrophotography. His work has been exhibited at the Tacoma Art Museum, G. Gibson Gallery, Greg Kucera Gallery, SOIL Gallery, and Gage Academy among others. Carillo's work is in the permanent collections of the Tacoma Art Museum, the San Francisco Museum of Modern Art, and the private collection of Sir Elton John. He is represented by G. Gibson Projects, Seattle; he is also the owner of Gallery Frames. **See page 136.** *Selected Daniel for the first iteration of the Riffs residency at PCNW, 2016.*

Elinor Carucci (b. 1971, Jerusalem; lives in New York) graduated from Bezalel Academy with a degree in photography. Her photographs are included in the

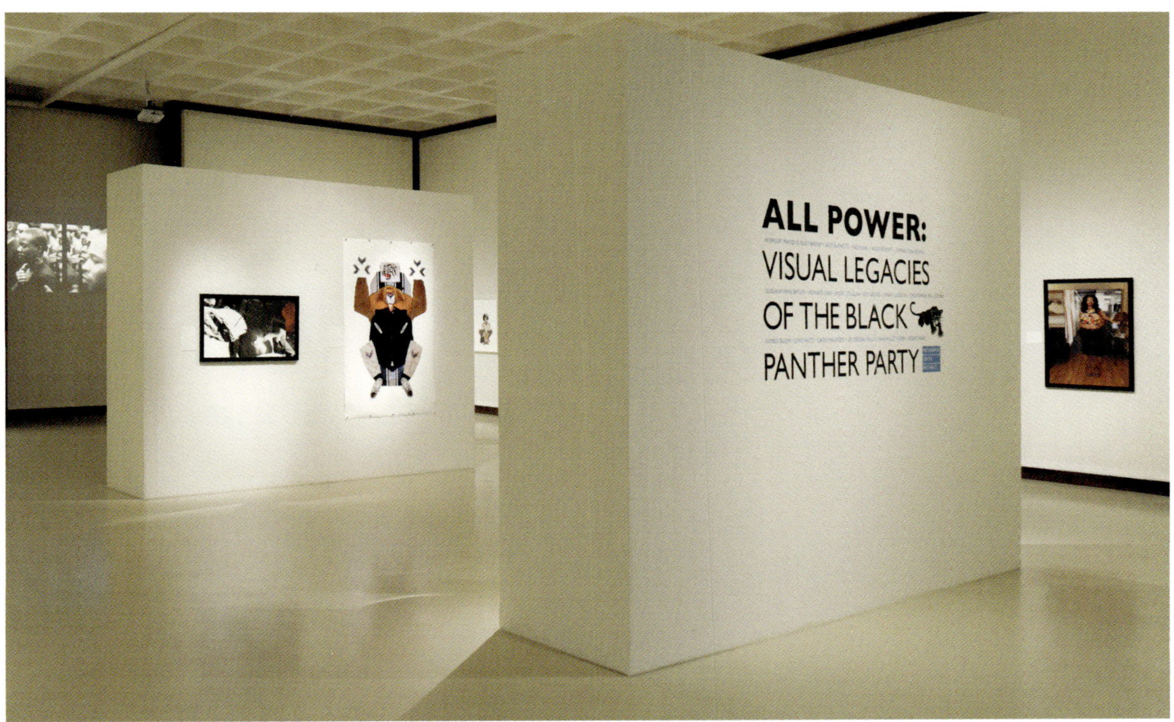

collections of the Museum of Modern Art, the Brooklyn Museum of Art, and the Museum of Fine Arts Houston, among others. She was awarded the International Center of Photography's Infinity Award in 2001, and a Guggenheim Fellowship in 2002. Carucci has four monographs to date. Her work is represented by Edwynn Houk Gallery, New York. **See gatefold, pp. 120–121.** *Acquiring editor of a revised edition of* Closer *(Chronicle, 2010); included her work in the exhibition* Notions of Home, *at PCNW September 14–December 10, 2017;* Closer, *designed by Roger Gorman, was exhibited in* By the Book: Nine Designers, *at PCNW September 10–December 13, 2018.*

Catherine Chalmers (b. 1957, San Mateo, California; lives in New York) holds a BS in Engineering from Stanford University and an MFA in Painting from the Royal College of Art in London. She has exhibited around the world, and has two monographs, both published by Aperture Foundation. Chalmers is the recipient of a Guggenheim Fellowship and a Robert Rauschenberg Residency. **See pages 84–85, 162.** *Designed the jacket of* Food Chain *(1999), and developed and designed* American Cockroach *(2004). Included Chalmers on a panel at the Palm Springs Photo Festival, 2009; included her work in the exhibition* Terminal: On Mortality and Beauty, *at PCNW January 8–April 4, 2015.*

Adrain Chesser (b. 1965, Okeechobee, Florida, lives in White Salmon, Washington) is a largely self-taught photographer who refined his practice with mentors Rosalind Solomon and Debbie Fleming Caffrey. Chesser's work is in the permanent collections of the Portland Art Museum, the Museum of Fine Arts Houston, the Norton Museum of Art, and many private collections. **See gatefold, pp. 120–121, and 129.** *Published his second monograph* I have something to tell you *(Minor Matters, 2018); included his work in issue 3 of* Latitude 47, *and in the exhibition* Notions of Home, *at PCNW September 14–December 10, 2017. Included Chesser in an online panel for the Palm Springs Photo Festival, 2021.*

William Christenberry (1936–2016) was an American photographer, painter, sculptor, and educator who drew inspiration from his childhood in Hale County, Alabama, focusing on the psychology and effects of place and memory. He was the recipient of a Guggenheim Fellowship, faculty at the Corcoran School of Art, and the author of multiple monographs. His work is held in many significant public collections. **See page 73.** *Christenberry participated in the Aperture West lecture series, 2006.*

Bruce Davidson (b. 1933, Oak Park, Illinois; lives in New York) has made indelible images documenting social inequality. He attended Rochester

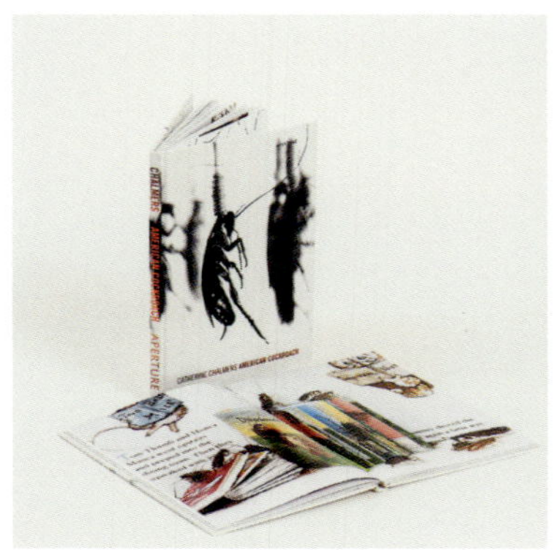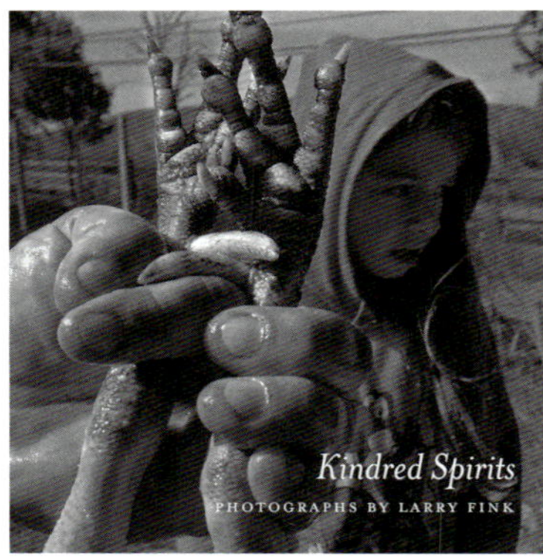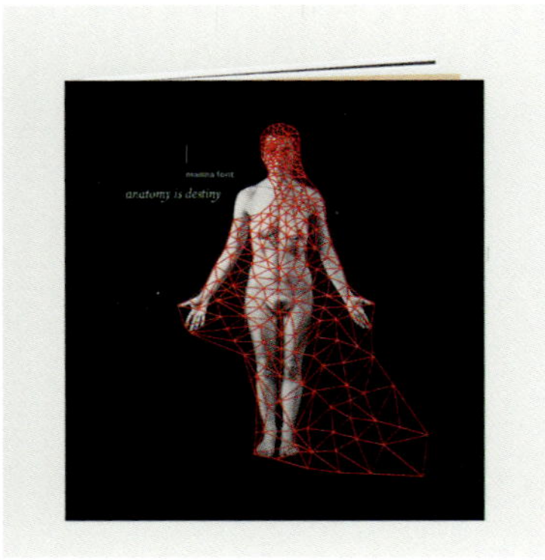

Institute of Technology and Yale University, where he studied with Josef Albers. He met Henri Cartier-Bresson, one of the founders of the renowned cooperative photography agency Magnum Photos, while stationed in Paris during his army service; he became a full member of Magnum in 1958. Work from his sixty-year career has been extensively published in monographs and is included in major public and private collections around the world. He is represented by Howard Greenberg Gallery, New York. **See pages 78-79.** *Davidson participated in the Aperture West lecture series, 2007, and in custom magazine events with Levi's and IC Lab, 2010. His work, along with that of his daughter Anna Mia Davidson, was included in the exhibition* Notions of Home, *at PCNW September 14–December 10, 2017.*

Jeff Dunas (b. 1954, Los Angeles; lives in Los Angeles) is best known for his portraits of musicians and entertainers made over his five decades in the field. His work has appeared in hundreds of magazines, album covers, and calendars, and he is the author of multiple books. In 2005, he founded the Palm Springs Photo Festival. **See pages 43, 163.** *Designed the book interior and exhibition graphics of* State of the Blues; *produced a custom magazine event in Los Angeles, 2007; and developed and participated in*

programming for the Palm Springs Photo Festival annually since 2005.

Larry Fink (b. 1941, Brooklyn; lives in Martin's Creek, Pennsylvania) has had solo exhibitions at the Museum of Modern Art, the Whitney Museum of American Art, the San Francisco Museum of Modern Art, the Philadelphia Museum of Art, Bene Taschen Gallery in Cologne, Fotografiska NYC, David Hill Gallery, London, and the Musée de l'Elysée in Switzerland, among others. His first book, *Social Graces* (Aperture, 1984), was followed by fourteen more monographs. Accolades include two Guggenheim Fellowships, and two National Endowment for the Arts Individual Photography Fellowships. He was professor of photography at Bard College for over twenty years, retiring in 2019. He lives with his wife, artist Martha Posner, on their farm. **See pages 101, above, 169.** *Fink participated in the Aperture West lecture series, 2007; included his photographs in* Terminal: On Mortality and Beauty, *on view at PCNW January 8–April 4, 2015. Fink was one of the "starting five" authors to launch Minor Matters in 2013;* Social Graces, *designed by Wendy Byrne, was exhibited in* By the Book: Nine Designers, *at PCNW September 10– December 13, 2018.*

Marina Font (b. 1970, Argentina; lives in Miami Beach, Florida) studied design, sculpture, and photography at the Escuela de Artes Visuales Martín Malharro, Argentina; photography at Spéos École de la Photographie in Paris; and earned an MFA in photography from Barry University, Miami. She has exhibited in numerous solo and group shows in galleries, cultural institutions, and museums. Her work is represented by Dina Mitrani Gallery, Miami. **See page 146 and above.** *Published her first monograph,* Anatomy Is Destiny / la anatomía es destino (Minor Matters, 2018).

Joe Freeman Jr. (b. 1981, Woodbury, New Jersey; lives on Vashon Island, Washington) has been exploring the energy of existing and imagined terrains for two decades. He holds a BFA from Rhode Island School of Design, and an MFA from the University of Washington. His work has been featured through *National Geographic* and in *Photograph* magazine, and has been exhibited in solo and group shows throughout the United States. **See pages 2–3, 154, 156-57, 161.** *Included his work in issue 3 of* Latitude 47, *and in the exhibition* Notions of Home, *on view at PCNW September 14–December 10, 2017; selected and wrote about his work for a feature on climate change in* Photograph *magazine, January 2020.*

David Hilliard (b. 1965, Lowell, Massachusetts; lives in Boston) received his BFA from the Massachusetts College of Art (MassArt), and MFA from the Yale University School of Art. Hilliard's photographs have been exhibited nationally and internationally, and are in many public collections. He is the recipient of both Fulbright and Guggenheim Fellowships. Hilliard is represented by Carroll and Sons Gallery in Boston; Jackson Fine Art in Atlanta; The Schoolhouse Gallery in Provincetown, Massachusetts; and Yancey Richardson Gallery in New York. **See pages 128–129.** *Published his second monograph,* What Could Be *(Minor Matters, 2014/2020); facilitated master-classes through YoungArts, Miami; wrote about his work for* Don't Take Pictures *magazine, issue 9, 2017.*

Eirik Johnson (b. 1974, Seattle; lives in Seattle) has exhibited at the San Francisco Museum of Modern Art; the Institute of Contemporary Art, Boston; and the Museum of Contemporary Photography, Chicago, among others. He has authored four monographs. He was the recipient of a J. William Fulbright Scholarship and the 2012 Neddy Prize through Cornish College of the Arts, Seattle. He is represented by G. Gibson Projects, Seattle, and Rena Bransten Gallery, San Francisco. **See**

page 136. *Introduced* Sawdust Mountain *for publication (Aperture, 2008); produced a custom magazine event in San Francisco with Crumpler and SF Camerawork, 2010; selected for the inaugural Riffs residency at PCNW, 2016; included in the exhibition* Notions of Home, *at PCNW September 14–December 10, 2017; published his third monograph,* Pine *(Minor Matters, 2018).*

Lisa Kereszi (b. 1973, Chester, Pennsylvania; lives in New Haven) received her BA from Bard College and her MFA from Yale University. She was awarded the Baum Award for Best Emerging American Photographer in 2005, and is the author of four monographs. Kereszi's work has been exhibited at numerous institutions, and is in many public collections; she is represented by Yancey Richardson Gallery, New York. Kereszi began teaching at Yale University in 2004; since 2013, she has been Senior Critic and Director of Undergraduate Studies in Art. **See pages 98-99, 164.** *Worked together in the Publications office of Bard College; edited and designed* Joe's Junk Yard *(Damiani, 2012); included her work in* Notions of Home, *at PCNW September 14–December 10, 2017; have lectured in several of her classes at Yale.*

Isaac Layman (b. 1977, Yakima, Washington; lives in Seattle) graduated

from the University of Washington. Layman's first solo museum exhibition, *Paradise,* opened at the Frye Art Museum in 2010. His works are included in numerous collections, and have been exhibited throughout the United States. He has been represented by the Elizabeth Leach Gallery, Portland since 2010. **See pages 145, 159.** *Designed the catalog to his 2010 museum exhibition; included his work in the exhibition* Terminal: On Mortality and Beauty, *at PCNW January 8–April 4, 2015; published his second book,* Homeschooled *(Minor Matters, 2016).*

An-My Lê (b. 1960, Saigon, South Vietnam; lives in Brooklyn) has exhibited work at the Museum of Modern Art, New York; Museum of Contemporary Photography, Chicago; and San Francisco Museum of Modern Art, among many others. She is a professor in the Department of Photography at Bard College. Lê is the author of two books, both published by Aperture: *Small Wars* (2006) and *Events Ashore* (2014), and has received many awards, including a Guggenheim Fellowship, and fellowships from the New York Foundation for the Arts, and MacArthur Foundation. Lê is represented by Marian Goodman Gallery, New York. **See pages 88-89.** *Lê participated in the Aperture West lecture series in 2006; facilitated her masterclass at YoungArts, 2018.*

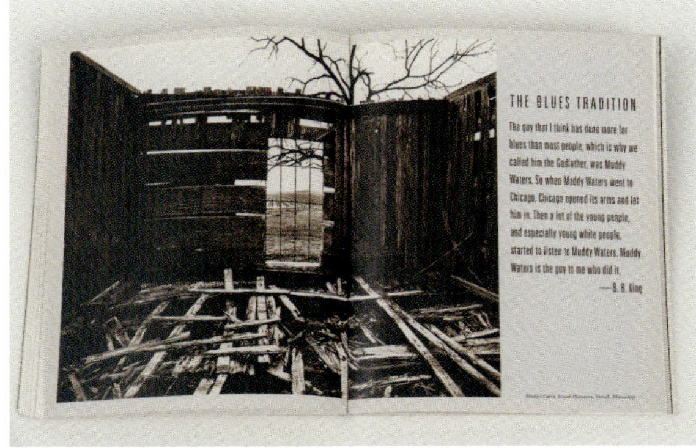

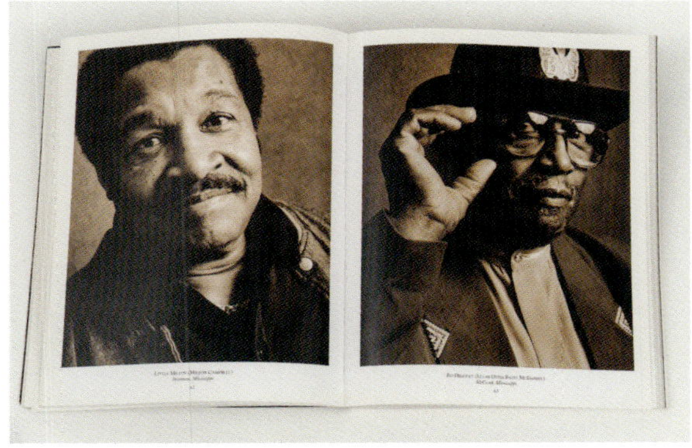

Mary Ellen Mark (1940–2015) had eighteen books of her photographs published in her lifetime; *The Book of Everything*, a comprehensive three-volume set edited by her husband Martin Bell (Steidl, 2020) expands upon previous volumes. Her work has been exhibited in museums worldwide, and was widely published in *Life*, *Rolling Stone*, *The New Yorker*, *New York Times*, and *Vanity Fair* among other publications. **See pages 62, 65.** *Invited her to lecture at Hammer Museum, Los Angeles for inaugural Aperture West public event, 2003; with Sandy Cioffi facilitated film screening,* Twins, *Seattle Central Community College, 2003; with Yoko Ott facilitated film screening,* Streetwise, *Frye Art Museum, 2006; custom magazine programs with IC Lab, Polaroid, USA Network, 2008–10; public lecture on her work, Seattle Public Library, 2016; her books* Exposure, *designed by Mary Shanahan;* American Odyssey, *designed by Wendy Byrne; and a group project,* Paradise, *designed by Roger Gorman, were exhibited in* By the Book: Nine Designers, *at PCNW September 10–December 13, 2018.*

Jim Marshall (1936–2010) was best known for his pioneering work in the music industry; his photographs appeared on the covers of over five hundred albums, and in countless magazines, including *Life* and *Rolling Stone*. At least seven monographs were published during his lifetime; his estate has produced six more to date. He is the subject of a feature-length documentary, *Show Me the Picture*. **See pages 114–115, 165.** *Acquiring editor of two books of Marshall's work through Chronicle Books: a limited edition of* Proof *(2004/2009), and* Pocket Cash *(2010). Lectured on his work at the Apple Store, Soho, New York, 2010; editor and designer of* The Rolling Stones 1972 *(2012); curator of an exhibition of the same name at Experience Music Project, Seattle, 2012; part of conception and design of the Jack & Jim Gallery, Austin City Limits Live, 2012, and lectured there on his work as part of "We Walk the Line," a tribute to Johnny Cash.*

Barbara Morgan (1900–1992) was one of the co-founders of *Aperture* magazine in 1951–52. Best known for her dance photographs, particularly her collaborations with Martha Graham, her later shift to photomontages and abstraction continued her expression of living energy. From 1919–23, she studied at University of California, Los Angeles (UCLA), and eventually taught there; they acquired her archive in 2016. **See page 39.**

Graham Nash (b. 1942, Blackpool, England; lives in New York), OBE, is a musician, songwriter, and photographer. With R. Mac Holbert he co-founded Nash Editions in 1989, and became a pioneer of fine art digital printing; their original Iris printer is in the permanent collection of the Smithsonian Museum of American History. Among other recognitions in music and photography, he is a two-time inductee into the Rock and Roll Hall of Fame. **See pages 110-111.** *Participated with him in panel organized by Marita Holdaway, 2004; facilitated limited-edition print with him through Aperture, 2007; acquiring editor for* Taking Aim *(Chronicle, 2009).*

Dorothy Norman (1905–1997) studied English and literature at Smith College, and at the University of Pennsylvania, Philadelphia. Norman met Alfred Stieglitz in 1927 at The Intimate Gallery in New York City; he encouraged her to make her own photographs. **See page 48.**

Sylvia Plachy (b. Budapest, 1943; lives in Woodhaven, New York) studied photography at the Pratt Institute. She has had solo exhibitions at the Minneapolis Institute of Arts, the Whitney Museum at Philip Morris, the Queens Museum, and in galleries around the world. She was a staff photographer at *The Village Voice*, *Metropolis*, and *The New Yorker*. She has authored six books, is the recipient of a Guggenheim Fellowship, the ICP Infinity Award, the Erich Salomon Award, and a Lucie Award, among other honors. Her photographs are in numerous public and private collections. **See pages 93, 94-95, 121, 122.** *Plachy participated in the Aperture West lecture*

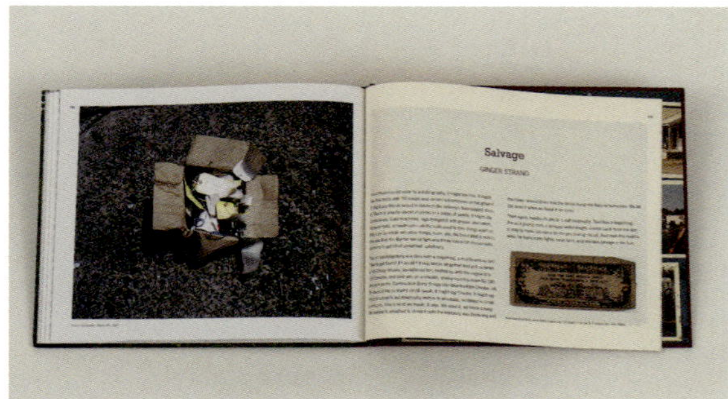

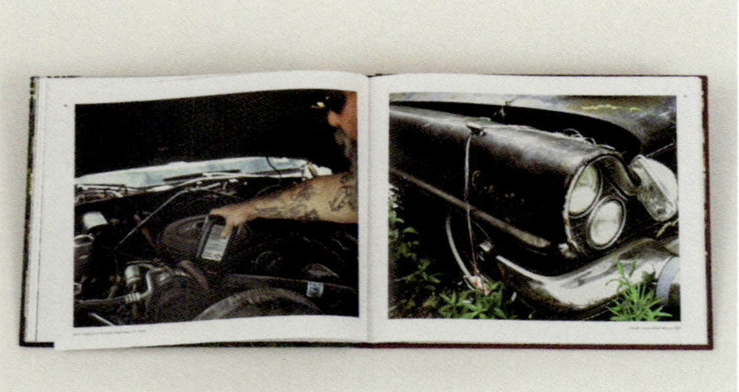

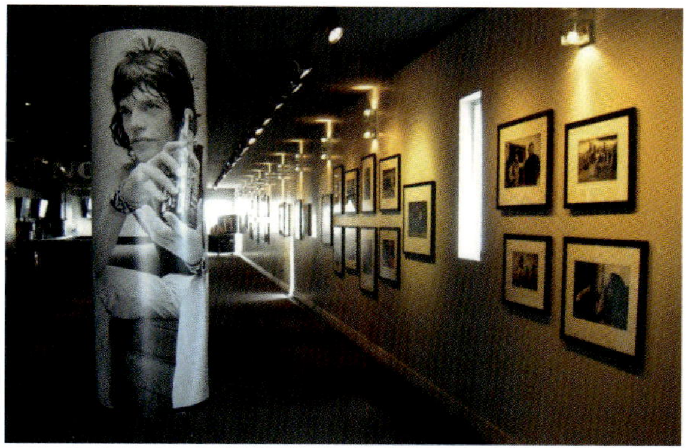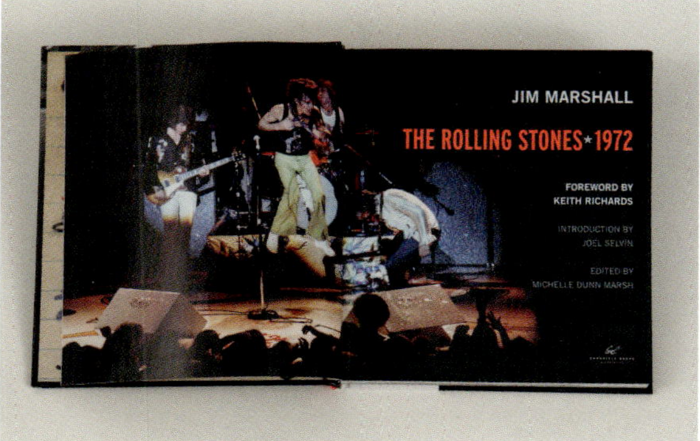

series in 2005; in the custom magazine programs "Character Project" with the USA Network in 2008–09 and Sony Photo Camp in 2011; included her work in Terminal: On Mortality and Beauty, at PCNW January 8–April 4, 2015, during which she also had an installation at Leica Store Bellevue; included her work in Notions of Home, at PCNW September 14–December 10, 2017; co-presented with her at YoungArts in 2017; the jacket of her first book, Unguided Tour, designed by Yolanda Cuomo, was exhibited in By the Book: Nine Designers, at PCNW September 10–December 13, 2018.

Eugene Richards (b. 1944, Dorchester, Massachusetts; lives in Brooklyn) studied photography with Minor White. In 1968, he joined Volunteers in Service to America (VISTA), and helped found a social service organization and a community newspaper, *Many Voices*. He has authored eighteen books to date, and completed seven short films. He has received the W. Eugene Smith Award, the Robert F. Kennedy Lifetime Achievement Journalism Award, a Guggenheim Fellowship, grants from the National Endowment for the Arts, the Kraszna-Krausz Photography Book Award for Photographic Innovation, the Leica Oskar Barnack Award, and countless other awards. His work is in many permanent collections,

including the Metropolitan Museum of Art, the Museum of Modern Art, The Smithsonian Museum of American Art, George Eastman House, and the Nelson-Atkins Museum of Art. **See pages 54–55, 105.** *Richards participated in the Aperture West lecture series, 2004; facilitated custom magazine program with Kodak, 2007; included his work in* Terminal: On Mortality and Beauty, *at PCNW January 8–April 4, 2015; curated solo exhibition of his work,* Enduring Freedom, *at PCNW September 8– November 16, 2016, during which he also had an installation at Leica Store Bellevue.*

Meghann Riepenhoff (b. 1979, Atlanta, Georgia; lives and works in San Francisco, California and Bainbridge Island, Washington) creates in collaboration with the landscape and the ocean; her cyanotypes are never wholly processed, and change over time. Riepenhoff received her BFA from the University of Georgia, Athens, and MFA from the San Francisco Art Institute. Her work has been featured throughout the United States and is in many permanent collections. She is the recipient of a Guggenheim Fellowship among other honors, and has had two monographs published, both by Radius Books: *Littoral Drift + Ecotone* (2018) and *Ice* (2021). She is represented by Haines Gallery, San Francisco and Yossi

Milo Gallery, New York. **See page 135.** *Selected her as one of ten artists for the inaugural PCNW Presents program, 2014.*

Charlie Rubin (b. 1986, New Rochelle, New York; lives in Brooklyn) received his BA from Haverford College, and his MFA from Parsons School of Design. He was recognized by *FOAM* magazine in its 2013 Talent issue and accompanying exhibition, and his work has been published by *VICE*, *The New Yorker*, and *The New York Times*, among others. **See page 119.** *Rubin's professor at Parsons School of Design, 2011; introduced his work to Ann Pallesen, who included it in* Process, *PCNW March 13–June 15, 2014; introduced his work to Paul Kopeikin, who presented a solo exhibition,* Intervention, *April 25–June 6, 2015 at Kopeikin Gallery, Los Angeles.*

Stephen Shore (b. 1947, New York; lives in Tivoli, New York) is a photographic prodigy. At age ten he received a copy of Walker Evans's book *American Photographs*, introducing him to a descriptive visual language of place; his work was acquired four years later by Edward Steichen at the Museum of Modern Art. Shore worked in Andy Warhol's studio, the Factory, from 1965 through 1967, and had a solo exhibition at the Metropolitan Museum of Art, the first accorded a living American

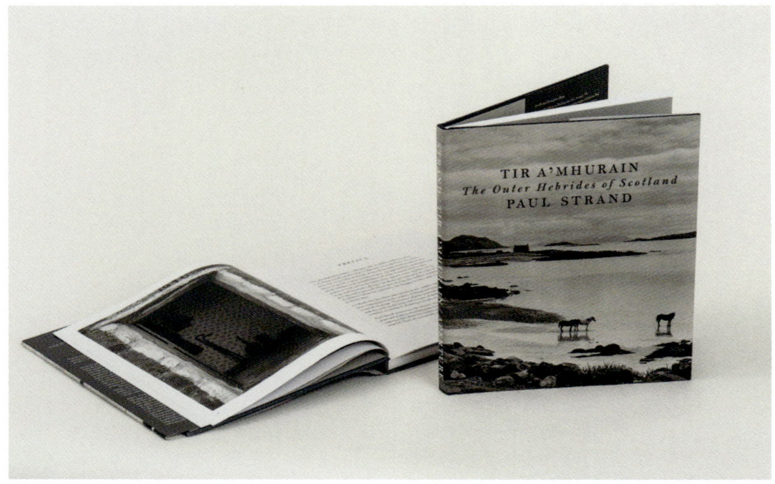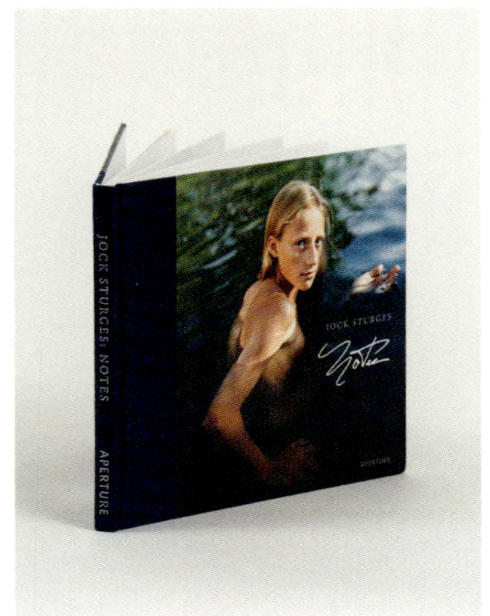

photographer, in 1971. In 2017, the Museum of Modern Art held a major retrospective spanning Shore's career. He has been widely exhibited, collected, and published. He is represented by 303 Gallery, New York. Shore has been the director of the photography program at Bard College since 1982. **See pages 30, 68–70.** *Shore participated in the Aperture West lecture series in 2004; his first book,* Uncommon Places, *designed by Wendy Byrne, was exhibited in* By the Book: Nine Designers, *at PCNW September 10– December 13, 2018.*

Jonathan David Smyth (b. 1987, Belfast, Northern Ireland; lives in New York) works with photography, video, and performance. His work has been exhibited throughout the United States and internationally, and has been featured in *Ain't-Bad* magazine, *Musée* magazine, and *Flat* magazine, among other publications. He holds a BA with honors in photography and film from Edinburgh Napier University, and an MFA in photography from Parsons School of Design. Smyth's debut monograph *Just One More* (2017) is followed by *Between You and Me* (2021), both published by bd studios. **See page 141.** *Smyth's professor at Parsons School*

of Design, 2013; introduced his work to Chieko Phillips, who included it in Me and My Selfie, *PCNW September 10– November 1, 2015; wrote introduction to his first monograph.*

Edward Steichen (1879–1973) helped facilitate public acceptance of photography as a fine art, working closely with Alfred Stieglitz on the seminal publication *Camera Work*, which also included many of his images. He was closely tied to the emergence of a department of photography at the Museum of Modern Art, where he organized the hugely influential *Family of Man* exhibition in 1955. **See page 34.**

Paul Strand (1890–1976) began studying under photographer Lewis Hine when he was seventeen; he was also mentored by Alfred Stieglitz. In 1915 he began working with a large-format camera, and the results contributed to the rise of modernism in photography. In the early 1950s, due to the conservative political climate in the United States, Strand moved to Europe, where he lived until his death. Dozens of books and museum exhibitions of his work have been presented internationally. **See pages 40, 51, and above.**

Jock Sturges (b. 1947, New York; lives in Seattle) studied at Marlboro College in Vermont, and later received an MFA from the San Francisco Art Institute. Sturges is represented by galleries throughout the world, and is the author of many books. His work is in the collections of the Philadelphia Museum of Art, the International Center of Photography, the Metropolitan Museum of Art in New York, the Denver Museum of Art, the Musée de l'Elysée in Lausanne, Switzerland, the Museum Ludwig in Berlin, and the Musée de la Louvière in Brussels, among others. **See pages 80-81, and above.** *Organized a book signing at NW Bookfest, 2002; Designed* Jock Sturges: Notes *(Aperture, 2004); included him in gallery representation program PCNW Presents, 2014; included his work in* Notions of Home, *at PCNW September 14–December 10, 2017.*

Carrie Mae Weems (b. 1953, Portland, Oregon; lives in Syracuse and New York) is an internationally recognized artist who has received numerous awards, grants, and fellowships, including from the National Endowment for the Arts, Anonymous Was a Woman, and the MacArthur Foundation. Weems was

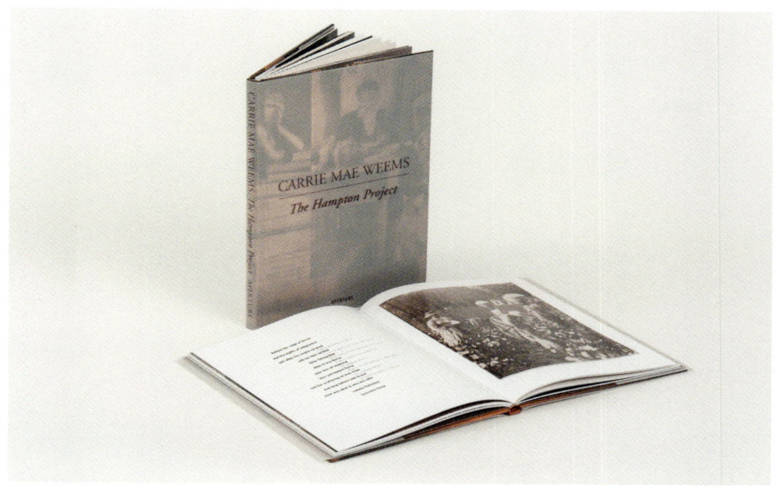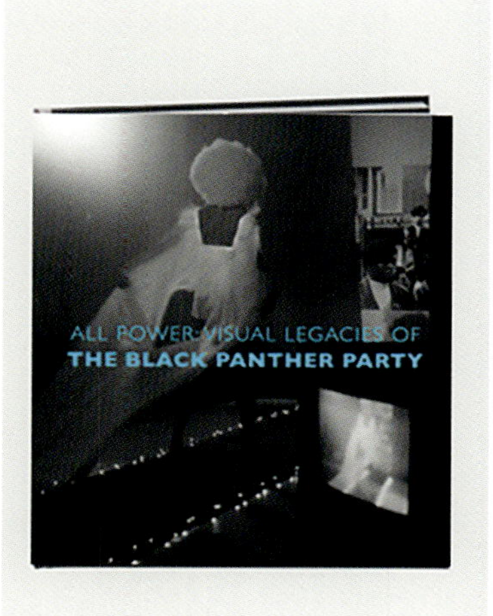

presented with one of the first US Department of State's Medal of Arts in 2012, and in 2013, the Congressional Black Caucus Foundation's Lifetime Achievement Award. Over twenty books have been published exploring her work, which is held in major collections nationally and internationally. **See page 47, and above left and right.** *Designed* The Hampton Project *(Aperture, 2001); facilitated masterclass invitation with YoungArts, 2015; included her work in the book and exhibition* All Power: Visual Legacies of the Black Panther Party *(Minor Matters, 2016 / exhibit through PCNW, 2018); online conversation with her for Palm Springs Photo Festival, 2020.*

Alice Wheeler (b. 1961, Kansas City, Missouri; lives in Seattle) grew up in Ralston, Nebraska, and moved to Hollywood at seventeen, an early devotee to punk rock music and culture. She worked as a photojournalist for many local and national publications. Wheeler's work has been featured on record covers and in museum exhibitions internationally. She holds a BA from The Evergreen State College. Since 1999 she has been represented by Greg Kucera Gallery, Seattle. **See page 132.**

Published Wheeler's first book Outcasts & Innocents *(Minor Matters, 2015).*

Minor White (1908–1976) was one of the founders of *Aperture* magazine, and its inaugural editor from 1952–75. He began his career in photography in Portland, Oregon, taking on assignments from the Works Progress Administration and exhibiting at the Portland Art Museum. At Ansel Adams's invitation he returned to the west coast, where from 1946–53 he formed the curriculum for one of the first creative programs in photography at the San Francisco School of Fine Arts (now the San Francisco Art Institute); he taught workshops and in formal programs throughout his career. **See pages 33, 127.**

Will Wilson (b. 1969, San Francisco; lives in Santa Fe) is a Diné photographer and trans-customary artist who spent his formative years on the Navajo Nation of which he is a citizen. Wilson studied photography, sculpture, and art history at the University of New Mexico (MFA, Photography, 2002) and Oberlin College (BA, Studio Art and Art History, 1993). Since 2012, Wilson

has been involved in the creation of the Critical Indigenous Photographic Exchange (CIPX). Using a large format camera and the wet-plate collodion process to create timeless historic photographs, he gives the unique objects to the subject, retaining a high-resolution digital file for his ongoing creative usage. He has pioneered his "talking tintypes" among other forms of presentation through this project. **See front cover.** *Facilitated invitation to Wilson to give a masterclass at YoungArts in 2019.*

Nancy Salguero McKay (b. 1979, Mexico City; lives in Federal Way) is the executive director of Highline Heritage Museum in Burien, Washington. She was selected as one of the most fabulous people in Washington state in 2020. McKay was born 80 percent deaf; she came to the United States at seventeen, got hearing aids in both ears, and was able to hear well for the first time. She is a mother, has taught in the Museum Studies program at the University of Washington, and has been recognized for her leadership in the museum and heritage fields.

Michelle Dunn Marsh (b. 1973, Seattle; lives in Seattle) is an American of Indo-Burmese and Irish descent; she holds dual citizenship with Ireland. She conceived, and with Steve McIntyre co-founded Minor Matters, a collaborative publishing platform, in 2013. They launched Book Pitch, an online consulting service for aspiring visual authors, in 2020.

Dunn Marsh led Photographic Center Northwest from 2013–2019, spent fifteen years in various roles with the nonprofit publisher Aperture Foundation, New York; was senior editor of art and design at Chronicle Books in San Francisco; and has worked in a freelance capacity with over twenty publishers and cultural institutions on books or public programming. She has produced more than ten fundraising events, meeting goals from $10,000 to $1M. A committed educator, she achieved tenure as a professor of graphic design at Seattle Central Community College in 2003, and has lectured at Parsons | The New School for Social Research, Yale University, Seattle University, and elsewhere on photography and publishing. She chaired the photography panel for YoungArts, Miami from 2015–2020, teaches workshops and masterclasses, and has conceived and moderated over forty public panels. Dunn Marsh has participated in national portfolio reviews annually since 2003. She holds a BA from Bard College and an MS in Publishing from Pace University.

Select Exhibitions Curated

Enlightened: Contemporary Photography by YoungArts Alumni, YoungArts campus, Miami, May 3—June 30, 2017

Here I Am: Photographs by Lisa Leone Bronx Museum of the Arts, New York, September 11, 2014 –January 11, 2015

The Rolling Stones 1972, Photographs by Jim Marshall, EMP Museum, Seattle, July 14, 2012–January 6, 2013

At Photographic Center Northwest:

With Maikoiyo Alley-Barnes and Ann Pallesen, *Seen: an exploration of the Inside and the Out, the Then and the Now, by the (still) Invisible Men,* January 16–March 8, 2014

Terminal: On Mortality and Beauty, January 8–April 4, 2015

Eugene Richards: "Enduring Freedom," September 8–November 16, 2016

All Power: Visual Legacies of the Black Panther Party, AIPAD Photography Show April 4–7; PCNW April 20–June 10; the Sarah Spurgeon Gallery, Central Washington University, Ellensburg, September 27–October 21, 2018

Jun Ahn: On The Verge, January 8–March 24, 2018

By The Book: Nine Designers, September 10–December 13, 2018

Select Lectures and Public Programs

Masterclasses, Seagull School of Publishing, Calcutta, Bengal, India, February 1–2, 2017, February 6–7, 2020

"Reading Photographs," PhotoIreland, May 28, 2019

"Photography: Still an Agent for Change," panel, Palm Springs Photo Festival, April 28, 2016, and SXSW, March 14, 2017

"The Legacy of Mary Ellen Mark," Seattle Public Library, October 5, 2016

"Representing: Successful Approaches to Visualizing Marginalized Communities," Seattle University, December 11, 2013

"Resonance and Reading Photographs," Jacob Lawrence Gallery, University of Washington, October 30, 2012

"Jim Marshall's *Pocket Cash,*" Apple Store Soho, New York, March 24, 2011

"Ten Things You Should Know about Magazine Publishing," panel, Photo Plus Expo, New York, October 2010

"The Pleasure of Print," keynote, Atlanta Celebrates Photography, October 2009

"Routes to Roots and Beyond: The Ongoing Evolution of *Aperture,*" Society for Photographic Education national conference, Portland, Oregon, 2004

Select Juries

Lucie Foundation Scholarship, Los Angeles, 2020

Oskar Barnack Award, Leica Camera, Wetzlar, Germany, 2017

"The Curator," *Photo District News,* New York, 2015

Sony World Photography Awards, London, 2010

Texas Photographic Society National Competition, San Antonio, 2007

Alaska Positive, Juneau, 2004

Select Press / Honors

Jean Dykstra, "The Curators: Michelle Dunn Marsh," *Photograph,* Vol. 15, No. 5, May/June 2018

Robert Ayers, "Truth in Beauty," cover story, *Pacific Northwest* Magazine, the *Seattle Times,* June 22, 2014

Visual Accord: The Photographic Book Design of Michelle Dunn Marsh, exhibition, Homer Public Library, September 5-November 5, 2007

First place awards in photography and in scholarly and reference books, New York Book Show, 2001

　　Larry Fink, *Cigar* (Michelle), Hellerton, Pennsylvania, 2013. Digital capture.

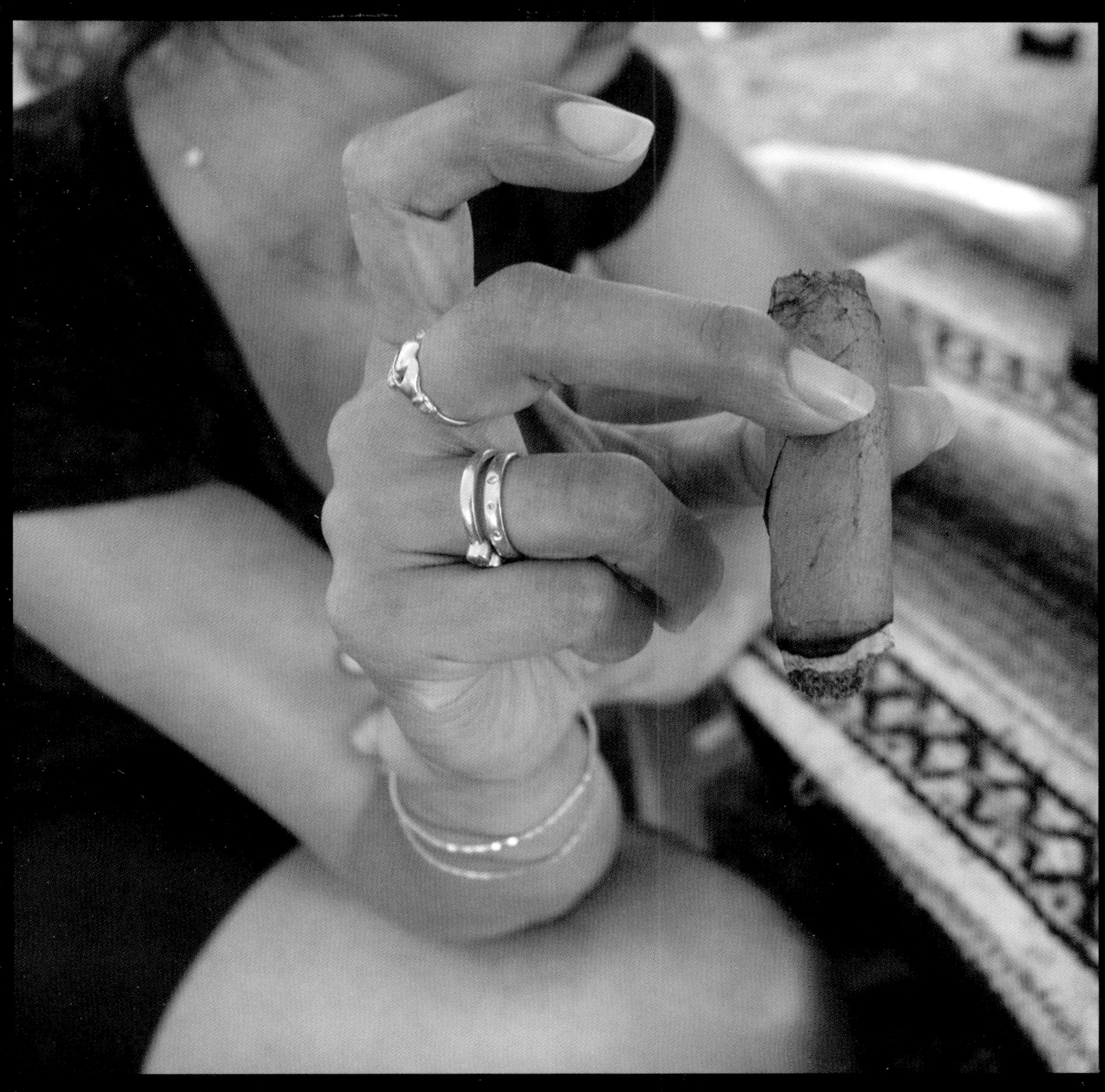

MINOR MATTERS

LEGACY PUBLISHERS

Caryl Baron

Ken Baron

Cynthea Bogel and John
Stevenson (1944–2020)

Wendy Byrne

Jeff Dunas and
Laura Morton Dunas

Marina Font
and Tomas Nores

Lee Grambush

John Jenkins III

Christopher and
Alida Latham

Lucia | Marquand

Dina Mitrani

New York Public Library,
Miriam and Ira D. Wallach
Division of Art, Prints,
and Photographs

The Seattle Public Library

Pat Soden

Rick Smith and
Gayle Green Smith

Dabi Stathakopoulos

Robert Tommervik

Anastasia, Steve,
and Otto Van Dyke

Freddie Yudin

Calvin Abe

In memory of Chinua Achebe

Doué Adler

Lisa Ahlberg and Geoff Mirelowitz

Margaret Albaugh

Brian Kilbride Allen

Lawrence and Renée Andrews

Mitchell Andrews and Edwina Davies

Nola and Walter Andrews

Margarita Anthoine
and in memory of Robert Anthoine

Matt and Lauren Appleby

Joseph Baio and Anne Griffin

Sunandini Banerjee
and Rick Simonson

Nancy Baron

In memory of Stevan A. Baron

Missy and Bruce Barth

Jake and Rachael Barth

Endia Beal

Claire Beckett

Lara Behnert

Miranda Belarde-Lewis

David Belisle

Abby Bender

Melonie Bennett

Sherrie Berger

Paul Berger

Nathan Bett, Amy Burmeister,
Olivia Bett

Dawoud Bey

Barbara and Arjun Bhatt

Nisha Bhukhan and Rana Dutta

Viveki Bhukhan

Meg Birnbaum

Walter Bodle and Lynne Iglitzin

Yadesa Bojia

Jeanette Borchers

James Bracher

Jane Andromache Brien

Constance Brinkley

In memory of Troy James Bryant

Mark Bryce

Barbara Bullock-Wilson

Gretchen Burger

Mark Bussell

Erin Callahan

Leah Canady Raney

Amybelle Capule

Stefano Catalani

Catherine Chalmers

James Cox Chambers

Tara Champion

Carrie Chase-McNamara

Alison, Johnson,
Miles, and Kiki Chen

Kimberly Cheng

Bruce and Odile Chilton

Amy Christian

Elizabeth Chucker

Sandy Cioffi

Mark Citret

Annie Claflin

Brian Paul Clamp

Annabel Clark

Gerhard Clausing

Rachel Cobb

David Colby

Christine Collins

Ephen Glenn Colter

Matt Connors

Thomas Corddry

John Cornicello

Dale Cotton

Chris Cox

Susan Coyle

Pio Dabrowski

Ricker Dahlgren

Alexa Davalos

Adam Paul Davidson

Anna Mia Davidson

Stacy Davis

scott b davis

Ben Davis

Amelia Davis and Bonita Passarelli

Maria Décsey Tan

Nicole M. de Jesús

Patrick DelliBovi

Rachel Demy

Jesse and Elana Diamond

Joan Dinkelspiel

Alice Dison

Aaron Dixon

Christopher Duenow

Joyce V. Dunn and in memory
of Richard J. Dunn

Kevin and Cecilia Dunn

Aidan Dunn

Conor Dunn

Lisa Dutton and Spike Mafford

John Eaton

Suzette Eby

Paula Ely

Esa Epstein

Elena Erber and Bernard Greenwald

D Lily Evans

Randy Faerber

Dee Fair-Barrett

Hossein Farmani

John Ficker

Larry Fink and Martha Posner

Peter C. Fisher

Michael Foley

Jack Foote

Andrew Fowler

Jona Frank

Hannah Frieser

Jeff Frost

Carole Fuller

The F-U Gang

Hal Gage

Nicholas Galanin
and Merritt Johnson

Michael Galloway

Susan Gans

Caitriona Gerber

Rosalyn G. Gerstein

Gail Gibson and Claudia Vernia

Kurt Giessel

Steve Gilbert

Helaine Glick

Paulo Gonzales

Roger Gorman

Simone Grace

Kris Graves

James Graves

Daniel Gregory and Lori Kane

Tim Greyhavens

Frits Habermann

Vicki Halper

Meg Handler

Amy and Thaddeus Hanscom

Ellen Harris

Randy Harris

Cynthia Hartwig

Ashraf Hasham

Chelsea and Jazmin Haven

Deb and Craig Haven

Liam and Toni Haven

Susan Hawes

Daniel Hawkins

Richard Hay Jr.

Emily Haynes and Sanjay Patel

Robin Held

Mark Hempel

Jorgen Henriksen

Bill Hensler and Jill Schoenleber

Highline Heritage Museum

David Hilliard

Steve Hoedemaker
and Tommy Swenson

In memory of Michael E. Hoffman

R. Mac Holbert

Marita Holdaway
and in memory of Fred Housel

William and Lisa Holderman

Stacia Horvath

Elisa Huerta-Enochian

Naomi Hume and Kenneth Allan

Peter Hunsberger

Samantha and Jessica Hurley

Melinda Hurst Frye

Josie Iselin

Deborah Jack

Ann Jastrab

Alex Jespersen-Wheat and Adam Gyi

Eirik Johnson and Heidi Hall

Russell Johnson and Barbara Ierulli

Marteinn Jonasson

Diane Jonte-Pace

Manny Kagan

Lola Kantor

Daile Kaplan

Andy Katz

Amy Kawadler and Dan Milnor

Dennis Keeley and Veronica Cotter

Sandra Kehoe

Samantha Kelly

Richard Kelly

Maureen and Adrian Kelly

Lisa Kereszi

Betsy Kerlin, and Peter,
Kerlin, and Jesse Pyun

Kat Kiernan

Rebecca Kiger

Douglas King

Naveen Kishore

Varun Kishore and Sharanya Dutta

Ben Ko

Paul Kopeikin

Harini Krishnamurthy

Elizabeth Krist

Julia Kuskin

Amina Lakhaney

Jason Langer

Stephanie Lara

Thea and Jasper Layman

Lisa Leone and Jimmy Bollettieri

Miriam Leuchter

Barbara Levine

Mark and Elizabeth Levine

Leah and Rob Levine

Drew Levy

Stu Levy

Thomas Lewis

Joan Liftin

Mike Lim

Kayla Lindquist

Joan Lobis Brown

Jim and Christina Lockwood

Lucie Foundation

Dolores Lusitana

Hannah Lynch

Berette Macaulay and Dale Woodard

David Maisel

Michael Maiura

Becci Manson

Wayne Marien

Alistaire, Jackie, Xavier, and Kai Marsh

Lynn Martin

Rania Matar

Annu Palakunnathu Matthew

Randy Matusow

Pete Mauney

George McClintock

Nancy McCrary

Enda McEvoy

Steve McIntyre and
Silvia Tornga McIntyre

Tim and Kathy McKamey

Shawna McKenzie

Michelle McLeod and
Darrin Dedmon

Yvette Meltzer

Rhonda Mitrani

Jaya Ferrandis Mitrani

Orli Ferrandis Mitrani

Martin Morfeld

Rachael and Adam Morrison

Linda Morrow

Margot Muir

Ursula Murphy

Christopher Myers

Erika J. Nesholm

Janet Neuhauser

Cree Nevins

Canh Nguyen

Jackson Nichols

Paul Nicks

David Nolan

Terry Novak

Bridget Nowlin

Kristine Nyborg

Jane Olin

The Olive House, Paso Robles

Arthur Ollman

Lori Ordover

Ara Oshagan

In memory of Yoko Ott

Marcy Palmer

Rebecca Palmer

Lydia Panas

Joe Park and Deborah Gassner

Nina and Zara Park

Roz Duavit Pasion

Susan Patrice

Debra Pemstein

Ibarionex Perello

Charles Peterson

Sandra Phillips

PhotoIreland

Chris Pichler and Maya Ishiwata

Donna Pinckley

Sylvia Plachy and Elliot Brody

Luna Posadas Nava

Dana Price Cheney

Patti Quill

Liz Quinlisk

Alan E. Rapp

Anna Ream

Brandon Remler

Anna Rheim

Kolya Rice and Nicole Wiggins

Meghann Riepenhoff

Molly Roberts

Susan Rosenberg Jones

Rosalie Rosenthal

Mark Richard Ross

Ben and Deborah Ruffins

Danielle Rustad

Philip Sager

Jenny Sampson

Jeff Schewe

Charles Schneider

Roger N. Scotland

Leonor and Dick Schorr

Karin Schorr

Jenifer Schramm

Thom Sempere

KC Serota

Amy Silverman

Ruta and Raj Singh

Preston Singletary and Åsa Sandlund

In memory of Karen Sinsheimer

Margaret Skiba

Gerald Slota

Giselle Smith

J. Sybylla Smith

Brian Smith and Fazia Ali

Jonathan David Smyth
and Rob Ritter

Heather Snider

Dave and Angie Snyder

Erin Spencer and Kaleb Kerr

Maria Sprowls

Sue Stigleman

Douglas G. Stinson

Diana C. Stoll

Jennifer Stoots

Jock Sturges

Mary Virginia Swanson

Jean-Marc Tallon

Anna Tamura

Anthony Tarricone

Rose Tatlow

Phyllis Thompson

Robert Tobin

Linda Troeller

In memory of Marilyn Trueblood

Tom Vani

Doug Vann

Albert Varady

David and Cookie Vigil

Patricia Vogel

Tarrah von Lintel

Robert Wade

Fiona Walsh

Irene Walsh

Sarah Walsh

Lauren Walsh

Kimberly and Bruce Ward

Peggy Washburn

Tariqa Waters

Dawn Watson

Bridget Watson Payne

Lewis Watts

Charlotte Watts

Adam L. Weintraub

Lauren Wendle

Glen Wexler

Allegra Wilde

Stephen and Bette Wilkes

In memory of Daniel L. Williams

Bryonie Wise

Roland Wolff

Tim Wride

Mark Wuscher

Frank Yamrus

Youth in Focus

Dorothy A. Yule

Daniella Zalcman

ACKNOWLEDGMENTS

When I sent Sylvia Plachy a PDF of the photographs in the Highline installation and asked if they were interesting together, I did not know that I'd end up here, two years and 176 pages later. I have named teachers, colleagues, institutions and inspirations throughout the text in recognition of the role collaboration plays in my life and work, and to give deserved credit to so many with whom I have worked. I am short on space for this very important last part, so will focus primarily on the constituents related to the book itself, and trust that the people in my life who I deeply love, and whose love I depend on, know who they are.

This book would not exist without the participation of the photographers featured within it. Thank you for your respect, support, and in many cases the gift of living with your work. You collectively gave up over $10,000 in licensing fees to this publication. Equally relevant, your generosity in doing so meant I had to see through the book when I was looking for excuses to stop. I am usually trying to get *you* paid, so accepting your in-kind contributions was difficult. *I am so grateful.* Special thanks to Meredith Lue and Julia Bezgin at Falkland, Inc., Kellie McLaughlin and Annette Booth at Aperture Foundation, Amelia Davis and Bonita Passarelli of Jim Marshall Photography LLC, and Sandy and Kate Christenberry.

To the additional people who have gifted me their artwork: Jun Ahn, David Belisle, Walter Bodle, Yadesa Bojia, Haley Bueschlen, Johnny Carrera, Pio Dabrowski, Anna Mia Davidson, Steve Davis, Jesse Diamond, John Divola, Colleen Fitzgerald, Neil Folberg, Nicholas Galanin, Robert Glenn Ketchum, Charles Lindsay, Beth Lipman and Ingalena Klennell, Joseph Park, Niv Rosenberg, Seeing With Photography Collective (Mark Andres and Peter Lui), and Preston Singletary—I appreciate you and your work so much, thank you for recognizing me and trusting me as a custodian of your creations. Likewise, a giant embrace to all the photographers, artists, and compatriots in publishing who have gifted or traded me books over the years. There are dozens of you and lest I leave anyone out, I will just acknowledge you collectively. You feed my favorite addiction.

Nancy Salguero McKay and Cyndi Upthegrove of Highline Heritage Museum are wholly responsible for demanding of me the installation that led to this book. Thank you, Nancy, for gently pushing me forward. You saw significance to my story that I did not. I see it now. As you led me, I hope to lead others.

A number of people stepped up to assist with promotion of the book during its pre-sales process. Thank you Jean Dykstra of *Photograph*, Jon Feinstein of Humble Arts, Andy Adams of FlakPhoto, and Joy Celine Asto of Photo Focus for your coverage of *Seeing Being Seen*. Ann Jastrab of the Center for Photographic Art, Maria Sprowls of Fotografiska, J. Sybylla Smith, and John Cornicello all invited me to speak during the pre-sales period, and created access to the audiences they cultivate—thank you. Other individuals went above and beyond in sharing with their networks, or purchasing copies in bulk for Seattle-based nonprofits, including Nancy Baron, Sandy Cioffi, Carrie Chase, Christopher Duenow, Sharanya Dutta, Cynthia Hartwig, Amy Kawadler, Dina Mitrani, Ruta Singh, and Freddie Yudin. Huge gratitude for your endorsement and support!

To the friends and family in my social media feed who are used to pictures of my shoes, or my travels, thank you for your good humor. So many of you joined in to publish *Seeing Being Seen*. The co-publishers of this book reflect every aspect of my life—my family locally, in Oz, and in Ireland; schoolmates I've known since kindergarten; family friends; fellow alum and staff of Bard College; colleagues from every professional position I have occupied; and board members from the nonprofit institutions I've worked with. Thank you all. It is a proud moment to review the co-publishers on every book Minor Matters has published, but it is particularly meaningful when there are so many familiar (and unfamiliar!) names in this one.

I have been working with separations master Thomas Palmer for over twenty years; it is always an education, and a joy. I offered to include his biography in this book, because his involvement in the reader's experience of black and white photographs in reproduction is that significant. He said no. I hope this acknowledgment sufficiently tweaks his modest New England sensibilities. Thank you for taking on the many different projects I toss at you, with little time and even less money, and consistently bringing your excellence.

Marteinn Jonasson read about Minor Matters in Conor Risch's *Photo District News* interview with us, our first, in 2013, and has been working with us since the beginning. Thank you for staying with us, working with our budgets, and pushing your teams to meet our vision of excellence in the printing of our books.

To Vicki Halper, my longtime curator-author-collaborator-friend, and Al Varady, Bardian through and through, thank you both for gamely agreeing to be my primary readers, and foraging through what I wrote, what I said, what I meant, and helping me get it all back into what I wrote. Susan Hood, thanks for the pinch hit! Lesley Martin, Ivan Vartanian, and Michael Lorenzini, thank you for diving back into your memories of our days at Aperture and assisting me in managing mine. Thank you Diana C. Stoll, editor of so many books I've designed, and joyous travel companion, for lending your eagle eye to this text and making time you don't have for conversations, and to Kathleen Pike Jones for consulting the *Chicago Manual of Style*, despite my occasional requests to override it. Jeff Dunas and Laura Morton made their oasis available to me for much-needed respite in 2021; its calm made possible at least three drafts of the book. So much love and gratitude.

To Marshy, Jax, Xav, and Kai; Tig, Steve, and Ottobot; Bunky and family; Mrs. Byrne; Aunt Bridget; Sylvia; Lin; Bets; Amy; Jake; Uncle Roger; Bhai, B, Owen and Audra; Vek, Nisha, and always Bella; Baby Tender and Jim; the Marvel house; the Gassner-Parks; the F-U Gang; Dabs; Mo and my bestie; Lisa (Lavish and Leone); Rick, Sunandini, and Naveen; Gail, Claudia, John, and Steve; Robin Held and Nicholas Polimenakos; Endia, Alain, Maxim and Victor; Esa; Lauren; Nicky-G, Merritt, and At Tugáni; Bee; Wal and Nola; Mitch and Eddie; Renée, Lawrence, Aston, and Samara; Ads, Alex and Owen; Sarah, Fionan, and Arlen; Fiona, Micky, Mitchy and Nathan; Irene and Ross; Enda; and Ms. Nora (aka Pangur Ban)—thank you for contributing to my well-being always, but especially these last two years. Sharon Tolson, I will never forget that you made room for me. To the loves that have been—peace. To the love that will be, I believe in you—I think I am finally ready. Honor and gratitude to the sustaining and universal Energy. Respect to the ancestors—Anastasia Patricia Walsh, Thomas Gabriel Dunn, Walter Fernandez Vallis, and my Nana Theodora Christenson Vallis—and to my mother Joyce Dunn, the bride of her Richard. Grateful for the blessing that is my father Dick Dunn. From the moment I first started writing, he treated my words as precious.

Steve McIntyre, thank you for saying yes to Minor Matters, and continuing to guide it with me. Who knew that a couple of small-town, cigar-smoking creatives could collaborate with friends and strangers around the world to make art books? I guess we did. I appreciate your family's ongoing support of our endeavor. Thank you to our authors (past and forthcoming!) who have joined as co-publishers to this book, and to others we have published. You make real the community I dreamed of living in. Thank you for making work that continues to provoke, and to inspire. To the thousands of friends, family, colleagues, and unknown allies who have co-published books through Minor Matters—nothing manifests without you. We're making history one book at a time. Thank you for taking part. To our Legacy Publishers, your trust in what we are cultivating keeps us going, thank you for fueling the flame.

Thank you to the curious and dedicated who have chosen me, as well as those assigned to me, in classes, workshops, and masterclasses, and to the individuals who invite me to teach, including at YoungArts, Seagull Publishing Institute, PhotoIreland, Palm Springs Photo Festival, Parsons | The New School, Yale, and others. Sharing knowledge with and learning from devotees is one of the most important exchanges of my life.

Finally, to the shy girls, and all the observers in the apple trees—I see you. Keep dreaming. And when you're ready to step into the world, work hard to make those dreams reality. You can do it. I believe in you.

—MDM

1995

Stephen Shore

Graduation, Bard College,
Annandale-on-Hudson,
New York
P. 30

Mary Ellen Mark

Elise Collins,
Union, South Carolina
P. 65

1997

William Christenberry

Green Warehouse,
Newbern, Alabama
P. 73

1998

Lisa Kereszi

Joe Jr.'s Belly
PP. 98–99

An-My Lê

Untitled, Tranh-Hoa,
from the "Viet Nam" series
PP. 88–89

2001

Eugene Richards

*A Firefighter Sits Alone
in the Rubble,*
World Trade Center site,
New York
PP. 54–55

2002

Jock Sturges

Vanessa,
Le Porge, France
PP. 80–81

2004

Catherine Chalmers

Hanging
PP. 84–85

2006

Alice Wheeler

Boy with Rabbit Ears,
Evergreen State Fair,
Monroe, Washington
P. 132

2007

Larry Fink

Sylvia Plachy,
Michelle Dunn Marsh,
and Charlie Harbutt,
New York
P. 101

2008

Mary Ellen Mark

Alex Londono and Chayanne
Yate, NYC Pride March,
New York
P. 62

David Hilliard

Boys Tethered
PP. 128–129

2010

Isaac Layman

Glass Plate Negative
P. 145

Joe Freeman Jr.

Tar and Asphalt
P. 154

2012

Charlie Rubin

I Love You, Rock
P. 119

Adrain Chesser

Untitled
GATEFOLD,
PP. 120–121

Sylvia Plachy

Michelle Dunn Marsh,
Woodhaven, New York
P. 121